# Beastly Folklore

St. Mary's H. S. Library
South Amboy, N. J.

## Joseph D. Clark

The Scarecrow Press, Inc.
Metuchen, N.J.  1968

Copyright 1968 by Joseph D. Clark

Library of Congress Card No. 68-12617

## Foreword

Our speech, sayings, superstitions, riddles, songs, stories, games, and pastimes tell us much about the animals that live among us. Like humans some of these animals are predatory and frustrating; others are distinctly useful and friendly.

As evidenced in the sketches in this text, the names of animals play an extensive role in the language of the English-speaking world. There are thousands of words and phrases that describe or qualify persons, their activities, plants, devices, processes, and so forth, in terms of animal characteristics.

The common folk, with rare humor and much common sense, have used their knowledge and understanding of the animal kingdom to criticize man himself, and not always in a gentle and inoffensive manner. Some of the stories are uproariously or subtly expressed; others are openly vulgar or bitterly caustic. Granted that folklore may attribute to animals many traits that are natural in preserving a balance in nature, it must be conceded that the tales usually succeed in exposing the weaknesses of human nature.

These sketches are presented in a popular and folksy manner, leaving the scientific information in the main to the biologists. It is hoped, however, that the series will stimulate the reader to look with renewed interest at the animals in their yards, in the parks, fields, forests, and elsewhere.

Credit is due to all the authors and publishers and the unnamed millions who have preserved and transmitted the animal folklore of this and other nations. A full measure of appreciation is extended to all the students, collectors, contributors, authors, and university presses that made possible the publication of the Motif-Index and the Frank C. Brown Collection of North Carolina Folklore, the primary sources of the superstitions recorded herein.

J. D. C.

## Table of Contents

| | Page |
|---|---|
| A Hog Is a Hog Is a Hog | 7 |
| To Get Your Goat | 20 |
| The Feast of the Buzzards | 29 |
| Raising a Stink (the Polecat) | 36 |
| Asses and Their Relatives | 40 |
| Out-Foxing Reynard | 51 |
| Playing Possum | 58 |
| The Hawk as Sharper | 62 |
| A Bird That Nobody Knows (The Starling) | 68 |
| Jaybird as Chatterbox | 71 |
| The Coon as Hand-Scratcher | 74 |
| That English Sparrow | 78 |
| Agile as a Squirrel | 80 |
| Black as Crows | 85 |
| The Owl as King of the Night | 92 |
| The Heart of an Ox | 99 |
| Bats in Belfries | 106 |
| King of the Birds--The Eagle | 111 |
| Wolf! Wolf! Wolf! | 117 |
| The Rabbit's Foot | 125 |
| Goosey Goosey Gander | 137 |
| Monkey See, Monkey Do | 149 |
| Bear in Mind | 159 |
| Baa, Baa, Black Sheep | 170 |
| Cattle on a Thousand Hills | 187 |
| Chickens on and off the Roost | 209 |
| Love Me, Love My Dog | 232 |
| The Way the Cat Jumps | 254 |
| Rats! | 277 |
| The Trail of the Serpent | 288 |
| A Horse of Another Color | 304 |
| Bibliography | 325 |

A Hog Is a Hog Is a Hog

In North Carolina all hogs and pigs are up four percent to 1,456,000 head, which is the largest increase in swine production in the U.S. of states with over 1,000,000. All other states except Kentucky in this size population showed increases in total hogs when compared to 1964. ---The News and Observer, January 10, 1966.

Let's face up to the fact that there are a lot of swine in North Carolina and other parts of this hog-eating world. Swine (Suidae), with a heritage of almost nine thousand years, were brought to the New World by Columbus, Cortez, the Pilgrims, and others. Swine, always a reliable source of food and other products, constitute a large segment of the economic and gastronomic indices of prosperity and delightful living.

The production of swine and the processing of pork products are subjected to all sorts of scientific, technological, and business research to make them more profitable and appealing. The animals are bred (sometimes four or more times a year) for less fat and more lean; they are medicated to prevent diseases and to promote quicker growth; they are fed wholesome and nutritious diets on a rationed basis; they are domiciled in portable houses and pig parlors; they are mechanically cooled or kept warm, watered and scrubbed, combed and pampered. Grazed in clover fields, handled with care and respect, the hogs have never had it so good.

But not for long. Soon the hogs are stuck, scalded, hamstrung, scraped, gutted, chilled, inspected, dissected, salted, peppered, smoked, sweetened, watered, and prepared in sundry customary ways for the feast. The poor creatures are truly hog-tied as they proceed from the hog-killing parties and the assembly lines to the dining-room table.

The array of pork products is unmatched for versatility of

cuts, tastiness, and economic and social uses.  Behold this outpouring of plenty:  hams, shoulders, loin chops, fat back or sidemeat (bacon), spareribs, backbone, jowl, liver, kidneys, heart, tongue, brains, feet, hock, skin, marrow, intestines, tail, and testicles (mountain oysters).  From the hogs come sausage stuffed in casings (entrails), lard, cracklings, chitterlings (chitlings), boiled or pickled pig's feet, souse, puddings, pon horse (corn meal cooked in stock from liver pudding), liverwurst, bologna, frankfurters, salami, bratwurst, and other mixtures of pork products with cereals and other meats.

Industrially, the bristles are used in brushes; the hair in cushions, felting, and insulation; pigskin in gloves, wallets, and other leather items.  Certain parts are sources of gelatin, cosmetics, roofing compound, and cleaning emulsions.  The bone, blood, lungs (lights), and other offal go into feeds and fertilizers.  It is trite but true that nothing but the squeal escapes the butcher.

Many superstitions attest to the efficacy of pork products in curing ailments, in foretelling the future, in assuring prosperity, or in warding off dire happenings.  Hogs on foot, moreover, can forecast the weather.

In large measure, the most revealing facet in this story is not the hog but man himself.  As recorded in the name-calling and sayings given hereafter, this hog-to-man adaptation is earthy and often scandalous.  Be that as it may, the hog remains unconcerned about man's low estimate of him.  In every respect the hog is himself, and his cleanliness can sometimes make a man blush.

The hog is an outcast among some religious groups and therefore has no benefit of clergy.  He has been proscribed and convicted by prohibitions and customs, be they ever so well-grounded on sanitary considerations in lands that had no refrigeration.  The Koran is against the hog, and so is the Bible.  In Leviticus (XI, 8) there appears:  "The swine is unclean to you.  Of their flesh ye shall not eat."  Matthew (VII, 6) says, "Neither cast ye your pearls before swine."  This dislike of hogs is implied in Jesus' parable of the Prodigal Son and in his driving of demons out of sick persons into swine.

One ought to question the castigation and mistreatment of the hog, now recognized as one of the most adaptable and most intelligent of the domesticated animals. The hog has been forced to root for his substance, to cool off in mud puddles, to wallow in his own excrement, to eat and drink everything in his uncooked swill, and to survive chiefly on his own. His very names--piggy, piggie, piglet, pigling, hog, sow, swine (also boar, gilt, barrow, and stag) --are qualified as nasty, dirty, greedy, piggish, and hoggish. And his places of shelter--pigpen, piggery, pigsty, hogpen, hoggery, and swinery--smell no better than they sound.

With laughter and contempt, man has turned his characterizations of swine against himself and his society. A man can be as happy as a pig in a puddle, and at other times as loud as one that has been caught in a gate. As a ham actor, he demonstrates the uselessness of shearing hogs for wool. Some call man a hog-grubber--narrow-minded, pig-headed or stubborn. And if you wish to see man at his worst, watch his maneuvering on the highways--as a road hog he is the hog-wildest. Nosiree, there is nothing hamstrung about this guy. Furthermore, his moral aspirations are hardly any better. For instance, if he is a swineherd he is usually stupid and sex-minded, notorious for visiting pigs (prostitutes) in pigpens (roadhouses). If he is a trader, you had better look out-- he may sell you a pig in a poke. This fellow wants all ham--and let the hominy go.

This lout, a hog in armor, can be a hog-head leading a parade of swine to the market, or a stump-rooter in the forest, or a sand hog tunneling under a river. His name is also associated with contraptions such as hambone (trombone), hog-caller (loudspeaker), hog (pulp agitator), hog-leg (six-shooter), pig-sticker (sword), pigbed (where molten iron is poured), sow (an ingot bigger than a pig ingot), pigpen (skillet), a pig for brushing or scrubbing pipes or ducts, or a pigskin (football).

Swine have a long history in the pastimes of Europe and the United States. For instance, "educated" pigs were taken on long tours in England before 1800, gaily clad pigs were used to entertain Louis XI of France, and hog-calling contests and greased-pig chases have long been a feature at country fairs.

One of the most spectacular sports, popular in England and on the Continent, is the hunting and killing of the wild boar. Once this vicious animal is brought to bay and dispatched by a gun, or preferably by a sharp spear, his enormous head is lopped off and prepared for the festivities. The head is placed at the center of a long board, decorated with holly or mistletoe and lighted by candles, and paraded through the streets or within the high-ceilinged halls of the mighty.

Another aspect of swinish amusement is observed in children's games, rhymes and stories. Wee pigs, suckling pigs, and pigs frisking about in clover have found a warm spot in the hearts of the very young. Children play such games as "Barnyard Chorus," "Grunt, Pig, Grunt," "Pigs in Clover" (a marble game), and the simple card game called "Pig." They recite and act out such rhymes as "Tom, Tom, the Piper's Son," "This Little Pig," "Pig in the Parlor," "To Market, to Market," "Black Eye Piggie Pie," "Pig-Tails and Pony-Tails," and "I Had a Little Pig." Children the world over have enjoyed "Three Little Pigs," a story far more delightful to them than Charles Lamb's "A Dissertation upon Roast Pig," which is better adapted to grown-ups concerned about the Chinese method of roasting pork by burning barns.

But when the pig becomes an adult he ceases to be a clean and innocent plaything. In the children's rhyme-game "Hog Drovers" the drivers are no cleaner than the hogs they tend. In the satiric and patriotic song entitled "Root, Hog, or Die," the satiric thrust is at Jefferson Davis of the Confederacy.

Regardless of the low estate of hogs, superstitious folk regard them, dead or living, as remarkable aids to mankind. For instance, fat meat or lard mixed with salt will rid you of your itch; fat meat and lard treated with kerosene or salt, or with goose manure stewed with sweetgum leaves, or mixed with fishing baits and other messy ingredients, are effective ointments to draw out poisons and fever in boils, to cure or eliminate colds, coughs, croup, diphtheria, mumps, rheumatism, snake bite, ringworm, toothache, warts, and whatever else that may be troubling you. If you are praying for a change in the weather, especially during a drought, keep your eyes on pigs or hogs that are squealing, playing noisily, running with sticks or socks or other cast-off things in their mouths--you'll soon discover that colder weather, wind and storms are on the way. If you are looking for greater prosperity in the coming year, make a pig of yourself on New Year's Day by consuming plenty of hog jowl. To supplement this, carry round hambones in your pockets, or pick up a coin lost in a pig's track, or nail a horseshoe to the trough of your fattening hogs. If by chance you are scared a witch will enter your home, put some money under a hogpen. She will get the cash, take off for a cemetery or some other ghoulish place, and thus will not disturb your nervous system. These and other remedies or magic rites, the folks maintain, can really make you admire any dirty hog.

In conclusion, domesticated swine exist primarily for big profits and much gustatory enjoyment, particularly when folk eat high on the hog. This epicurean view is well expressed by Horace (65-8 B.C.) in his Epistles IV: "When you have a mind to laugh, you shall see me, fat and sleek, in Epicurus' herd."

Man or hog? Ugh! In a pig's eye... Oinck! Oinck! Oinck! Bro-ther, pass some more of that Carolina barbecue.

## Derivative Names

ham: piece of pasture land

ham actor: inferior, flamboyant actor (probably from practice of using ham to remove make-up)

hambone: trombone; spurious Negro dialect

ham-cases: trousers

ham-joint: cheap restaurant

ham-meat: ham

hammy: something flavored with ham

ham-pilot: clumsy pilot in British RAF

hog: greedy person; early American ten-cent piece (also six pence); light railroad engine; agitator to stir paper pulp;

machine used in cutting small bits of lumber; student in St. John's College, Cambridge, England; to clean bottom of ship

hog-backed: having a back like a hog's

hog-caller: loudspeaker

hogfleece: fleece from first shearing of sheep

hog in armor: lout in fine clothes

hog it: to snore, sleep soundly

hogg: British shilling

hogged: horse's mane cut to be bristly

hog-grubber: ignorant, narrow-minded, sneaking person

hog-head: railroad engineer that often leads parade of hogs to market

hog jowl: jowl used as food

hog-leg: six-shooter used by trail drivers

hog Latin: imitation language

hognut: nut from pignut hickory

hogshead: large cask (63 to 140 gallons); source unknown

hog shearing: great ado about nothing

hog's pudding: mixture of flour, currants, etc., stuffed into casings (entrails)

hogtie: secure by all legs

hogwash: swill, slop, nonsense

hog-wild: irrational

pig: fat and sloppy person; prostitute; policeman; brush or swab for cleaning a duct or pipe; flask for distillation of liquids in laboratory; pressman (see pigsty); to damage or spoil

pig bed: sand bed into which molten iron is poured to make iron pigs

pig between two sheets: sandwich

pigboat: submarine, so named from sucking pigs nosed against

# Hog

    tender

pig, in: pregnant

pig in blanket: frankfurter baked in biscuit dough

piggin: iron pot or skillet with two ears

piggyback (pickaback): carried on back or shoulders or on transportation facilities

piggy bank: savings bank shaped like a pig

pig-headed: stubborn

pig iron: crude iron, cast into masses called pigs

pigpen: roadhouse; shelter for pigs

pig-poker: swineherd

pig salve: lard

pigskin: football; saddle

pigstick: hunt wild boar with spear

pig-sticker: bayonet

pigsty: pigpen; pressroom of newspaper or printing plant

pigtail: braid of hair; twist of tobacco shaped like a pig's tail

porker: sword

"Porkopolis:" Cincinnati, Ohio, in 1880's

porkpie hat: hat with low crown and flat top

razorback: thin, long-legged hog

road hog: selfish driver

sand hog: tunnel worker

shoat: young hog

sow: channel or runner to conduct metal into molds; ingot larger than a pig

sow-belly: salt pork

stump rooter: wild hog

swinehead: person given to stupid and sensual life

swineherd: person tending swine

swine-backed: having a back shaped like a hog's

## Proverbs and Proverbial Phrases

Bleeds like a stuck pig.

Common as pig's tracks.

Crooked as a pig's tail.

Dirty (drunk, fat, filthy, gluttonous, greedy, hungry, lazy, lousy, muddy, nasty, potty, proud, selfish, sloppy, stingy, stubborn) as a pig (hog). Also, eats (grunts, smells, squeals) like a pig (hog).

Fat as a pig.

Fist like a ham.

Frisking about like pigs in clover.  Happy as pigs in clover.

Good as a pig eating slop.

Good-natured as a sucking pig.

Happy as a pig in a puddle.

Happy as a dead pig in the sunshine.  Cf. Happy as a dead pig in paradise.

Independent as a hog on ice.

Like a pig (hog) in a squall (storm).  (Out of his senses)

Loud as a pig (hog) caught in a gate.

He cares as much as a hog about Sunday (holiday).

Naked as a scraped hog.

He has no more use for it than a pig needs the New Testament.

He has no more use for it than a hog has for a sidesaddle.

On the hog: broke or having no funds.

Pussy (swollen) and prosperous as a prize pig just before killing time.

# Hog

Scared like a hog in killing time.

Slick as a greased pig. Cf. Slippery as a greased pig.

Snore like a pig (sow) in the sun.

Sour enough to make a pig squeal.

Useless as tits on a boar.

He waits like one hog on another.

Root, Hog, or Die. (Title of song, meaning to be independent or suffer the consequences; evidence of hog's capacity to survive.)

Don't buy a pig in a poke (bag).

Go the whole hog. (To spend lavishly on entertainment, to spend entire sum of ten-cent piece or six pence; British hogg is shilling.)

Bring home the bacon. (To win a greased pig at a chase or fair; earn a living.)

Eat high on (off) the hog. (To live well; switch from salt pork to loin chops and roasts.)

Having boiled pig at home. (Being master in one's house.)

No ham and all hominy. (No pay and all work.)

Pull (get) the wrong pig (sow) by the ear. (Make a mistake.)

Ham-string. (Cripple an animal by cutting tendons behind the knees or hocks.)

Hog-tied. (Tied by all four feet; precluded from doing anything.)

In a pig's eye. (Expression of disgust for somebody's nonsense.)

In less than a pig's whistle. (Short time.)

Enough to make a hog blush.

When a pig flies. (Improbable action.)

When a pig plays a flute. (Improbable action.)

When the hog gets his snout under the gate. (Look out; he's in or out.)

The greediest hog is the poorest.

St. Mary's H. S. Library
South Amboy, N. J.

The still hog (sow) gets the hogwash. (The still pig gets the swill.)

Selfish hog in the manger. (One that thinks he owns the hogpen.)

Make a sow's ear. (Commit an error.)

You can't make a silk purse out of a sow's ear.

## Superstitions and Motifs

### From the Brown Collection

Tie a bullet that a hog has been shot with around your neck, and you will stop bleeding. (VI, 1895).

Fat pork used on boils will draw out inflammation or fever. (VI, 916).

Goose manure stewed with sweetgum leaves and hog lard, strained and made into an ointment, is good for burns. (VI, 997).

Go to a barn, lie down, and roll over three times. Then get up and walk backwards thirty-three steps, and the chicken pox will be cured. (VI, 1026).

Place on chest a piece of red flannel soaked in hog's-feet oil, kerosene, and salt. For best results, do not remove flannel suddenly; let the flannel disappear or be lost. (VI, 1140).

Grease chest with hog's feet oil and cover with flannels to cure coughs and colds. (VI, 1128).

Use hog's-feet oil for the croup. (VI, 1256).

Old remedy for diphtheria is salt pork applied to the throat to draw out poison and to form blisters, which may be lanced or allowed to break open. (VI, 1282).

To cure mumps, rub the grease of the jawbone of a hog on the swollen glands, and make a cross mark on jawbone with a piece of charcoal. (VI, 1831). Cf. To cure mumps, take a jawbone of a hog, cook it, get marrow out, and rub patient with it. (VI, 1828; cf. 1829-31).

To cure a pain in the neck, rub your neck where a hog has been scratching his back. (VI, 1838).

For rheumatism, one should stew baits (fishing worms) with hog lard, and use as an ointment. (VI, 1968). Cf. If you go to a tree where a hog has rubbed, and then rub and squeal, your rheumatism will be cured. (VI, 1983).

# Hog

Ringworm: Make a salve by boiling house leek down to a gravy and mixing this with pure hog lard. (VI, 2740).

Place fat pork over a snake bite to draw out poison. (VI, 2137).

Powdered hog lice is good for sore eyes. (VI, 1368).

The right-hand jawbone of a hog is used to rub and cure risings. (VI, 2312).

A certain bone from the head of a hog, hung on a red string around the baby's neck, will make the child cut teeth. (VI, 359). Cf. If you pull an old tooth, and a cat or dog or hog finds it, the tooth that comes back will resemble the tooth of the animal finding it. (VI, 393).

If a hog's tooth is carried in the pocket, the bearer will never have a toothache. (VI, 2348).

To cure warts, rub with meat, meatskin, or stolen meat. Then hide meat under rock, bury it, dispose of it in some manner, or give it to someone (who will get the wart). (VI, 2462ff). Cf. To cure warts, rub them with salt meat. (VI, 2474). To cure warts, wash your hands in warm pig's blood. (VI, 2475).

Pig with straw in its mouth indicates colder weather. (VII, 6283). Cf. If you see a hog running with leaves in its mouth and squealing, it is a sure sign that a cold snap is coming. (VII, 6284). If hogs take socks, sticks, and the like in their mouths, it is a sure sign of cold weather. (VII, 6286). If one sees a pig making a bed, there will be cold weather to follow. (VII, 6285).

If you see a hog with a stick in his mouth, it is a sign of bad weather. (VII, 6178). Cf. Pigs squeal before bad weather. (VII, 6180). Horses, cows, and pigs running, kicking, and being especially playful are a sign of wind. (VII, 6988). When it's cold and windy, pigs will squeal. (VII, 6287). Fighting hogs foretell storms. (VII, 6922).

Hogs see the wind. (VII, 6986). Cf. Suck a blue sow and see the wind. (I, 479). If you drink a sow's milk, you will be able to see the wind. (I, 479).

It is good luck to cook hog's head on New Year's. (VI, 2826). For New Year's dinner have corn bread, peas, and hog's head. Then you will have food all year round. (VI, 2830). If you have hog jowl and peas on New Year's Day, you will have peace and prosperity the whole year. (VI, 2828). To insure having food the whole year, you must have pork of some kind with cabbage. (VI, 2833). Cook peas and hog jowl on New Year's Day, and you will have plenty of money the rest of the year. (VI, 3405).

Carry a round bone of ham in your pocket for luck. (VII, 5805).

To find a coin in a pig's track is good luck throughout life. (VI, 3423).

If a horseshoe is nailed to the hog trough, no ills will befall the fattening hogs. (VII, 7690; cf. 7674).

William Geston, failing to kill anything with his gun, accepted the popular advice by pouring corn over it and feeding hogs on it. He found it better than ever. (VII, 7906).

Bury a dime under the hogpen to keep witches away. (VII, 7675).

To dream of fresh pork out of season is considered a sign of death. (VII, 5237).

If you eat the end of a hog's tongue, you will always tell lies. (VI, 3681).

A man by the name of Hog, who felt many of the barbs of his neighbors, had his name changed legally. Thereafter the wags of the community yelled:  Hog by name,
Hog by nature,
Hogue by act of the Legislature.

From the Motif-Index

Boar has nine tusks in each jaw. (B15.7.8).

Boar refuses to fight with lowly ass. (J411.1).

Earth made of mud shaken off primeval boar. (A822).

Man transformed to boar. (D114.3.2).

Wild boar as ogre. (G352.2).

Wild boar given permission to squeal before wolf eats him. (K551.3.4).

Hog goes to bath, but wallows in mud. (U123).

Why hog lives in sty. (A2433.3.6).

Revenant as woman riding a hog. (E425.1.5).

Jesus drives evil spirits into hogs. (A2287.1ff).

Pig attempts to imitate goat's tricks. (J2415.6).

# Hog

A god's urine was used to make pig.  (A1871.0.1).

Literal numbskull kisses a pig.  (J2461.2.1).

The stingy parson and the slaughtered pig.  (K343.2.1).

The pig's blood enchants.  (D766.2.1).

Divination from pig liver.  (D1311.10.2).

A sow saves pigs from wolf coming to baptize them.  (K1121.2).

The cat brings suspicion between eagle and sow.  (K2131.1).

Swine magically kept from fattening.  (D2089.3.1).

Clerics were expelled in shapes of swine.  (Q226.2).

Eaters of swine were not allowed to enter Venus' temple.  (J1447).

## To Get Your Goat

Went out to milk and I didn't know how,
I milked the goat instead of the cow.
                    --Turkey in the Straw

    Dispensing with the kid gloves, one should recognize the goat as a paradox in fact and fiction: he is endearing and repulsive, gentle and rambunctious, good and evil.

    To children, he is a delightful plaything; to some of them and many grown-ups, he is a devilish character. No farm youngster would ever mistake this animal for a cow. Shucks alive! He knows too much about the peculiarities of farm stock, both the friendly and the mischievous. He has heard many a yarn about the exploits of the goat and he recalls all of them--the time the pesky billy goat snatched Grandpa's nightshirt from the clothesline and ate it with grinning mockery, or when another goat debarked all the young apple trees in a new orchard, or when a stranger ventured into the pasture and had the daylights knocked out of him in a briar patch, or when the goat swallowed six red flannel shirts, was beaten and tied to a railroad track, and finally coughed up the shirts and flagged down the oncoming train. So, unless you are on friendly terms with your goat, the farm boy advises you to keep your shirt on and your pants well insulated for social security.

    Let us take a look at the goat, which has a useful place in the economy of some European nations, in the East, and in some areas of the United States. Often associated with sheep and antelopes, the goat (genus <u>Capra aegagrus</u>, family <u>Bovidae</u>) is an uncultivated billy goat in other parts of the world, but here he is a pet, and may his god Pan never forsake him. Behold him--hollow horns that arch backward, straight hair and no wool on his thin body, a grandfatherly tuft on his chin, rickety and shaggy legs supposedly given him by the wolf. Possessor of a mimicking independence, agile and active, he betrays none of the timidity of the other flocks or herds. In a pasture, he keeps the sheep spread out and moving--in some packing houses he escorts the sheep to the slaughter, and in consequence is called the Judas goat.

This is not the type that domestic and commercial fanciers talk about. Poet Carl Sandburg of Flat Rock, North Carolina, cherished his flock and attributed much of his vigorous health to goat milk. The scientists, breeders, and producers of goats, especially in Switzerland, value carefully bred and nurtured flocks as sources of excellent food. Though the flesh, chiefly that of the kid, is deliciously edible, the goat is prized largely for its human-like milk, which is readily digestible and free of tubercular germs. Much richer than cow's milk, it yields cheese of top quality. A well-developed goat may produce as much as eight quarts of milk daily and in a period of ten months some fifty or more pounds of butterfat. Dairy goats, bred occasionally six months after birth, are often cross-bred, dehorned early, medicated, comfortably housed, nutritiously fed, and milked in modern and sanitary sheds. Under these conditions, to say nothing about the kindly attitudes of the owner, the goat can be as gentle and clean as a house cat.

The most widely propagated types of goats are the Swiss Taggenburgs, with females weighing 100 to 125 pounds and bucks (often 36" in height) weighing 150 to 200 pounds, in shades of brown from light-tan to black; the Swiss Saanens, larger than the Taggenburgs, pure white or slightly cream in color; the scarce Oriental-British Nubians (originating in Africa), with very short hair that is white or tan or dark-brown and with established records for the highest and richest production of butterfat; and the very popular, large breeds, French, Rock, and Swiss Alpines (seldom seen in America), known to be hardy and great producers of high-quality milk. Minor breeds are the Scandinavian Norskas, the Spanish Murcianas, and the Maltese, all of them important to the economy of their respective nations.

Well-informed champions of the goat consider him a blessing of mankind. One American enthusiast, Frank R. Coutant, has said:

"Every dairy goat is a personality. They are high in intelligence, mischievous but never malicious, anxious for human companionship, appreciative of all you do for them, faithful to their friends, and dependent upon their owners for protection."

On the other hand, in folklore the goat is not reputed for exhilarating aroma, elegance, or respectability. He is considered smelly and stinking, lustful and adulterous, tricky and blasphemous --half-man, half-demon, half-god. He is a teaser, deceiver, lecher, harlot, goatsucker, swindler, and all-round diabolical creature. And his goatishness, used to satirize the human species, is qualified as goat-bearded, goat-drunk (lecherous), goat-eyed, goat-eed, goat-footed, goat-hoofed, goat-horned, goatish (awkward and lustful), goat-kneed (knee-sprung), goat-toothed, and so forth. Shakespeare has this to say in King Lear: "An admirable evasion of whoremaster man, to lay his goatish disposition to the charge of a star." In another astrological reference, he calls this damned goat an arrogant fool: in disclaiming his being born under the sign of the kid, he asserts that he was born under the sign of the goat.

To allow this record to be unchallenged would be goatishness itself. The name goat or kid is often kindly utilized to specify certain actions and objects, or to identify plants, herbs, and flowers. (See the list below.)

In the main, however, the goat is having a hard time living down his outlandish reputation in folklore as a wicked spirit. For thousands of years, in scriptures and mythologies, the goat has been, if not a devil, at least one of his relatives or agents. For instance, in the account of the last judgment in Matthew XXV, the goats on the left (awkward, sinister or evil) side are separated from the sheep on the right (dexterous and holy) side, each group being sent to the places prepared for them. Traditionally, this hellish goat is similar to the one mentioned in Leviticus XVI and alleged to have borne away the sins of the people into the wilderness. This sin-bearer was dubbed a scapegoat in 1530 by the scholarly John Tyndale, and this particular goat is still frequently employed.

Since medieval times, the phrase "that old goat" has signified a sensual or lecherous person, usually a man. In general, this lascivious and stinking old man gets people's goat because he is the epitome of goatishness.

Hard on the heels of this foolish man is the monstrous, demonic goat of mythology. As portrayed in the natural-unnatural bestiaries, he is a grotesque creature of the first order. As a devil with goat's feet he rides a goat. As a witch he also rides a goat. And, to show what a blasphemous guy he is, the witch sometimes wears a rosary made from the pellets of sheep dung. At other times in his kaleidoscopic movements, he is a ghost, or a man with shaggy legs, arched horns, and a goateed goat head; sometimes he is a rollicking satyr, often appearing as a gargoyle.

By way of contrast is that smiling and solicitous goat-god, Pan, who has the legs of a goat and often the horns and ears too. Embodying goodness and gentility, this wood spirit protects the forests, streams, fields, flocks, and shepherds. At times he is a bit impish, but withal he is a friendly spirit.

All of this explanation may sound like so much goat's wool, but it is in our folklore, in our Bible, in our mythologies, and in our great literature. No kidding!

## Derivative Names

billy goat: male goat; goatweed

buck: grown male goat

doe, doeling: female goat

goat: old and wornout car used by hot-rodders; fool; lecher; inferior race horse; junior officer in World War II; yard engine (Canadian) that shoves and pushes around railroad cars

goat antelope: intermediate animal between goats and antelopes, such as a chamois

goatbrush: Oregon box

goat bush: bitter-barked shrub

goat chaffer: European goatsucker

goatee: pointed or goatlike beard

goat fever: Brucellosis

goat fig: one of several wild figs, caprifig

goatfish: any of several fish of mullet family

goat grass: annual grass related to wheat

goat-god: Pan, a wood spirit that protects fields, forests, wild animals, flocks, and shepherds; represented with legs of goats and sometimes their horns and ears

goat gunner: mountain gunner

goatherd: tender of goat herds

goathouse: brothel

goatling: young goat

goat lock: chin whiskers, suggestive of goat's beard

Goat Major: British lance corporal in charge of regimental goat

goat milker: goatsucker, harlot

goat moth: European moth

goat nut: jojoba in western United States

goat owl: goatsucker

goat-pox: virus disease of goats

goatroot: European yellow-flowered herb

goatsbeard: herb with small white flowers, plant of chicory family, herb of rose family

goat's-chicory: pilewort, figwort, fireweed

goat'sfoot: South African plant with bluish-yellow flowers

goat's-hair: bundle of short, white cirrus clouds portending rain

goat's-horn: herb in shape of southern European pod

goatskin: skin of goat, leather, container for liquids

goat's-leaf: European honeysuckle

goat's marjoram: wild marjoram, goat's organy

# Goat

goat's pepper: chili

goat's-rue (goat's-eye): plant of pea family in southern Europe

goat star: Capella

goat's-thorn: thorny shrub

goatstone: type of Old World orchid; bezoar of goat, used as antidote

goatsucker: nocturnal bird supposed to suck the milk of goats

goatweed: West Indian plant

goatweed emperor: brown and orange butterfly

goat willow: great sallow of Europe

goat's wool: something non-existent

kid: to tease, make fun of, deceive, fool; to bind in bundles; seed pod of legume; small wooden tub used by sailors

kid brother or sister: younger brother or sister

kidcote: shed for goats

kidd (variant of kid): swindler

kidded: brought forth young

kidder: teaser, deceiver

kidskin: skin from kid, leather

nanny-goat: parimutuel or totalizer

nanny-goat sweat: inferior whiskey

scapegoat: person taking blame for another; the goat that carried away the sins of the people into the wilderness (Leviticus XVI, 8-10). The scholarly John Tyndale is credited for first using scapegoat in 1530. There are similar accounts of casting out demons by having a goat breathe in the sins of a person

## Proverbs and Proverbial Phrases

The goat must browse (bleat) where she is tied: Poverty or hardship forces man to endure.

Get one's goat: To anger, annoy, or frustrate. Cf. Get one's nanny. (Archaic)

The goat gives a good milking, but she casts it all down with the feet: Good service is spoiled by later misbehavior.

Play the goat: Play the fool. Cf. Play the nanny-goat: Play silly tricks.

Be the goat (scapegoat).

Be the goat's toe: Be pre-eminent in British Isles.

Hot (free) as a mountain goat: wildly sensual. Cf. Hot in love as goats.

Handle with kid gloves: To exercise care or tact.

Look at goats and monkeys: To gaze lecherously.

Mischievous as a goat: Playful and tricky.

Ride the goat: Be initiated into a secret society.

As much sense as a billy goat.

Kid oneself: Delude oneself.

Kid stuff: Anything childish or immature.

Separate the sheep from the goats. (See St. Matthew, XXV, 32-33).

Smell like a goat. Cf. Stinks like a goat. Stynken as a goot (Chaucer).

Old goat: Sensual or lecherous person, usually a man; any old and disliked person who is mean, stingy, stubborn, and unsympathetic toward young people.

You can't get wool off a goat: None to get. Cf. It is a task to spin wool still on a goat's back. As many stars as hair on a goatskin.

Almost as swift and agile as goats.

The goat eats while the camel talks.

The fool thinks that the goat mimicks him.

The herd's spirit is in the last goat's tail: The tail is used for magic.

Goat

The pig imitates the tricks of the goat: After the goat returns decked out with ornaments and plenty of food.

## Superstitions and Motifs

### From Brown Collection

Goat dung made into a tea will cause measles to break out. Gargle the throat and drink. (VI, 1805). Cf. Drink nannygoat tea to cure measles. (VI, 1806).

Goat grease is used to cure rheumatism. (VI, 1979).

When sheep and goats bleat loud and long, you may expect rain. (VII, 6673).

### From Motif-Index

Goat's liver heals blindness of raja in India. (D1505.14.1).

Devil as goat. (G303.3.3.1.5).

Devil's mother rides a goat. (G303.11.3.1).

Devil writes faults on goat skin. (G303.24.1.2). (Swiss)

Devil has goat feet. (G303.4.5.4).

Goat is transformed to a person. (D334). (India)

Antelope becomes a goat. (D411.4.2). (India)

Ghost (revenant) as a goat. (E423.1.9).

Dwarfs with goat feet. (F451.2.2.3).

Goat as child's nurse. (B535.0.3). (Jewish)

Husband transformed to goat so as to watch wife's adultery. (K1531).

Man with goat head. (B24.2).

Man carried on goat horns. (B557.1).

Treasure comes from goat entrails. (B119.2).

Woman bears goat. (T554.6).

Goat heads show curse of Ham. (A1614.1.2). (Irish)

Pan, the wood spirit, is part man and part goat.  (F442).

Witch as goat.  (G211.1.5).

Witch rides on goat.  (G241.1.2).

Witch's rosary made of goat dung.  (G243.2.1).

Goat's tongue pierced and witch becomes sick.  (G252.2).

Goat's legs shaggy because wolf tore them.  (A2371.2.8).

Goat and hog as friends.  (A2493.22).

Goat as sacrifice.  (V12.4.5).

Goat declares he was born under the sign of the goat, not under the sign of the kid in the Zodiac.  (J2212).

## Quotations--Literary and Otherwise

How many stars in the heavens? --As many as the hairs on a goatskin.  Motif-Index (H702.2).

What goes round a button and round a button? -- Billy goat.

Like the goat, you'll mourn for your beard. -- Aeschylus.

If you think that to grow a beard is to acquire wisdom, a goat is at once a Plato. -- Lucian.


The pride of the peacock is the glory of God.
The lust of the goat is the bounty of God. -- William Blake, <u>Marriage of Heaven and Hell</u>.

My men, like satyrs gazing on the lawn,
Shall with their goat feet dance the antic hay. -- Christopher Marlowe, <u>Edward II</u>.

## The Feast of the Buzzards

> I am a gentleman, though spoiled i' the breeding. The Buzzards are all gentlemen. We came in with the Conqueror. -- Richard Brome, <u>English Moor</u>.

Not too many years ago in some rural communities where sanitation was neglected, one could see an amazing and morbid spectacle--the repulsive feast of the buzzards. It had only one redeeming aspect--it rid the countryside of a large animal body that had been left in an open field to rot and swell under the blazing sun.

Observers can hardly forget the sight of a lone buzzard high in the sky as he scouted the land for carrion. Aided by keen vision and an extraordinary sense of smell, he soared slowly and gracefully until he located the object of his search, then he circled the sky above it several times. By some mysterious method of communication, he was soon joined by his hungry brothers. The encircling continued--the circles became bigger and bigger, sometimes horizontal and sometimes tilted at forty-five-degree angles. Around and around the buzzards floated, until all the hungry were included in the flight. Then they descended with a sure and placid timing to take their positions about the deserted carcass.

Jumping up and down, they preened themselves, they jostled one another with their sharp beaks and cumbersome wings, they spread out at comfortable distances in semicircles. They were now ready for the feast. They pulled, they tugged, they gouged, they ripped, they tore huge hunks from the mass that nature had provided for them. Protruding eyeballs, hair matted with blood, puffy skin, swollen and putrid flesh, ligaments, and offal--it was there in awful abundance. The vultures consumed this fetid stuff in great gobs, cramming themselves as long as they could. Then they waddled off, lifted themselves wearily to the limbs of the trees nearby, and for a long period drooped and dozed. Having digested their meal, back they came with ravenous strength to tear and glut some more. If need be, they roosted in the trees for the night and resumed their work next morning, sometimes repeating the grim process day after day until the ravage was complete. Once the rites were over, the buzzards winged off in triumphant splendor, upward and upward, circle upon circle, back to their secret places in the forest. It was a ceremony well ended--and the sole evidence of the buzzards' coming was the disjointed and scattered bones, soon to be washed clean by the rains and whitened by the glaring light of day.

The buzzard that feasts in this revolting manner is the turkey buzzard (<u>Cathartes aura</u>), observed chiefly in the Americas. Seldom seen north of Pennsylvania, it is blackish-brown in color, has a red foreneck and a nearly naked and wrinkled skin on the head. Its wing span is almost five feet and its flight is elegant and rhythmic. Its only food is carrion.

This bird of prey (<u>busard</u> in Old French and Middle English) belongs to the hawk family, a large and slow-flying clan whose members include the red-tailed hawk, the red-shouldered hawk, and the broad-winged hawk. Buzzards (genus <u>Buteo</u>) are frequently called hen hawks. The term <u>buzzard</u> also applies to other species such as the bald buzzard (osprey), moor buzzard (marsh harrier), the honey buzzard (European short-winged hawk), and the turkey buzzard. In the Orient there is the buzzard eagle, a bird of prey somewhere between the buzzard and the eagle. Some classify the condor of the Andes as a member of this great family.

As his manner of feasting suggests, the buzzard is unquestionably nasty, filthy, and repulsive. He stinks, he becomes sick, he vomits and he pukes. He is reputed to be quarrelsome on his roost or at his meals, and he is stark blind to his natural habits in devouring the rotten carcasses of this earth.

A graphic illustration of how this nastiness is directed to the human species is the common expression "old buzzard," a euphemism for "old bastard." It connotes a high degree of gulli-

Buzzard

bility, stupidity, and foolishness, and wields a humorous and satiric thrust in the reduction of a dunce to his proper status.

The word buzzard, singly or in compound forms, provokes much humor of an unusual sort. For example, a buzzard score is two strokes above par on a hole in golfing, an ex-buzzard is a useless hawk, a buzzard-lope is an uncertain and awkward run, buzzard bait is poor and unsavory food, a buzzard's roost is a dirty joint or hideout, a buzzard cult is a cheap organization whose members cockily wear insignia such as eagles and other artifacts, and a buzzard colonel has spread eagles on his shoulders in contrast with the less important symbols of a lieutenant colonel. Buzzard is chicken or turkey served at army, prison, or college meals. The list below also reveals that the term is applied inoffensively in naming certain plants and other objects.

According to various beliefs, the buzzard can bring babies, catch thieves, forecast the weather, cure ailments and diseases, and portend good or evil fortune. His feathers, properly worn as charms, will prevent fever and rheumatism. Grease from his body will cure smallpox and rheumatism; it will also ease teething pain. His flight over houses heralds the coming of visitors, and if one imitates a buzzard's flopping he will be assured of seeing his lover. Moreover, if one wishes upon seeing a buzzard, his wish will come true. But the bird is not always a guardian angel: he may be a trumpeter of misfortune--the shadows of an unseen buzzard over a household may indicate an early death in the family.

Although you may have some doubts about these beliefs, it must be obvious that the turkey buzzard in spite of his grotesqueness manages with great efficiency to purify and cleanse the landscape.

### Derivative Names

buzzard: stupid, contemptible person; dunce or blockhead

buzzard: turkey or chicken served at meals in army, prison, or college

buzzard: golf score of two strokes above par on a hole

buzzard: scavenger that cleans and purifies, a general belief of the North American Pueblo Indians

buzzard: noisy insect such as the moth or cockchafer

buzzard: thief finder

buzzard: eagle insigne as used on army clothing, etc.

buzzard, ex: useless hawk

buzzard, old: filthy and unkempt old man, originally euphemism for "old bastard"

buzzard bait: very poor or rotten food

buzzard colonel: full colonel wearing eagle insignia

buzzard curlew: long-billed curlew

buzzard cult: Southern cult whose members wear insignia such as eagles

buzzard grass: pearl millet

buzzard lope: running in an awkward, loose-jointed manner

buzzard's-berry: bearberry

buzzard's roost: nasty, dirty joint or hideout

buzzard sweep (wing): large sweep of shovel

## Proverbs and Proverbial Phrases

Between hawk and buzzard. (Not quite master or mistress, nor quite a servant; to advance or recoil is problematic)

Blind as a buzzard. Cf. "I read each a blind buzzard."-- William Langland, The Vision of Piers the Plowman.

A buzzard is called a hawk by courtesy.

Filthy as a buzzard.

To make buzzard talk. (To quarrel)

The kite will never be a good hawk.

Nasty as a buzzard.

An old man's shadow is better than a buzzard's sword.

# Buzzard

Ragged as a buzzard.

Sick as a buzzard.

Stinks like a buzzard.

Vomits (pukes) like a buzzard.

## Superstitions and Motifs

Buzzards' feathers are effective as charms.

Buzzard's grease will cure smallpox.

A bag of buzzard's feathers is sometimes tied around a baby's neck to ease pain of teething.

In Wintun legend the two Hus brothers that created death had the shape of a buzzard. -- Gertrude Jobes, Dictionary of Mythology, Folklore and Symbols.

Origin of buzzard's head: Hopi Indians state that buzzard's head became red when he raised the sun a bit, and when he raised it farther it burned the feathers on his head. -- Funk and Wagnalls, Standard Dictionary of Folklore, Mythology and Legend.

## From Brown Collection

Children are told that babies are laid in hollow stumps by buzzards and hatched in the sun. VI, 4.

It is bad luck to kill a buzzard. You will have chills and fevers. VI, 1085.

Wear a string of buzzard feathers around the neck to keep off the fever. VI, 1412.

Wearing a buzzard feather behind the ear will prevent rheumatism. VI, 1971. Cf. Buzzard grease is used to cure rheumatism. VI, 1972.

If a buzzard flies over you and casts his shadow over you, it is a sign of bad luck. "Run, Negro, run, don't let the buzzard's shadow fall on you" is an old slave saying. VII, 7284.

If you look at a buzzard flying overhead, you'll pay for it. He'll throw up (vomit) or puke on you. VII, 7285.

If a buzzard is flying over a church at the time of a wedding, misfortune will soon come to the married ones. VI, 4852.

If a buzzard sits on a chimney of the house of a sick person, the person will die. VII, 5007. Cf. When a buzzard pitches on a dwelling house, it is a sign that some member of the family in that house is going to die. If you see a buzzard's shadow and not the buzzard, you will hear of a death. VII, 5290 and 5299.

Flapping like a buzzard is a sign of seeing a lover. VI, 4508-13.

A buzzard flying over the house is a sign that visitors are coming. VI, 3967-78. Cf. 8547.

If buzzards sit on trees with outspread wings, it is a sign of rain. VII, 6708. Cf. To see buzzards forming Job's coffin means rain in forty-eight hours. VII, 6709. Buzzards always fly before a storm in the direction that it is going. VII, 6229. The wind is going to blow when buzzards fly high. VII, 6993.

Make a wish before the sailing buzzard moves his wings, and it will come true. Cf. If you see a buzzard, make a wish, and if it flaps its wings, the wish will come true. VII, 7281. Cf. 7282-83.

From Motif-Index

Rescue of man from hole (tall tale): Several buzzards were lassoed and tied together; when ropes were suspended into the hole, the buzzards became frightened and pulled man out of hole. B547.2.1.

Buzzard transformed to door flop. D423.4.

Witch as a buzzard. G211.4.5.

Buzzard steals coyote's eyes while the coyote is throwing them up into the air. K333.3.

Buzzard hatched by hawk for fouling his nest. Q432.1.

Quotations--Literary and Otherwise

Mr. Buzzard
"O Mr. Buzzard, don't fly so high,
Yo can't make a livin' aflyin' in de sky."
-- Funk and Wagnalls, Standard Dictionary of Folklore, Mythology and Legend.

Turkey Buzzard
"Where you gwine, turkey buzzard,
Where you gwine, crow?"

"Gwine down in the new ground,

To get the grub and hoe."
-- Brown Collection, III, 139f.

Raising a Stink

Whew! For skunkiness, the skunk has no equal. This creature, which exhibits no courtesy, can be characterized as a first-class stinker or essence peddler.

In Europe and parts of Asia this mammal is known as a polecat, a name derived from the MF poul, pol, "cock," plus the ME cat, probably because of his preying on poultry. He belongs to the carnivorous family Mustelidae and he is closely related to the albino ferret. When domesticated, he has white stripes on his back from head to tail. In the wild state he is dark brown above and black below, his face variegated with white. His fur, long and coarse, is of little commercial value.

The polecat of the Americas is classified as a skunk of the genus Mephitis mephitis. Kin to the carnivorous weasels and minks, he is a black and bushy-tailed mammal with a white stripe along his back, head, and tail. He has an overall length of almost two feet and is possessed of a long and pointed muzzle. He walks leisurely, hunts at night, and feeds on fowl, frogs, fish, and so forth. When frightened or attacked, he ejects a secretion from his perineal or anal glands--the strong and unpleasant stench may engulf a neighborhood for days. Automobiles that have run over a skunk may have to be abandoned for something longer than a coffee break. Some people declare that the only way to rid clothes of the odor is to burn them.

Folklore about the skunk, though not extensive, concentrates on the subject matter--every bit of it is poly-saturated and raised to the nth degree of offensive odor. As supported by the lists below, the evidence is against this beast--the only way he could escape from a courthouse would be to let loose on it as he does on the countryside.

His name is given to persons, other animals, or plants that

also smell and raise a stink. A human skunk is expert in beating his bills, he routs his opponents with a complete knock-out, and he cheats or betrays in his social enterprises. In the plant kingdom, the skunk cabbage is a low-growing weed that flourishes in moist earth and gives off a putrid odor. In like manner, the skunkbrush (skunkbush) is a shrub having a bad odor similar to that from the bear brush or squawbush. The presence of these and other related plants, as well as some animals whose names are prefixed with skunk, is a warning to pull on your gas mask or take your date to a higher altitude.

What is a skunk good for anyway? His value is at least four-fold: 1. Skunk oil, say the folk, when rubbed in will cure numerous muscular aches. 2. The fur, after deodorizing and uniform dyeing, does pass on the market as a decent sort of fur to keep meticulous ladies warm, satisfied, and chic. 3. The animal is rated as an affectionate pet if de-scented, that is, if his perineal glands are shut off by a veterinarian. 4. The skunk has contributed about a score of the most malodorous words and phrases in the English language--for in word and deed, he stinks, stinks, stinks. (But his lucky cousin, the mink, is welcomed in the best society.)

### Derivative Names

polecat coffee: inferior brand of coffee

polecat dance: a dance once popular among Creek Indians

polecat tree (polecat wood): yellow buckthorn

polecat weed: skunk cabbage, as defined below

skunk: fur of skunk; mean, contemptible person; common palm civet; prostitute; boy whose duty it is to wake up workers on next railroad shift; unidentified target, detected visually or by radar

skunk bear: wolverine

skunkbill (skunktop): surf scoter (duck with rank odor)

skunk bird (skunk blackbird): bobolink

skunkbrush (skunkbush): shrub with bad odor

skunk cabbage (swamp cabbage and skunkweed): broad-leafed, low plant that grows in moist ground; it has cowl-shaped, brownish-purple spathe with unpleasant smell

skunk currant: eastern U.S. wild currant, with offensive-smelling red fruit

skunkdom: domain of skunks

skunk egg: onion

skunkery: place where skunks are bred and raised

skunk grape: fox grape

skunk grass: strong and rank grass of genus <u>Eragrostis</u>

skunk-haul: small catch of fish (off Grand Banks)

skunk-head (skunkhead coot): Labrador duck

skunklet: small skunk

skunk mushroom: death cup, rank and poisonous

skunk oil: oil from skunk, with supposed curative power

skunk porpoise: speckled, black-and-white porpoise

skunk spruce: white spruce

skunktail (skunktail grass): squirreltail

skunk turtle: musk turtle

woods pussy: polecat, essence peddler

## Proverbs and Proverbial Phrases

Skunk: to beat bill for payment; to cheat someone out of something, to betray, to welsh in betting; to defeat completely in games.

Skunky or skunkish: to be like a skunk.

Drunk as a skunk.

Smells (stinks) like a skunk (polecat).

Kill another skunk: to create a new scandal.

Polecat 39

> Let every man skin his own skunks: that is, do his own unsavory chores, etc.

## Superstitions and Motifs

<u>From Brown Collection</u>

Skunk oil is good for certain muscular troubles.   VI, 1835.

<u>From Motif-Index</u>

Bad smell of skunk.   A2416.3.

Color of skunk.   A2411.2.4.

Walking of the skunk.   A2441.1.6.

Why skunk is disliked.   A2522.4.

## Asses and Their Relatives

A long time ago, by some kink of evolution, an ass or two started this whole business of jackassness, and it's been creeping along ever since.

The Egyptians recognized jackasses as early as 4000 B.C. and had a high regard for their capacity to bear great burdens and make life easier for struggling humanity. Sometimes they were mistreated, as illustrated by Balaam's conduct during the flight from Egypt. (See Numbers, 22-24.) This prophet beat and cursed his ass, but instead of getting a blistering kick in the pants, he got a blessing. In Hebrew history kings, judges, and prophets (including Jesus) considered asses symbols of peace and salvation; asses were hailed with so much respect that the later Greek and Roman writers accused the Jews of being idolators of the ass. Asses were as popular among the people of Israel as were the regal cavalry horses among the Babylonians, Assyrians, and Egyptians. It is debatable whether asses or horses have done more in advancing civilization, but let's drop this intriguing question and consider the asininity of more recent times.

You ought to know that the ass, a quadruped, is called asinus in Latin and belongs to the genus Equus. A domesticated animal, he is further qualified as Equus asinus, to distinguish him from the domesticated horse known as Equus caballus.

The ass looks somewhat like a horse. He is smaller, however, has longer ears and perhaps longer years, a shorter and stiffer mane, and a distinct tuft of hair on his tail. He moves leisurely, is sure-footed and patient, and under most conditions is hardy and dependable. In a few farfetched superstitions, he is a vampire and a devil, he can give signs of falling weather, he is extremely jealous of the status of the horse, and he thinks that he bears a divine image. As applied to the human predicament, he

# Ass

is a blockhead and dunce who makes an ass of himself, brays in the faces of people whenever it is safe, laughs from sunrise to sunset, wags his ears to appear wise, climbs ladders to the tops of castles with gold, and comes down to eat thistles and straw mattresses. As a perverse and ornery cuss, he has no hope of being anything except an ass. In view of his scornful reputation, it is apt to quote: "He that makes himself an ass must expect to be rode."

Incidentally, an ass in some Spanish-speaking areas is called a burro, which though smaller than the usual breed runs true to form as a capable pack animal. His name has been given to the grunt, a fish, and to a species of shrub.

The donkey is a Xerox duplicate of the ass, both animal and human. Occasionally called a donk, he too kicks, laughs, and brays. The word donkey as a prefix in compounded words indicates an auxiliary machine or contrivance, such as donkey cart, donkey doctor, donkey engine, donkey pump, donkey smokestack, etc. A donkey act is a mistake. The donkey, traditional symbol of the Democratic Party, is also employed in naming slow-sailing ships or parts of them and is further associated, less complimentarily, with spotted bats, herbs that smell, a penguin that brays, a kingfisher that laughs, and a jack rabbit that flaunts his big ears. In human society, the donkey has its parallels in those arrogant fools who can be evaluated by the following quotation: "If an ass goes a-traveling, he'll not come home a horse."

Next in the procession is the jenny or jenny ass, somewhat smaller than the jackass. She is meek, rather shy, and dependable as a bearer of burdens as well as of little asses. Probably because of these qualities, her name is not taken in vain--except to designate a man who meddles in women's affairs. Similar to the use of donkey in compounding, her name is prefixed to the names of birds to indicate the feminine sex such as jenny howlet and jenny wren. Capitalized, as in Jenny or Jennie, her name is a popular one for human females. She has given her name to an airplane, a spinning jenny, a traveling crane, a small derrick, a scaffold, and other business and industrial items. In general folks respect her maternal and useful role and thus refrain from casting aspersions at her.

The last in the series is the mule, a name derived from the Latin <u>mulus</u>, <u>mula</u>, male and female. He is a hybrid with no hope of posterity, born of an ass and a horse. His parents are most commonly the jackass and the female horse, but he may also be the offspring of a stallion and the jenny ass. As such he is known as a hinny, which both neighs and whinnies. The mule has a large head, long ears, small hoofs. About the same size as the horse, he has shorter and stubbier hair in the mane and on the tail. He is known for endurance and steadiness as well as excellence of work--except when balky. Although he is half-brother to the horse, that does not mean that his mule sense is only half horse sense.

The mule is extremely popular in folklore. His name is borne by such diverse items as a sexually impotent man, plane handler, jack rabbit, spinning frame, mixed coin design, small tractor, blanket chest, and low-grade liquor. The mule has inherited chiefly the qualities of the ass: he is balky, braying, contrary, headstrong, kicking, obstinate, stout, strong, stubborn, and tough. A blue mule is nice, a humped-back mule is crazy, and a mule skinner swears.

Some of the superstitions about the mule may be of help to you. For instance, if you kiss a mule's nose you won't have scarlet fever; you can know when lightning will strike by watching a mule's behavior; you can get your wishes if you tag gray mules; you can have prosperity, money and a lover if you count a hundred gray mules and tag them properly; and you can secure much cash if--when you see a white mule--you kiss your right hand and then stamp it on the left hand. But beware, beware, of picking up a mule's lost shoe, and never dare to kill a mule--bad luck awaits just around the corner.

Since asininity is highly unpredictable in scope and quality, you should be warned: "If an ass kicks you, never tell it."

### Derivative Names

ass: dolt, blockhead, stupid person

# Ass

ass: weight in Sweden, U.S.A., and Britain

ass: journalist's compositor

asininity: quality of being stupid and foolish

asses' bridge: fifth proposition in the first book of Euclid--a source of great difficulty for beginners

burro: donkey or ass, especially small one used as pack animal

burro: any of several species of grunts, fish; a species of plants and shrubs of genus Cappario

donk: short for donkey; whiskey, especially raw, homemade corn whiskey

donkey: same as ass

donkey: stubborn, silly, or stupid person, an ass

donkey: section man on railroad

donkey: support for paper, etc. in bathtub

donkey: symbol of Democratic Party

donkey: workbench on which machine cuts veneers

donkey act: blunder or mistake

donkeyback: on a donkey

donkey boiler (also donkey): secondary boiler

donkey boy: driver of donkeys

donkey cart: pony cart

donkey crosshead: crosshead driven by crank

donkey doctor: mechanic keeping donkey engine in repair

donkey engine: (also donkey): small steam engine

donkeyish: like a donkey

donkeyism: asininity

donkeyman: operator of donkey engine

donkey oats: common sorrel

donkey party: game involving blindfolded players

donkey pump (also donkey): auxiliary pump

donkey puncher: operator of donkey engine

donkey sled: foundation frame or support for donkey engine

donkey stack: auxiliary smokestack

donkey's breakfast: straw mattress

donkey's-eye: sea bean

donkeywork: plodding, routine work

jackass: male ass, donkey

jackass: blockhead, dunce, dolt, fool, stupid person

jackass: to ride a jackass

jackass: hawse bag (nautical)

jackass bark (also brig): sailing vessel with rig in usual order

jackass bat: large, spotted bat in southwestern U.S.A.

jackass clover: fur clover; rank-scented herb

jackass copal: Zanzibar copal, a resin of various colors used in veneering, etc.

jackass deer: kob antelope; mule deer

jackassery: acts of stupidity

jackass fish: morwong in Australia, New Zealand, and Tasmania

jackass frigate: slow-sailing vessel

jackass hare: jack rabbit

jackassification: making an ass of someone

jackass kingfisher: laughing jackass

jackassness: quality of being an ass, asininity

jackass penguin: penguin of South America and South Africa, whose notes suggest braying of jackass

jackass rig: any rig, usually a minor one (nautical)

Ass

jackass rigged: rigged as such

jenny: female ass

jenny: prefixed name to denote female, as jenny ass, jenny howlet, jenny wren, etc.

jenny: short for spinning jenny

Jenny (also Jennie): female name; nickname for Jane

Jenny: airplane used in training

jenny: traveling or locomotive crane

jenny: steam-blasting machine used to clean grease from surfaces

jenny: a man who busies himself with women's affairs, a "betty"

jenny ass: female ass

jenny cutthroat: the whitethroat (British)

jenny howlet: female owl

jenny scaffold: one that may be taken apart after use

Jenny spinner: labeled artificial fly

jenny winch: small derrick

Jenny wood: hard and strong wood from timber tree along Amazon River; also name of tree

jenny wren: female wren

long jenny and short jenny: terms designating sockets in billiards (British)

spinning jenny: textile machine

mule: stubborn or cranky person

mule: hybrid in biology, usually sterile, as noted in crossing of canaries and other birds

mule: spinning machine for simultaneous drawing and twisting of cotton, wool, etc. into yarn, thread, and for winding into cops

mule: chilblain

mule: sharp-sterned variety of coble (boat) off northeast England mule: day hand in composing room

mule: hybrid coin that is a mixture of designs from other coins

mule: minor who procures or sells narcotics

mule: plane handler on aircraft carrier

mule: railroad brakeman

mule: sexually impotent man

mule: to shoe one's mule, to embezzle

mule: ladies' backless slipper

mule: small tractor or electric engine used to pull vessels along canal

mule: translation of literary work, a pony

mule: bootleg whiskey

mule armadillo: South American type of armadillo

muleback: back of mule

mule chair: cacolet (two-seated chair mounted below hump of riding animal)

mule chest: blanket chest

mule deer: long-eared deer of western U.S.A., larger than Virginia deer

mule-ears: plant of genus Wyethia

mule fat: California herb

mule foot: box tortoise; also having solid hoof like mule's or mule-footed

mule frame: spinning frame

mule-jenny: female mule

mule-killer: any of several animals supposed to kill livestock, such as scorpion, walking-stick insect, mantis, wheel bug, etc.

mule mark: striped mark like that on mule

mule pulley: adjustable guide pulley for belt

# Ass

mule rabbit: jack rabbit

mule skinner: mule driver

muleteer (also mule skinner, muleman): driver of mules

mule twist: cotton or other yarn spun on a mule

mulewort: fern of genus <u>Hermionitis</u>

mulish: stubborn or obstinate

mulishness: quality of being mulish

Brown's Mule: brand of chewing tobacco

white mule: diluted or flavored grain alcohol used as liquor; cheap or bootleg whiskey (probably from the "kick" of the drink)

## Proverbs and Proverbial Phrases

An ass in a lion's den. (Aesop)

To make an ass of oneself.

To ass about: to fool about.

To have ass ears: to have ears of a fool.

Every ass loves to hear himself bray.

There is many an ass with two legs.

The ass knows well in whose face he brays.

Well! Honey is not for the ass's mouth: persuasion will not convince fools.

The ass waggeth his ears: he who talks wisely but has little learning.

A living ass is better than a dead doctor.

An ass is not called to court but that he bears sacks.

The ass's hide is used to the stick.

He that makes himself an ass must expect to be rode.

When an ass climbs a ladder, we may find wisdom in women.

An ass loaded with gold climbs to the top of the castle.

An ass laden with gold overtakes everything: a rich fool is thought to be wise.

The ass loaded with gold still eats thistles.

It would starve to death like the ass between two bundles of hay. Cf. I am like Buridan's ass between two piles of hay.

If an ass goes a-traveling, he'll not come home a horse.

When an ass kicks you, never tell it.

Laughs like a jackass.

Makes more noise than a jackass in a tin stable.

Stubborn as a jackass.

From jackass to jackass: morning to night, from laughing jackass that utters his laugh at daybreak and nightfall.

Donkey's years: very long time, probably alluding to long ears of the donkey or ass.

Better a lame donkey than no horse.

Mule carrying corn escapes while one carrying gold is robbed. Motif-Index, L453.

Blaze-face mule is always a fool.

A mule's gallop is soon over.

He who wants a mule without fault must walk on foot.

He reminds me of the south end of a north-bound mule.

White mules never die; they turn into Baptist preachers. Brown Collection, VII, 7149. Cf. Gray mules never die; they turn into Baptist preachers.

Balky as a mule.

Brays like a mule.

Cantankerous as a mule.

Contrary as a mule.

Crazy as a hump-backed mule.

Headstrong as mules.

Ass

Kicks like a mule (also Kentucky mule).

Looks as nice as a blue mule.

More than one mule in that stable (unfaithful wife or girl friend).

Obstinate as a mule.

Ornery as a mule.

Stout (strong) as a mule.

Stubborn as a bob-tailed mule.

Swears like a mule skinner.

Sweat like a mule.

Tough as a mule (also mule's hide).

## Superstitions and Motifs

From Brown Collection

If a mule can roll all the way over, it proves that he is strong. VII, 7669.

If you kiss a mule on the nose, you will never have scarlet fever. VI, 2091.

Warts: Use feather of white turkey to rub grease, taken from left side of buggy drawn by a gray mule, for three days until half past three o'clock and wart will disappear. VI, 2569.

A horse or mule draws lightning. VII, 7009.

The first person you shake hands with after you have counted one hundred white horses and mules will be the one you marry. VI, 4476.

Wish on a mule. VII, 7143. When you see a gray mule, make a wish, wet your thumb, and stamp your hand. VII, 7144. A wish will be granted if, when you see a gray mule, a wish is made, and the mule is tagged. VII, 7145.

Kiss your right hand, "stamp" it twice on your left hand when you see a white mule, and you will find money. VI, 3421. When a person sees one hundred gray mules and tags them on his left side, he will find money after. VI, 3422.

Count all the gray mules that you see, and when you have reached a hundred good luck will come to you. VII, 7146.

If you find a mule's shoe, pass it by, because it is the sign of bad luck. VII, 7147.

It is bad luck to kill a mule. VII, 7148.

From Motif-Index

Ass's behavior predicts the weather. B141.3.

Vampire has ass's ears. E251.4.2.

Ass that carries divine image thinks people bow before him. J953.4.

Laughing ass that lost part of his upper lip laughed at the horse that lost his tail. J1169.5.

Ass thought to be a devil. J1785.3.

Ass jealous of horse until he learns better. L452.

Ass jealous of horse, but later sees horse working in a mill. L452.1.

Ass jealous of war-horse until he sees him wounded. L452.2.

Lions despise what ass admires. V149.1.

## Out-Foxing Reynard

A fox went out in a hungry plight
And he begged of the moon to give him light,
For he'd many miles to go that night
Before he reached his den-O.
-- The Gray Goose

For thousands of years and in numerous lands, the fox has been a perennial source of amazement and frustration. His career as a predator is depicted in games, rhymes, songs, proverbs, tales, sermons, sports, and other aspects of the artistic and social interests of mankind. With unabashed piety and clever fraudulence he has convinced many a victim that it was for his advancement to be stripped of his feathers and eaten. For lack of superior opposition he has played havoc in more than one chicken roost. If, however, you succeed in diverting him from his prey, he will always plead sour grapes. Dismiss the guard, and he'll come again with the nightfall.

Some decades ago the fox was classified as any of the small, flesh-eating animals of the family of dogs (Canis). Now he has been restricted to the genus Vulpes, which embraces the following types: (1) the blue fox, an arctic inhabitant whose fur has a bluish cast; (2) the cross fox, whose spine and shoulders are marked with a dark cross; (3) the silver or black fox, whose black fur is banded or tipped with white hairs; and (4) the red fox, the European and American species, whose fur is reddish-brown and whose tail is very bushy.

The red fox, best known to most English-speaking people, is recognized as one of man's worst enemies, especially as a destroyer of flocks. With all sorts of diabolical gimmicks, he shams death, he comes as a scholar in disguise and flaunts his learning, he disguises himself with a sheepskin, he licks the lamb to show his friendship. If he loses his own tail, he induces others to whack off theirs. If the goose gets away, he'll accuse him of larceny, bring him into court, and have himself elected foreman of the jury. Of one thing we can always be sure--"When the fox turns preacher, the geese had better not go to night meetings."

The folks regard Reynard as crafty, cunning, sly, spry, and wise. He may grow gray, but he tarries not in his pursuit of poultry and mutton. He plies his trade in field and forest, in chicken coops and barnyards, ranging far and wide from his burrow. He is the epitome of egotism, patience, malice, subtlety, piety and penitence, quick-wittedness, thievery, and gnawing hunger.

Because of his widespread appearance and devilish reputation throughout the world, his name is used in numerous ways. It is associated with plants, herbs, or trees, such as foxbane, foxchop, fox-glove, foxgrape, and foxtail lily. It is a part of the names of animals, such as foxbat, foxfish or fox shark, fox goose, fox snake, fox sparrow, fox terrier, and fox wolf. A fox is a fur, an artificial sore, a sword, an Algonquian Indian, a demon or goblin, and a crafty person. To fox means to discolor with spots, to fool or deceive or outwit, to repair the upper parts of shoes, and to become exceedingly drunk (perhaps derived from the excessive, gnawing hunger of the fox).

Well! Well! This legendary son of a bitch! What can you do about his treachery toward the innocent, the helpless, the unsuspecting, the foolish, and the gullible? Sermonize all you will concerning his quick-wittedness and depravity, the fox retains his foxiness. He aches with hunger and he will continue to nab your chickens, geese, and sheep.

One obvious way out of your difficulties is "to catch a fox," that is, to drink yourself into oblivion and pay the fox no mind. Or, according to one superstition, you may let him retire as a broken penitent to a monastery that will give him a free meal-ticket; you may donate him to a zoo; you may castrate him or you may provide the necessary pills for his mate. Thus you may eliminate or cripple just two of the thousands of red and gray foxes, all of which are well trained to be foxy from the days of their youth.

Fox 53

With the desperate youngsters coming along, you may have to resort to religious gimmicks--you may damn them and ban them or excommunicate them. Shucks! You will still have your foxes. The best procedure is offered by the adage: "Let every man skin his own foxes."

In the first place, never be fainthearted. Police your premises adequately and place safeguards around your sheepcotes and poultry houses. Continue your use of steel traps, shotguns, and fox hounds. Get on the ball and install hidden contraptions of the year 2000--radar clocks that detect prowlers and stop them in their tracks, nuclear bombs planted along all paths and lanes, clawprinting to identify the types of predators, breathalizers to establish the percentage of alcohol in tipsy foxes, computers that visualize their movements from trees toward chicken domiciles, and a staff of foxy psychologists to coordinate known techniques and to institute better ones. Be prepared to reduce your sleeping hours and increase your vigil. If you expect a food product, forget it--fox meat does not make good sandwiches or fox-burgers. You may, however, be rewarded by an undamaged fur and a happy wife. Be patient--subtle--ingenious! Reynard does respect superiority.

### Derivative Names

fox: fur; sly and crafty person; symbol of sagacity in heraldry; demon or goblin; Indian of Algonquian tribe, formerly of Wisconsin; rope-yarn twisted and tarred for sizings, mats, etc.; small rope made by hand of two or more rope-yarns; artificial sore (British); sword

fox: to discolor with stains, spots, etc.; to intoxicate; to repair shoes; to fool or outwit, to trick by sly and crafty act, to cheat and rob; to become sour during fermentation (beer)

foxbane: European herb, wolfsbane

fox bat: flying fox; fruit bat

foxberry (fox plum): bearberry; mountain cranberry; cowberry

fox bolt: anchor bolt

fox-chase: fox hunt

foxchop: fig marigold

fox docken: common foxglove

fox dog: hound dog or fox hound with keen sense of smell, trained to hunt foxes

fox earth: burrow of a fox

foxed: badly discolored, as a fabric

foxed (fox-drunk): intoxicated or tipsy. Cf. Catch a fox: to become very drunk

foxer: one who repairs shoes

foxery: fox-like cunning

fox farm: place where foxes are bred for commercial use

foxfeet: fir club moss

foxfire (fox light): Ignis fatuus, phosphorescent light from foxed or rotten wood such as foxwood, given below

foxfish: European dragonet, fox-shark

foxfurred: trimmed with fox fur

fox geranium: herb Robert

foxglove (fox-and-leaves): plant with tall stalks, having many bell-shaped flowers, genus Digitalis, symbol of insincerity; a birthday on August 31

fox goose: Egyptian goose

foxgrape: any of several species of American grapes, especially northern foxgrape

foxhole: protective hole in ground for soldier

foxily: slyly or craftily

foxiness: slyness or craftiness

fox key: cotter secured by fox wedge, as given below

fox lathe: lathe used in turning brass

fox mark: brownish spot caused by foxing

fox moth: grayish-brown European moth

Fox

fox paw: faux pas

fox poison: spurge laurel

fox rose: Scotch rose

fox-shark: thresher shark or sea-fox or foxfish

fox skin: cap made of fox skin

fox snake: rodent-eating snake

fox sparrow: large American sparrow

fox squirrel: arboreal squirrel

fox-tail: tail of fox; mustache; grass with brushlike spikes of flowers resembling a fox's tail

foxtail barley: squirrel-tail

foxtail grass: any of several grasses or ground pines; the last cinder in the refining of metal

foxtail lily: plant of genus <u>Eremurus</u>

foxtail millet: coarse grass used as grain

foxtail pine: low pine with dense head of foliage

foxtail saw: dovetail saw

fox terrier: small, active dog of breed once trained to hunt foxes

fox tongue: talisman that provides nervous man with courage

fox trot (fox walk): dance with short, quick steps; music for it; pace of horse between walk and trot

fox wedge: wedge used to open end of bolt, cotter, etc.

fox wedging (foxtail wedging): process of fastening with fox wedges

fox wolf: South American wild dog

foxwood: decayed, foxed, phosphorescent wood or foxfire

foxy: like a fox, crafty; discolored; strong-smelling

foxy red: reddish hair as on certain Europeans

fox and geese: board game using symbols of fox and goose as opposing markers

## Proverbs and Proverbial Phrases

Crafty (cunning, dumb, gray, sly, smart, wise) as a fox.

Light on the foot as the fox.

Sly as a fox when he is going to rob a hen roost.

Slyer than a fox.

Catch a fox: to become very drunk.

He does not know a fox from a fern-bush.

The fox preys farthest from home.

He that hath a fox for a mate hath need of a net at his girdle.

The fox smells his own stink first.

The fox may grow grey, but never good.

The sleeping fox catches no poultry.

It is an ill wind to see a fox lick a lamb.

It's easy finding the fox when you get sight of his tail. Cf. The tail is enough to betray the fox.

Like Aesop's fox, when he had lost his tail, he would have all his fellow foxes cut off theirs. -- Robert Burton, Anatomy of Melancholy.

Set a fox to keep one's geese: to entrust one's confidences and/or money to a sharper. Cf. He sets the fox to keep his geese.

When the fox preacheth, then beware your geese.

When the fox turns preacher, the geese had better not go to night meetings.

A fox should not be on a jury at a goose's trial.

An old fox need not be taught new tricks.

An old fox is hard to catch.

At length the fox turns monk.

The old fox is caught at last.

At length the fox is brought to the furrier.

Fox

When the fox failed to get the hanging grapes, he said that they were sour anyway. (Aesop) Cf. It is easy to belittle what you cannot get.

The fox's wiles will never enter the lion's head.

The fox fares best when he is banned (cursed).

Let every man skin his own foxes.

There is little to choose when the fox and the goat fall out.

### Superstitions and Motifs

Foxes go mad with the coming of the new moon.   Clark, 1356.

### From Brown Collection

If you have the hiccoughs, think of a fox with no tail.   VI, 1633.

Hunting: Foxes are easily trailed of a warm, foggy morning after a visit to the farmer's henhouse. VII, 7884. Fox trails are picked up around locust trees. VII, 7885. A good place to pick up a fox trail is around persimmon trees. VII, 7886. If a dog is running a fox, and the fox turns and barks at him, the dog will never catch him. VII, 7887. If a fox is killed in a drive, and his tongue hangs from the left side of his mouth, the one who killed the fox will kill one in the next drive.   VII, 7888.

A foxfire seen at night denotes cold.   VII, 6275.

### From Motif-Index

Fox about to be hanged asks to be allowed to see the geese. J864.2.

Fox in coffer was thought to be a devil.   J954.2.

Fox is disguised as a scholar.   K362.5.1.

When fox shams death, he catches a crow.   K827.4.

Fox in sheepskin gains admission to the fold and kills sheep. K828.1.

Fox leads an ass to the lion's den, but he himself is eaten. K1632.

Fox confesses to the cock and then eats him.   K2027.

### Playing Possum

> De possum am a cunning thing,
> He trabbles in de dark.
> Nuthin' 't all disturbs his mind
> Twel he hear ole Ranger bark.
> -- Brown Collection, III, 208.

One of the lesser known animals is the opposum or possum, a name of probable Algonquian origin and of somewhat limited usage in the Americas and Down Under. The people of the British Isles and Europe are aware of it largely by hearsay, and even where it is known the folklore about it is minor as compared with the more popular animals. However one salient characteristic of this creature is immortalized in a folk expression, commonly used to describe a type of behavior in tight places.

The possum (Didelphus marsupialis) is related to kangaroos, wombats, bandicoots, and others that carry and feed their young in pouches. This marsupial roams the land from the central part of the United States to the northern section of South America and is found also in Australia and Papua.

The American possum is usually grayish, chiefly nocturnal, and an omnivore, living on birds, fish, insects and fruits. Its overall length is almost two and one-half feet and its body is covered by a coarse and heavy fur. Its nose, ears, and tail are long, the tail being scaly and nearly naked. Generally the species is prolific, with six to sixteen in a litter, carried by the mother in her pouch. Though its flesh is never seen in a supermarket, some folks do relish its greasy, yellowish meat when served with baked sweet potatoes and corn bread. Its fur, properly treated and dyed, adorns a host of ladies throughout the world.

The names associated with this animal are highly derogatory. A possum is a pretender, a paltry fellow, a dupe or a simpleton;

Possum

and a possum-guts, in Australia, is a very low specimen of humanity. Poor folks may drink possum toddy, made from persimmons, or try to exist on possum fat and hominy.

The expression "to play possum," meaning to sham illness, ignorance or inconvenience, plays tribute to the possum's habit of feigning death when caught or hemmed in. Since this animal dares not fight back at an overpowering opponent, he hopes to escape the consequences by playing dead. Many a person has used a similar technique to get around harsh reality. Occasionally the trick has worked to his advantage, but sometimes his head has been lopped off at once without ceremony.

### Derivative Names

opossum mouse: any of several Australian phalangers resembling opossums; a type of flying mouse

opossum-rat: South American marsupial

opossum shrimp: shrimp-like crustacean, the female of which carries her eggs in a pouch behind her legs

opossum wood (opossum tree or possum wood): the silver bell and the name of the close-grained, hard, pinish wood as well as the name of the Australian timber tree; the light wood of the sandbox tree; the persimmon tree

possum: to feign death, pretend; to hunt possums; dissembler or paltry fellow; dupe or simpleton as used in Australia

possum: to ring-in or put ring in or around something as done in Australia

possum belly: bag under rear end of wagon for supplies, etc.

possum berry (grape or haw): chicken grape; shrub with hairy leaves and red berries; southern U.S.A. shrub with small white flowers

possum fat and hominy: a food once popular among Indians and Negroes

possum-guts: derogatory epithet in Australia

possum hunt (hunting): men and dogs in pursuit of possums

possum toddy: sort of beer made from persimmons

## Proverbs and Proverbial Phrases

Come to possum over (to deceive).

Gray as an opossum.

Grayer than a possum's hair.

Grins like a possum (also, a baked possum).

Happy as a possum up a 'simmon (persimmon) tree.

Having your tail in a split stick (carrying a possum on back).

Like a possum up a gum-tree (happy and contented).

Play like a possum.

## Superstitions and Motifs

### From Brown Collection

If a possum (terrapin) bites one, he will not turn "aloose" till it thunders. VII, 7013.

In country districts it is believed that the male possum copulates with the female through the nostrils, and that the birth of the young is also through the same openings. VII, 7893.

Talk of killing a possum and you'll die. VII, 7892.

If you have cold shivers down your back, you may be sure a possum has run across the place where your grave is to be. VII, 5238.

Hunt the possum in the dark of the moon; he can't see you. VII, 7889. Cf. If a dog trees up a little tree, it will be a big possum; but if up a big tree, a feisty possum. VII, 7891.

Opossums rove between sunset and ten o'clock at night. VII, 7890. Cf. Big possums walk late at night. Clark, 1357.

A sign of a cold winter is the thickening of the fur on the possum's back. VII, 6077.

### From Motif-Index

Deer, opossum, and snake each render indispensable aid to man. J461.4.

Marriage to person in opossum form. B641.8.

Possum

Why opossum has bare tail. A2317.12.

Why opossum has large mouth. A2341.2.1.

Why opossum plays dead when caught. A2466.1.

## The Hawk as Sharper

If you have ever spent much time near barnyards and chicken coops, then you have seen the savage attacks made by hawks on defenseless chickens unable to fight back or escape to an enclosure. You may recollect how a hawk, sometimes in company with a few others of his breed, sailed across an adjoining field, darted in crisscross manner from tree to tree, located the reservations for poultry, and then with lightning speed swooped upon his prey. He clinched his sharp talons around the squirming body of a baby chick or a half-grown one and hustled off to dispose of his dangling loot.

The mother hen spread her wings in wrath, cackled in three octaves of excitement, and scurried here and there in desperation. Her cries of anguish aroused the neighborhood. All the barnyard residents took up the hue and the agony: they hissed and cackled, they barked, they grunted, they bawled, they neighed--a notice to heaven and earth that murder had been committed. But soon they put away their grief and resumed their daily routines despite the lurking danger, for surely the hunger of the hawk would drive him back, as it had also driven the fox, to gorge himself upon the young and the helpless. You might have been inspired to frighten away the voracious intruder by hanging dead hawks on posts, barns, and chimneys, by burning chicken feathers, or by erecting numerous scarecrows. No use--the enemy will come again in the fullness of his greed.

This bird of prey, rather indefinite in classification, belongs to the genus Accipitridae, which does not include vultures and eagles. In a more restricted sense, it also excludes buzzards, falcons, harriers, caracaras, and kites. It does, however, include sparrow hawks, pigeon hawks, chicken hawks (the sharp-shinned and Cooper's hawks), and the goshawks, the largest breed.

In relating the hawk to the falcon (genus Falconidae) in liter-

# Hawk

ature and folklore, it is helpful to remember that falconry or hawking was a popular sport among the gentry of the Middle Ages. This pastime involved the breeding and training of the hawks of the lure (the game falconets and tercelets or tercels), which were hoodwinked, belled, and chained to the hunter's wrist or fist until released in the fields to pounce upon other birds and small animals. The falconer or hawker thus had at his command the combined power of a shotgun and a bird dog, to say nothing about the beauty of the falcon as typified by the male peregrine falcon, the female falcon-gentle, or the noble hawk of the lure.

Hawks in general are arboreal and diurnal; they are omnivorous, feeding upon birds such as pigeons and chickens, mice, rats, reptiles, insects, fruits, cereals, and so forth--in some ways they are useful to the economy. The chicken hawks that Americans know best have long legs, short rounded wings, hooked or curved-down bills, large, strong, curved claws, and long tails. They are characterized by keenness, quickness, ferocity, rapacity, and glamorous movements.

The use of the word hawk, alone or compounded, is extensive. As a verb it means to serve as a decoy, to annoy or embarrass, to hunt as in falconry, to peddle goods (usually without a permit), to gossip or spread rumors, and to swoop like a hawk. As a noun it is a mortar board with two handles, a bailiff or constable, a grasping person, and a swindler. The word is incorporated in the names of plants such as hawkbit, hawk's-eye, hawk's-feet, and hawkweed. As related to animals and insects, it includes the following: hawk cuckoo, hawk eagle, hawk fly, hawk moth, hawk parrot, hawks-bill turtle, and hawk swallow. Hawking is also a dyeing process; hawked means spotted; and hawkeys are spots or streaks. Then there are the hawker's gag (displaying shoe laces to avoid the charge of begging), the hawk nose, the hawkshaw (detective), and the war hawk.

The most impressive quality of the hawk is his sharpness. He is canny and watchful, a swindler of the first order. He hawks and peddles his contraband on the sly. He is a kibitzer and sharper, a thieving trickster who will jump on your last undersized chicken if you are not steady in guarding it. Let the British cry of "Ware! Hawk" be your watchword with this keen and hungry predator.

## Derivative Names

hawk: bailiff, constable

hawk: grasping person; a swindler

hawk: small board or metal sheet, with two handles, for molding mortar

hawk: to act as decoy

hawk: to annoy, tease, or embarrass

hawk: to clear one's throat, to spit with difficulty

hawk: to hunt, as in falconry or hawking

hawk: to peddle goods; to gossip or spread rumors

hawk: to swoop

hawk at: to fly in search of prey

hawk bell: small, spherical bell attached to hawk's leg

hawk-billed: shaped like a hawk's beak

hawkbit: fall dandelion

hawk call: that of hawk or bailiff

hawk cuckoo: Asiatic cuckoo resembling hawk

hawk eagle: bird between hawk and eagle

hawked: crooked like beak of hawk; spotted

hawker: falconer; one who sells hawks; peddler; sharper at cards

hawker's gag: boot-laces carried as excuse for begging

hawkery: place where hawks are kept

hawk-eyed (also hawk-eye): having sharp eyes and keen vision

hawkey (also hawkie): dark cow with white face, any cow

Hawk

hawkeys: white spots or streaks

hawk fly: robber fly

hawking: sport of falconry; dyeing process

hawkish (also hawky): being like a hawk

hawk moth: large moth with long body and narrow wings; hummingbird

hawk nose: nose curved like hawk's beak

hawk of the lure: noble falcon

hawk of the fist: ignoble falcon (reluctant to take off from fist)

hawk owl: north European, Asiatic, and American bird resembling hawk

hawks: an advantage

hawk's-beard: plant of the chicory family

hawks-bill turtle (also hawk's-bill or hawkbill, hawk's-bill tortoise): sea turtle with mouth shaped like a hawk's beak and whose horny plates furnish tortoise shells

hawk's-eye (also hawk-eye): blue variety of tigereye; golden plover

hawk's-feet: garden columbine

hawkshaw: detective

hawk swallow: common European swift

hawkweed: plant of chicory family; a symbol of quick-sightedness

war hawk: keen and vigorous fighter; an advocate of super-war attack

### Proverbs and Proverbial Phrases

Eyes like a hawk's.

Eyes as bright as a hawk's.

Fierce as a welk hawk.

Game as a hawk.

Hungry as hawks.

Keen as a hawk.

Like being between hawk and buzzard: perplexed and undecided.

Quick as a hawk.

Sails like a hawk.

Sharp as a hawk.

Sharp as a hawk's claws.

Took to her from the word go, like a hawk does to a chicken.

Wild as a hawk.

Look at one another as wild as hawks.

Like a blue-tailed hawk watching a chicken.

Hawk and pigeon: villain and victim.

Hawk! Beware: a warning when bailiff or constable is nearby.

Hawk one's brawn: to show strength instead of brains.

Hawk it: to be a prostitute on the streets.

Hawk one's meat: to peddle or display one's charms.

Hawk one's mutton: to be a prostitute.

He jumped on it like a hawk on a chicken.

He's a hawk of the right nest: a good falcon.

Know a hawk from a handsaw (Hamlet, II, ii, 405): to be discerning (handsaw not clear but perhaps corruption of hernshaw, a heron).

Hawks (crows) will not peck out hawks' (crows') eyes.

## Superstitions and Motifs

Gold hawk: sun deity.

Hawk: bird of clouds, storms, and sun.

Hawk on a lion in Egyptian heraldry represents the might and power of the sun.

Buzzard is hatched by a hawk and is ejected for fouling its nest.

Hawk

In "Hawk and Nightingale," by Aesop, the nightingale was caught by a hungry hawk and, begging to be let go, pleaded his tininess. The hawk replied that it was better to have a little one (in his claws) than a big one not caught. Cf. A bird in the hand is better than two in the bush.

In Buriat myths, a hawk stole the secret of firemaking from the porcupine that invented it; later the hawks told the secret to the gods, who in turn gave it to man. Cf. the exploit of Prometheus, who stole fire from the gods in heaven and gave it to man.

From Brown Collection

If you make a smoke before sunrise on the first day of May, it is a sure fact that the hawks will get all your chickens. VII, 7475.

To drive hawks away, hang one you have killed in a tree or on a pole. VII, 7476.

Burn chicken feathers to keep hawks away. VII, 7477.

Put a cabbage head up the chimney to keep hawks away. VII, 7478.

Other methods of keeping hawks away from chickens: string egg shells and hang in chimney; put flint rocks in fireplace; place rock on gate post; put white flint in the spring; place horseshoes in fire; put steel in fire; hang bottle of salt on a pole; hang scarecrow on a tree or post; put dead crow or hawk on the barn. VII, 7479ff.

To see a white hawk flying near the ground in winter is the sign of foul weather. VII, 6195.

From Motif-Index

Hawk persuades doves to elect him their king. K815.8.

Hawk flies away with geese on a line. X1267.1.

## A Bird That Nobody Knows

In the late nineteenth century some folks had an idea--North America and Down Under needed one more bird, to wit, the starling (*Sturnus vulgarus* of the family *Sturnidae*), a sort of blackbird well-known and admired in northern Europe and parts of Asia. This omnivore, about the size of the thrush, has in summer an iridescent plumage that gleams with purple, green, and steel-blue; during most of the year its feathers are dark brown, like the fur of a beaver. However, the importers of this lovely bird did not bring along any guidelines to control it. Today, with all our enlightenment, someone should be able to institute a program for its discipline.

The starling, probably because of its comparatively recent arrival, is almost non-existent in the proverbial and superstitious lore of the British and American people, and there are only a few descriptive adaptations of its name to man and his world. The word *starling* is a beaver and a beaver-brown color; it is the name of piles as well as a structure of piles erected to protect and support the piers of a bridge; it is a marked man, such as a British policeman. It appears in compounded forms such as starling stone, a petrified fossil whose colors resemble those of the starling, and starling's-egg green, a court color. And perhaps suggested by the promiscuous habits of starlings, the British speak rather contemptuously of Brother Starling, a man who shares another person's mistress.

These birds, according to the thrifty farmer and meticulous urbanite, are entirely too sociable. Oh, yes, they do eat insects, but their bad manners lead them into the grain-producing areas cultivated for hungry people. Once they have crammed their stomachs from dawn to dusk, off they fly in swirling black clouds, not only to trees but to warm barns and other man-made structures. They

have become more and more judicious about their roosting places--
they like especially tall courthouses with wide ledges of granite and
marble. Myriads of noisy starlings squat like self-appointed decorators on the best of Greek and Roman architecture--to chatter and
chatter until the sunrise. And after another day of foraging they
come again in foreboding clouds to resume their nightly hubbub.

Farmers, businessmen, and government officials are nonplussed by this bird of gorgeous plumage. To kill or not to kill?
To sterilize or not to sterilize the male? To issue or not to issue
contraceptive pills to the females? To be for or to be against the
sociable starling? Nobody has the answer. No use for the city
fathers to pass a law decreeing that no starling shall be allowed to
rest in comfort on the courthouse after dusk.

Still, there are a number of measures to try. Tear down
those buildings with broad ledges for shelter and erect structures
without cozy roosts for unwanted company. Flood all buildings with
tear gas. Install automatic guns to spray the exteriors of tall buildings from dusk until curfew. If these methods fail, call the whole
thing quits and move to a bomb shelter. And therein hold a caucus
to select a topnotch candidate for the Ph.D. in ornithology to complete and publish a thesis, within the next five years, on the subject "The Promiscuity of Starlings."

To indicate the frustration and despair of the whole situation,
the following quotation from Drew Pearson's Washington column of
March 27, 1966 is indeed appropriate.

> President Johnson has been able to pass a medicare
> bill, an anti-poverty bill, a massive program for Appalachia and education, but he has been a flat failure
> when it comes to the lowly starling. He has been able
> to sweet-talk or scare Congress into passing the biggest
> legislative program in history, but he hasn't been able
> to either sweet-talk or scare the starling away from
> government buildings.
>
> The Johnson administration has tried all sorts of devices. At one time it scared birds away by playing
> recordings of distress calls by other birds. However,
> the starlings soon got used to these calls and ignored
> them. Then the government changed the distress call,
> making it louder and shriller. This worked for a while,
> but the starlings got accustomed to the new call. The

administration tried another recording. Again it worked for a while, again the birds became acclimated.

"Starlings and blackbirds annually cause millions of dollars of damage to agriculture," John S. Gottschalk of the Interior Department's Wildlife Service told a House Appropriations Subcommittee. "We are still seeking more refined methods of dealing with this menace."

## Jaybird as Chatterbox

As springtime is being heralded in a thousand ways, the birds are flying back to our neighborhoods. Among the returnees is the jaybird (genus Garrulus glandarius). He is distantly related to the crows (Corvidae) and closely akin to the European and Canadian jays, but to most of us in eastern North America he is nothing but a plain jay or blue jay.

Smaller and more graceful than the crow, the jaybird has a handsome black-and-white crest, a colorful elongated tail, and wings with light-blue and grayish-white markings. Being an arboreal omnivore, he domineers over the wren, the sparrow, the cardinal, and any other birds that are smaller than he and beneath his dignity. His arrogant selfishness is set forth in the proverb "One cherry tree sufficeth not two jays." Moreover, he is restless and roving, noisy and chattering, harsh and loud, saucy and impertinent, pugnacious and confident of his ruling the roost. This bold invader destroys nests, eats the eggs of lesser birds, and frequently does away with their young. He seems to tell all competitors, including those of his own breed, "I dare you!"

The jay is properly classified by the ornithologists as Garrulus. This chatterbox is also deceptive and demonic. For instance, in the motifs of our oral literature, he is fond of borrowing the skins of cuckoos and peacocks to achieve his ends. Superstitious lore also portrays him as a dependable ally of the devil--on Fridays he is nowhere in sight because he is busily carrying twigs and grains of corn or sand to replenish the necessities of Hell.

Other folklore about this bird is incisive in its application to mankind. He is an inferior actor, an inexperienced person, a greenhorn, an easy victim for sharpers, a nag or scold, an unscrupulous windbag, and a coarse and loud woman. Like a country bumpkin, unacquainted with city customs, he jaywalks and violates other traffic regulations. He is also a jayhawker that fights ferociously from ambush--a characteristic of the Jayhawkers of Kansas, who carried on guerrilla actions during the Civil War. The only complimentary expression derived from the jay is jayhawk, in its meaning of an unusual or extraordinary person, prominent and influential.

The jaybird and his exploits are also recorded in a few of our popular songs, including the vulgar ones associated with the gossipy barbers of the late 19th century. The following selection is illustrative of the folks' humorous contempt for this chatterbox.

>             The Jaybird
> Jay bird died with the whoopingcough,
> Black bird died with the colic;
> 'Long came a toad-frog with his tail bobbed off
> And that broke up the frolic.
>
> He winked at me and I winked at him,
> I picked up a piece o' brickbat and hit him on the chin.
> He says, 'Oh, little man, don't do that again!'
> And that broke up the frolic.
>                                 -- Brown Collection, III, 201

### Derivative Names

blue jay:  road monkey

jay:  amateur or inferior actor; inexperienced person

jay:  country bumpkin, greenhorn; gullible and easy victim for sharpers; gawky and stupid person

jay:  gaudily dressed person

jay:  nag or scold; impertinent chatterbox; coarse and loud woman

jay:  wanton person; unscrupulous windbag

jayhawk:  to make predatory attacks

jayhawk:  unusual or extraordinary person

Jayhawker:  native of Kansas; plundering marauder; anti-slavery guerrilla during the Civil War

jayhawker:  a variety of ferocious hawks

Jaybird

jaypie: European jay

jayteal: European teal

jaywalk: to cross streets diagonally or in violation of traffic rules

jaywalker: one who jaywalks; one unacquainted with city ways

## Proverbs and Proverbial Phrases

Happy as a jaybird.

Naked as a jay (jaybird).

Naked as a picked jaybird.

Saucy as a jaybird.

To get along about as well as a jaybird with a "sparrer" hawk.

To flap a jay (to play or scalp one for a jay): to fool or swindle.

She slings her feet as spry as a jaybird in wild cherry time.

One cherry tree sufficeth not two jays.

## Superstitions and Motifs

### From Brown Collection

The unusual screeching of a jaybird is a sign of rain. VII, 6718

Jaybirds go to hell on Friday with a grain of corn. VII, 7252

You never see jaybirds on Friday because they are so busy carrying twigs to Hell. VII, 7253

Every Friday jaybirds carry a grain of sand to hell. VII, 7254. Cf. 7255

"Jaybirds as the Devil's Servants" (a tale). I, p. 633

### From Motif-Index

Jaybird borrows cuckoo's skin. A 2241.6

Jaybird in peacock's skin is unmasked. J951.2

## The Coon as Hand-Scratcher

For a coon's age--in fact, much longer--it has been a delightful sport in North America and southward to chase the raccoon, known to scientists as Procyon lotor. It was the Algonquians that first noted this animal and named him arakunem, literally "one that scratches with his hands," or "hand-scratcher." Later the Virginians called him arakun, further shortened to kun, then popularized to coon.

This mammal, an eater of flesh and fruits, is largely arboreal and nocturnal. His fur is coarse and varies from yellowish-brown to grayish-brown, with black-and-white markings. He has a black patch on each cheek and a masklike formation across his eyes. His tail is heavily bushed, with black-and-white circles or stripes. His disposition is amiable. Aside from the fun that he has given hunters, he has provided a fur that is quite comfortable on wintry days.

According to the folk, the coon steals, walks and dances, waddles along with a shuffle, climbs crouchingly upward, washes his face, and appears to have much cooniness or know-how. He is credited with being alert, sly, shrewd, and wise. For years the Australians have used his name to designate an aboriginal, and Americans have given his name, often derogatorily, to the Negro, who has traditionally enjoyed hunting coons with coon dogs. The term is compounded to describe animals or objects that have coonlike qualities, such as the following: coon bear (giant panda), coon-can (card game like rummy), coon cat (domesticated Angora cat), coon grape or raccoon grape (fox grape), coon oyster or raccoon oyster (small type eaten by coons), coon shouter (black-faced minstrel), coon song (once sung by southern Negro), coon-striped shrimp, raccoonberry (the May apple), raccoon perch (yellow perch).

Coon                                                                    75

The proverbial expressions, chiefly North American, are noteworthy in characterizing the coon and any person like him. For instance, a coon is safe and happy when he is up a tree, inside or outside. If he is a "gone coon," he is in serious or hopeless difficulty and may soon be "as dead as a skinned coon." He may be an extravagant coon, the black sheep of some family, that "goes the whole coon" as does the prodigal that "goes the whole hog." And this kind of fun and wastefulness may go on for "a coon's age," unless the hunters and sharpers put an end to the foolishness.

In reality, the coon is a fairly respectable animal, as evidenced in rhymes, songs, tales, and mythologies. The stories told by the American Indians present the coon as neither a dupe nor a fool, and seldom are the tables turned upon him as they are on the coyote and other predatory animals. Furthermore, the coon is not a creator or transformer as are most of the tricksters. Something of the same generous attitude is manifested in the old minstrel songs of the South, as illustrated by the following selection:

>             The Raccoon Has a Bushy Tail
>
> Raccoon got a bush tail,
> The possum's tail is bare;
> The rabbit got no tail at all,
> Just a little bunch of hair.
>
> Chorus:
>     Git along home, Cindy,
>     Git along home, Cindy,
>     Git along home, Cindy,
>     Ise bound to join the band.
>
> Possum up the 'simmon tree,
> Raccoon on the ground,
> Possum shake the 'simmons down,
> Raccoon pass 'em around.
>                     -- Brown Collection, III, 209

### Derivative Names

coon:   short for raccoon

coon:   to climb or creep crouchingly upward like a coon

coon:   to steal

coon: sly and shrewd man

coon: rustic, eccentric, and undignified person, often stupid and easily swayed; brutal person with little brains

coon: an American Negro, probably so called because of his expertness in hunting coons in the South; term frequently derogatory

coon: an Australian aboriginal

coon bear: giant panda

coon bug: black-and-white Australian bug

cooncan: a game of cards similar to rummy; term probably a corruption of conquian

coon cat: domesticated Angora cat, with long, fine, silky hair; cacomistle (See raccoon fox.)

coon dog (also cooner, coonhound): sporting or coon-hunting dog

coon grape (also raccoon grape): fox grape; woody vine with bluish fruit and foliage

cooniness: giving appearance of savviness and general know-how

coonjine: to walk, dance, or carry something with a sidling and waddling shuffle

coon oyster (also raccoon oyster): mangrove oyster, an undersized type eaten by coons

coonroot: bloodroot

coon shouter: black-faced minstrel

coon song: song once sung by southern Negro

coonskin: fur of coon, often made into overcoats, etc.

coon-striped shrimp: large, edible shrimp found off coast from California to Alaska

coontail: the hornwort

coony: showing astute and clever closeness; cagey and canny, sly or foxy

raccoonberry: fruit of May apple

raccoon dog: small, short-muzzled wild dog, native to Asia and

Coon

    having thick tail and raccoonlike rings about eyes

raccoon fox: cacomistle. Cf. coon cat

raccoon perch: yellow perch

### Proverbs and Proverbial Phrases

To be coon: to be wise and alert.

Coon a log: crawl on a log like a coon on all fours.

A gone coon: a person in serious and hopeless difficulty. Cf. I'm a gone coon. A gone gosling.

Coon's age: a very long time, since coon is notably long-lived.

There is a coon in every family.

It's as dead as a skinned coon.

To drop like a catamount on a coon.

To go the whole coon. Cf. To go the whole hog. The <u>hog</u> was an early American coin worth ten cents or six pence; and when won and completely spent at fairs, it was called going the whole hog.

Cross as a coon when it is cornered.

Happy as a coon in a hollow tree.

Safe as a coon up a hickory tree.

### Superstitions

If a coon hunting party hears an owl laugh as they are setting out for the night, they will go back home. But if it halloed "coon," they will have good luck. Brown Collection, VII, 7899.

Children are told that an old mother coon finds babies in the woods and takes them to people's houses. Brown Collection, VI, 2.

## That English Sparrow

In 1851 a little bird was brought to this country from England. Speculate as you will about the motives for importing this creature, we Americans have a steadily growing problem on our hands.

This small bird, known as the house sparrow (<u>Passer domesticus</u>) and commonly called the English sparrow, belongs to the family <u>Fringillidae</u>. Closely related to several weaver birds and to those of the finch family, it is also kindred to other sparrows classified as chipping, hedge, sage, song, savannah, tree, and so forth. Its body is predominantly striped with dark and light brown, its head has alternating marks of white and brown. A mere chirper, it lives by industriously gathering seeds, insects, worms, and the droppings of animals. And despite keen competition from larger and more aggressive birds, it thrives and multiplies.

Although the sparrow has been depicted in song as a symbol of God's love ("His eye is on the sparrow"), our countrymen rate this bird as a scratcher and fighter, lawless and lustful. Yet with all of this lack of affection, there are no recorded crisp expressions about the sparrow in American folklore. The known expressions are almost entirely British and generally as uncomplimentary as any that Americans might have coined. To illustrate the sparrow's sauciness, the British say, "As pert as a sparrow." To indicate his aggressive and fighting spirit, they have the proverb "Two sparrows on one ear of corn make an ill agreement." And to show his stealthy character, the folks Down Under have the phrase "To come in on a sparrow's ticket," that is, to gain illegal admission to an entertainment. Furthermore, in the list that follows, the British direct some pointed jabs at human beings, such as weedy persons, policemen out of favor, and pygmies with large mouths.

# English Sparrow

## Derivative Names

sparrow: mouse-gray

sparrow: active and self-reliant person

sparrow: small, undersized, weedy person (Australia)

sparrow: beer or beer money given to dustman; milkman's secret customer

sparrow bill: sparable (shoemaker's small headless nail)

sparrow catching: walking the streets in search of men

sparrow cop: policeman in disfavor with superiors and thus assigned to guard the grass

sparrow crow, at: at daybreak

sparrow dust: small gunshot

sparrow-grass (also sparragrass and sparry-grass): asparagus

sparrow hawk: small European hawk with short wings

sparrowish (also sparrowlike): like a sparrow

sparrow-mouthed: like a person with a large mouth

sparrow owl: pygmy or small owl

sparrow-starver: collector of dung from off the streets

sparrow-tail (also sparrow-tailed): swallow-tailed

sparrowy: frequented by sparrows or resembling sparrows

sparrowwort: South African heath or shrub

## Superstitions and Motifs

An infallible sign of the great white visitor (snow) is when sparrows swarm about the house. Brown Collection, VII, 7067

A sparrow intervenes in the elephant quarrel. Motif-Index, J2143.1

The sparrow is taught to sing by the lark. Motif-Index, A2271.2

The crow appropriates the sparrow's nest. Motif-Index, J684.2

Agile as a Squirrel

The gray squirrel (Sciurus carolinensis) is popular among all sorts of people on the North American continent. He has delighted millions of children and adults in the parks, at the zoos, in revolving cages by the wayside, and in their home areas. He has been the subject of rhymes and games, as illustrated at the end of this sketch. Ever since colonial times he has been the prey of hunters and marksmen, who enjoyed a pastime that also provided delicious food and comfortable raiment.

Squirrel hunting prepared many a man to be an expert rifleman and soldier. The rank and file of those who defeated the British army at King's Mountain, North Carolina, were skilled in trapping and killing wild animals. During the first World War there were a goodly number, like the famous Sergeant Alvin C. York of Tennessee, who having already learned to draw a bead on rabbits, turkeys, and squirrels had little to learn about sharpshooting from infantry officers.

The epithet squirrel tail was applied to the American Revolutionary Scout, who proudly bedecked himself with the squirrel's fur and tail. From that era to this the squirrel's tail, like the rabbit's foot, has been displayed as a talisman on bicycles and other vehicles to assure safety and good luck on the journey.

This squirrel of the folk belongs to the family Scuirridae, a group of tree-dwelling rodents varying in size from that of a mouse to an ordinary cat. The chief species are the gray, red, fox, and European squirrels, including numerous relatives such as the chipmunk and the flying phalanger of Australia. They are fairly prolific, having three or four in a litter during the spring. Adults have heavy gray, reddish, or brown coats; their tails are bushy; and their ears are tufted. Being omnivorous, they live on fruits, nuts, mice, insects, tender twigs, the eggs and young of birds. Oh,

Squirrel

yes, they also burrow in green lawns, they tear up attics, and they frequently get more than their share of the nuts.

Apart from their ravaging, they have much to their credit. In fact, our favorite, the gray squirrel, has an exemplary character. Despite the vagaries of weather and food supply, he is active, frisky, chipper, resourceful, and independent. On the ground or up a hickory or beech tree, he barks and snarls as he chips and grates the hardest nuts. He is the essence of curiosity, dignified gracefulness, thrift, flirtatious playfulness, nimbleness, surefootedness, and withal a shrewd timidity. With these superior qualities he has often outwitted his pursuer.

But man has tarnished the reputation of the squirrel in the use of his name to define such human situations as caching something stealthily, and weaving like a mad man from lane to lane while driving, or to describe a prostitute, a crackpot ("food for the squirrels"), a conformist that hates the company that he has to associate with, or a psychologist or psychiatrist that examines "nuts." In many respects man is squirrelly, that is, extremely odd and peculiar.

There is little disparagement in the compounding of squirrel with other words, such as squirrelfish, squirrel hake, squirrelmonkey, squirrel mouse, squirrel cup (hepatica), and squirrel grass.

As you might expect in view of the great popularity of the gray squirrel, a fairly sizable number of superstitions about him are in the records of the folk. Although he may be an omen of bad luck when he crosses your path, he may herald the weather and the proper time for planting crops. And the products of his body may be indispensable remedies for poor appetites, toothache, painful teething, and other ailments. Squirrel teeth, if placed under your pillow with the proper accompanying incantation, may reveal who your true love is to be.

## Derivative Names

squirrel:  fur of squirrel

squirrel: to hunt squirrels

squirrel: to cache something

squirrel: to weave in and out while driving a car; a reckless driver

squirrel: to climb to the top of a railroad car and set the brakes

squirrel: a harlot

squirrel: an Australian phalanger

squirrel: whiskey (rarely used today)

squirrel: psychologist or psychiatrist who examines "nuts"

squirrel: conformist in a group that he dislikes

squirrel: crazy person

squirrel, seam: body louse, a cootie

squirrels, food for the: stupid or crazy person; stupid job, task, or scheme

squirrel cage: display cage with inner portion that is rotated by squirrels

squirrel-corn: plant with cream-colored flowers, having roots with yellow, grainlike buds

squirrel cup: hepatica

squirrelfish: any of several brightly colored fish, reddish and having large eyes and rough scales

squirrel food: death camass, a plant poisonous to livestock

squirrel frog: small tree toad

squirrel grass: grass having bushy spikelets

squirrel hake: a fish

squirrel hawk: rough-tegged hawk

squirrelly: extremely odd and peculiar

squirrel-monkey: marmoset

squirrel mouse: dormouse

squirrel phalanger or opossum: Australian flying phalanger

Squirrel

squirrel plague: tularemia

squirrel rifle: inferior rifle

squirrel shrew: arboreal insectivore, having similarity to squirrel

squirrel's-foot fern: fall fern

squirrel tail: tail that is arched and vertical above anterior base

squirrel tail: American Revolutionary scout

squirrel-tail: squirreltail grass

## Proverbs and Proverbial Phrases

Chipper as a squirrel in the fall time.

Climbs like a squirrel.

Jerky as a squirrel.

Quick as a squirrel.

Roguish as a chip squirrel.

Squirrel's cracking a nut: a maxim denoting that one should pierce below the husk of the eternal.

Thrifty as a squirrel.

## Superstitions

In Buddhism the squirrel tail wards off carnal affections and spiritual foes.

Squirrels carrying acorns is a sign of hard winter. Brown Collection, VII, 6078. Cf. 6079-80.

Hunt squirrels before sunrise. Brown Collection, VII, 7902

To keep a baby from having serious trouble cutting teeth, rub its gums with the brains of a squirrel. Brown Collection, VI, 369

Squirrels bring good luck to the traveler. Brown Collection, VI, 3875. Cf. 3876-79 as omen of good luck and bad luck.

If a squirrel crosses your path, you will have bad luck. Brown Collection, VII, 8546. Cf. with rabbit.

Planting corn is effective when poplar leaves are as big as squirrel ears.  Brown Collection, VII, 8138

Squirrel stew is good for the sick.  Clark, 161

The fat of the gray squirrel is used for the toothache.  Brown Collection, VI, 2347

Catnip tea with squirrel liquor is good for a sick child with no appetite.  Brown Collection, VI, 275

If a woman sees a skinned squirrel before childbirth, she'll be confined too soon.  Brown Collection, VI, 18

When you kill a squirrel, pull its teeth and put them under your pillow, saying:

> Ninny, ninny, little squirrel
> That chatters in the tree,
> Tell me who my true love is to be.
> -- Brown Collection, VI, 4365

### The Squirrel in Game and Song

Chase the Squirrel--A steeplechase-type children's game, played to the accompaniment of this rhyme:

> Let us chase the squirrel
> Up the hickory, down the hickory;
> Let us chase the squirrel
> Up the hickory tree.
> -- Brown Collection, I, 80

### It's All Night Long

Of all the animals in this world
I'd rather be a squirrel.
I'd climb upon a telephone pole
And peep all over this world.

> It's all night long,
> It's all night long.
> -- Brown Collection, III, 214

## Black as Crows

According to legend, the crow was white until he ate the eyes of a snake. As partial support of this notion, the Chinese declare that a white-winged crow is an omen of evil and bad luck. Be that as it may, the crow now is obviously black, both in appearance and reputation. Don't damn him too much, for he helps maintain the balance of nature by destroying insects and carrying away carrion. As a token of respect for the eagle, humorously called crow, the captains or chiefs of the U.S. Navy include his image on their insignia; and the British, in the sense of being a "regular crow," indicate that he is a great success.

The crow belongs to the genus Corvus of the family Corvidae, which include magpies, coughs, ravens, jays, jackdaws, and other relatives. Found in many parts of the world, they are identified largely by their eating habits. In England there are carrion crows and hooded crows that feed on carrion, small birds, birds' eggs, and insects. Both groups, which interbreed in overlapping areas, migrate back and forth with the seasons from southern Scotland to the north Adriatic Sea. In India, there is the house crow, observed to be very prolific, easily domesticated, and dependable as a scavenger. In America, there are three principal kinds: the so-called carrion crow or black vulture; the fish crow (Corvus ossifragus), which lives on fish, molluscs, and garbage, but does not bother crops; and the American crow (Corvus americanus), widely prevalent in Canada and the United States. This last species, gregarious and migratory, feeds on insects and grain, and is highly unpopular with farmers.

Our American crow has a brilliant glossy-black plumage that in the full brightness of the day reflects tints of violet and green. The bird has an overall length of fifteen to twenty inches. Its shrill, harsh cry or cawing is gutteral, hoarse, and raucous--

seeming to say, to the human observer, "You damned fool!" This bird, along with his relatives, is reputed for his tremendous straight-flying speed, his tale-bearing, his thievery, and his capacity to live by cunning and wit. As for making an honest living, he can survive all kinds of hardships for several decades. His longevity attests to his talent for maintaining good health. If man only knew his secrets...

The crow is not an especially edible creature, except when figuratively consumed. Crow meat has never been a delicacy, whether raw or cooked. If perchance you are lazy, you may be called a **crow-eater**. If you "draw the crow," you have a raw deal or bad luck. If you must "eat crow," you are compelled to endure some sort of punishment or embarrassment, to apologize, or to make good for a failure or mistake. If someone has "a crow to pick with you," you must explain or make the necessary retractions.

The crow, in our superstitious lore, is disputatious about his blackness. The mother crow brags about her little ones being the blackest. Since those days of "some long-remembered wrinkle or crow's foot," the quality of blackness has been applied in several ways. A crow is an ugly and unpopular woman or girl, a depraved and unsightly object in a gutter, and a person that does not know the difference between another person and a crow.

This same blackness has been applied to the Crow Indians of Montana, to their missionaries, who were called crows because of their black garments, to an assemblage of British clergymen dressed in black and called a crow-fair, and often, with some unfairness, to the American Negro. The derogatory term **Jim Crow** has long been associated with segregation and its attendant evils. When white politicians attempt to win the Negroes' votes, the procedure is known as Crow Jimism.

The crow, though honored by the constellation Corvus in the southern sky, is still earth-bound, particularly in designating man's world of plants, tools or devices, persons, and so forth--such as crowbar, crowbill (a surgical instrument), crow's-nest, crowflower (lines supporting an awning), crowfoot or crowtoe (buttercup and other plants whose leaves are shaped like a crow's foot), crow tracks (chevrons), and crow's-foot (the wrinkles diverging from the human eye).

Call the crow a chicken, if you will, but he is not one in action. He never crows or exults as does the rooster. He is far less outspoken with his tricks as a gambler in competition with man and beast. He does, however, fend for himself in dialogues with owls concerning the merits of vision by day and by night. Sometimes in the guise of a ghost or demon, he robs the wren's nest, he kills the dove trying to protect her brood, he tears up the sparrow's nest, and when he has the right instrument he destroys the snake. Puffed up by these and other exploits, he struts and mimics the partridge's walk. He is quite a guy in the folk tales.

So what can you do with this bird? Eat him? Not unless you have to. Wish on him when you see him flying with a flock? Perhaps, if you believe in magic. Scare the devil out of him with a scarecrow? Yes, as long as you can fool him. Use him as a prophet of good harvesting time, rain, and foul weather? Certainly, if your weatherman is no better. Assume that his raucous cawing is a sure prediction of illness or death? Better call in a doctor, unless you prefer an undertaker. In other words, depend upon your own resources instead of on this creature of darkness.

## Derivative Names

crow: chicken

crow: Corvus, constellation in southern sky

crow: the shrill cry of rooster

crow: to exult, to utter cry of pleasure or victory

crow: eagle in various U.S. Navy insignia; chief or captain wearing such insignia

crow: a fluke, unexpected luck

crow: professional gambler

Crow: Indian; black-garbed missionary to Crow tribe

crow: mesentery of animal, especially when used as food

crow: old, useless, mean or ugly horse

crow: unpopular or ugly girl or woman

crow-bait: carrion; a scraggy, old horse; an aboriginal in Australia

crowbar: long metal bar, usually pointed at one end, used as lever, etc.

crowberry (also black crowberry): low, hardy evergreen in northern regions; black, edible berry; large cranberry

crowbill: horn pile; crow's-bill (surgical instrument)

crow blackbird: the North American grackle, especially the purple grackle

crow corn: colicroot

crow-eater: lazy person (Australia)

crow-fair: assemblage of clergymen wearing black garments

crowflower: lines used in supporting an awning

crowfoot (also crowtoe): buttercup or other plants having leaves shaped like a crow's foot; the bird's-foot trefoil

crowhop: rigid posture of a bucking horse

crow in working rig: seagull (naval)

crowkeeper: scarecrow

crow tracks: chevrons (army)

crow's-foot: a wrinkle at the outer corner of the eyes

crow's-nest: masthead lookout on ship

Jim Crow: poor man, common or average person; practice of segregation of Negroes from whites, etc.

Crow Jimism: illustrated by the politician who courts the Negroes for their votes

regular crow: a great success (British)

# Crow

## Proverbs and Proverbial Phrases

Black as crows.

Cunning as crows.

Every crow thinks its own young ones are the whitest.

Every mother crow thinks her crows are the blackest.

A crow is never the whiter for washing herself often.

Crows of a feather will flock together. Cf. "Birds of a feather flock together."

Draw the crow: to experience bad luck. (Australia)

Eat crow: to be forced to do something very disagreeable and humiliating, such as retracting a statement or taking punishment for failing. Cf. use in Great Britain: "To eat humble pie." (Umbles, unsavory innards of deer)

Eat boiled crow.

Have a crow to pluck (pull or pick): an unpleasant experience to be settled.

He cares no more than a crow cares for Sunday.

Hoarse as crows.

Like a crow in a gutter.

No carrion will kill a crow: applied to grass eaters and tough persons.

Not to know someone from a crow: not to know at all.

Poor as a winter crow.

Some long-remembered wrinkle or crow's-foot.

Straight as the crow flies: that is, in a straight line.

Thin as a crow.

## Superstitions and Motifs

A white-winged crow is a Chinese bird of evil omen.

The crow's cry is a warning of death or illness.

Crow on the fence, rain will go hence.
Crow on the ground, rain will come down.

From Brown Collection

A crow calling is a sign of death.  VII, 5292

When you hear crows cawing, it will rain.  VII, 6711. Cf. 6710, 6712-14.

Crows flying in flocks presage bad weather.  VII, 6187

When the crows caw, it is going to turn cold.  VII, 6291

Wish on a flying crow; if he flaps before he goes out of sight, the wish will come true and so forth.  VII, 7287ff.

To keep harmful birds away, nail a dead crow or hawk on the barn.  VII, 7493. Cf. 8334, 8331f.

Use scarecrow to keep away crows and other birds.  VII, 8323

When three black crows fly east over the field, it is time to harvest corn.  VII, 8157

From Motif-Index

The crow's house is full of wren's eggs.  H1129.9

The crow appropriates the sparrow's nest.  J684.2

The crow kills the dove that sings to save her brood.  U31.2

The crow drops a stolen necklace into a snake's hole and kills the snake.  K401.2.2

Crows and owls dispute over merits of day and night vision.  B299.2.1

The crow tries to imitate the partridge's walk.  J512.6

The crow is a bird of ill-omen.  B147.2.2.1

The ghost appears as a crow.  E423.3.8

### Said the Blackbird to the Crow

Said the blackbird to the crow,
"What makes white folks hate us so?"
"Oh, ever since old Adam was born
It's been our trade to pull up corn,
And that's why white folks hate us."
     -- Brown Collection, III, 203

## The Owl as King of the Night

During a fiery debate in the United States Senate over the war in Vietnam (the hawks wanted to escalate and the doves were trying to extricate us as soon as possible), Senator George Aiken of Vermont was reported to have said: "I'm not very keen for doves and hawks. I think we need more owls." Senator Aiken might have checked with Athens, where there is an oversupply of owls. The Greeks have a phrase for useless endeavors: "Like bringing owls to Athens."

Now, as in ancient times, the owl is a conspicuous and dubious bird. Aside from his occasional harmful excesses, he is one of our most useful predators. The folk, however, do not like this creature. This bias may be due in part to his unpretty appearance, but is more likely related to the owl's way of making an honest living for himself and family. During his nocturnal operations, he is quite aggressive in his quest for food--and he does so with outlandish clamor, an omen to the folk of bad luck and demonic influence.

Distantly akin to hawks and eagles, owls are of the genus Striges, a suborder of the family Strigidae. Throughout the world there are some 200 species, ranging in overall length from five to twenty-four inches. The principal types are the eagle owl, prevalent in Europe and Asia; the long-eared (woodland) and short-eared (diurnal) owls in Europe and North America; the great horned (barred) owl, seen often in the Americas; the snowy (white) owl of the Arctic; the barn (gray) owl of North America; and the North American screech (hoot) owl. Owls have large heads, ears, and eyes (forwardly directed); their bills are short and sharply hooked; their talons are long and strong, with reversible outer toes; their plumage is soft; and encircling their eyes are those distinctive disks of radiating stiff and shafted feathers.

Almost completely nocturnal, they roost in attics, trees, barns, and other places where they are not easily molested. Some of the folk say that owls prefer old and deserted houses, thus accounting for a bit of their demonic reputation. Excepting the great horned owl, which is highly destructive of poultry, they are usually harmless. In fact, they do much to preserve the balance of nature by devouring insects, mice, voles, shrews, rabbits, and so forth. By cocky and courageous efforts, they bring many a rat or crow or hawk to bay in preparation for the kill. They are sure in attack, their big eyes are keen.

Traditionally, they symbolize meditation, silence, and wisdom as illustrated in the phrase "wise as an owl." Apparently this characterization arose from the way the inactive owl sits on his roost during the daytime--solitary, solemn, looking like a judge or some other knowledgeable person. In this position, he may be thinking about his plans for the night, but he tells you not one confounded thing. He may be gathering data for his own computer as he stares and stares or as he twists his neck to evade the light of day. This taciturn repository of wisdom, so say the folk, is shrewd in holding onto his hard-earned knowledge. They declare that he is a first-class listener that gains more by keeping his mouth shut. Oh, yes! The truth is that his eyes cannot stand the glaring sunlight. And thus he is characterized as loony, sleepy, blind, drunk, or stewed.

This so-called intoxicated bird stands up well in man's use of his name. He is aptly dubbed the king of the night. When owl-light (dusk) comes, he is on the prowl with noiseless flight for his prey. He keeps late hours, he is a harlot on the dark streets, he is a smuggler of contraband. And his owlishness by night is mirrored by the names of dark creatures such as owlhead (black-bellied plover), owl monkey (night ape), owl parrot, owl swallow (night-jar, a jarring goatsucker), and owlet moth.

Closely linked to this dark image is the demonic owl, yellow-eyed and jealously malevolent. Owl-blasted, he has drunk much of infernal brews. Granting that he is sometimes a herald of good or foul weather, his shivering and hooting are tokens of malaria, chills, fever, and death. He is devilish and in league with bats. Now he is a witch, now a harlot, and now a vampire that only a silver bullet will kill. He is a thing of the underworld, moping and shrieking and tolling his bell for you. Go to the common folk; they'll tell you in no uncertain terms. They shudder when they hear his screeching, hooting, snarling, and hissing clamor. They trust him no more than do the kites and the crows, the mice and the rats, and all others with which he is in constant deadly warfare. This folk estimate breathes something of the fury of Macbeth in his closing hours:

> "It was the owl that shriek'd, the fatal bellman,
> Which gives the stern'st good-night."

## Derivative Names

owl: to hoot or stare like an owl

owl (also night-owl): person accustomed to work long hours at night; to sit up late at night; open for business at night

owl: to smuggle

owl: blow or punch on the head

owl: harlot

owl: breed of pigeons having an owl-like head, related to turbits and satinettes

owl (also owl car): street car that is operated at night

owl: wireless operator with headgear giving appearance of an owl

owl-blasted: bewitched

owl butterfly: large South American butterfly

owler: a person and/or vessel smuggling sheep from England to France

owlery: haunt or abode of owls

owlet: small owl; also type of European owl

owl-eyed (also owly-eyed): purblind; drunk

owl-fly: neuropterous fly

# Owl

Owlglass: jester or buffoon

owlhead: black-bellied plover

owlish (also owly): grave, stupid, night-prowling

owl-light: dusk or twilight

owl midge: fly of the family Psychodidae

owl monkey: night ape, so-called because of its large, yellow eyes

owlet moth: Brazilian moth of the family of Noctuidae

Owl Nebula: great planetary body, in figure suggesting an owl's face

owl parrot: kakapo

owl swallow: nightjar of the family Podargidae

owl's-clover: California herb of figwort family

owl's-crown: Confederate rose

owl-wide: wide as an owl's eyes and as unseeing

## Proverbs and Proverbial Phrases

Blind (or drunk) as an owl.

Drunk as a boiled owl.

Feel like a stewed owl.

Ignorant as an owl in a storm.

Like an owl in the desert (that is, mournful and crying). (See song titled as such in Brown Collection, III, 359.)

Like an owl in an ivy bush: having a large wig or very bushy hair; a stupid blunder; forced to be in the ivy bush with many chattering birds.

Loony as an owl.

Sleepy as an owl.

Solemn as an owl.

Stare like an owl in a thunder shower.

Still as the flight of an owl.

Wise as an owl.  Cf. Taciturn as an owl.

An owl was a baker's daughter.  (Saying based upon story told in Gloucestershire, England.  Jesus asked a baker to give him some bread.  The baker made a very large loaf for him, his daughter protested and was turned into an owl.)

Like bringing owls to Athens.  Cf.  Like carrying coals to Newcastle.

To catch the owl (that is, to play a country trick).

To live too near a wood to be frightened by an owl (not to be frightened at all).

An owl is the king of the night.

To take the owl (to become angry).

To walk by owl-light (to fear arrest).

When the owl sings, the nightingale will hold her peace.

## Superstitions and Motifs

In Greece, the worship of Athena was associated with owls.

In Rome, the owl was a bird of ill omen: it predicted the death of Augustus; its screeching preceded the death of Caesar.

Since the Norman Conquest, the owl's hooting has presaged death; thus owls are feared.

In Europe and America, where owl is omen of bad luck, his evil hooting may be counteracted by turning your pockets inside out or by tying a knot in a handkerchief or by throwing salt into the fire.

From Brown Collection

Do not allow an owl to sit in trees near your house and hollow (hollo); if you do, you will not be very prosperous.  VI, 3381

If you hear an owl hooting near your house, someone in the family is going to have chills and fever.  VI, 1087

The direction from which you hear the first owl halloo in the spring is a sign that you will travel that way most of the year.  VI, 3709.  Cf. Bad luck to hear a hoot owl on a journey.  Clark, 691

Owl

To hear a shivering owl near the house is a sign of sickness. VI, 714. Cf. 711f.

When an owl hoots for three nights near your house, you are going to have malaria. VI, 1797

If an owl appears on your place when someone is ill there, that person will die in two days. VII, 5008f. To hear a shivering owl is a sign of death. VII, 5303. Death to him who shoots an owl. VII, 5314. If you hear an owl hooting, the weather is going to be cold. VII, 6294f. If an owl hoots on the west side of a mountain, it denotes good weather. VII, 6389. If an owl hoots on the east side of the mountain, it denotes bad weather. VII, 6190. When owls hoot a lot, it is the sign of rain. VII, 6719. If the owl hoots at night in the summer time, it will rain. VII, 6723

Owls hooting in a tree foretell a north wind. VII, 6995

It is bad luck for an owl to come near a dwelling, on top of it, and so forth. The bad luck may be counteracted by turning over your shoes or turning your pockets inside out. VII, 7258-62, 7264-71

If you start out hunting and hear an owl, you might as well come back for you will not have good luck. VII, 7860

If a coon-hunting party hears an owl laugh just as they are setting out, they will go back home. But if he holloes "Coon," they will have good luck. VII, 7899

Witch's brew: seven hairs from blood snake, seven scales from rattlesnake, seven bits of feathers from owl, a hair from the head of a person you desire, and a bit of nail paring; cook these for seven minutes over a hot fire in the first rain water caught in April. Sprinkle the concoction on the clothes of the person to be charmed. It cannot fail. VII, 5555

From Motif-Index

Baker's daughter punished for stinginess toward Jesus. A1958.0.1. (See explanation above in proverbs.)

The owl is a bird of ill-omen. B147.2.2.4

The owl is made king over the peacock. J515

The owl thinks his hoots echo praise. J953.16

The owl avoids daylight. A2491.2

The devil appears as an owl. G303.3.3.3.6

Friendship exists between owl and bat.   A2493.3

Lawsuit arises between owl and kite.   B270.1

Lawsuit arises between owl and mouse.   B270.2

Witch appears as an owl.   G211.4.4

Owls and crows dispute over day and night vision.   B299.2.1

Enmity exists between owl and other fowls.   A2494.13.4.1

Vampire has the eyes of an owl.   E251.4.3

War is carried on between crows and owls.   B263.3

### Quotations--Literary and Otherwise

"It was the owl that shriek'd, the fatal bellman,
Which gives the stern'st good-night."
             -- Shakespeare, Macbeth

"A falcon, tow'ring in her pride of place,
Was by a mousing owl hawk'd at and killed."
             -- Shakespeare, Macbeth

"Save that from yonder ivy-mantled tower
The moping owl does to the moon complain."
             -- Gray, Elegy Written in a Country Churchyard

"The owl, for all his feathers, was a-cold."
             -- Keats, The Eve of St. Agnes

### A Wise Old Owl

"A wise old owl sat on an oak,
The more he saw the less he spoke;
The less he spoke the more he heard;
Why aren't we like that wise old bird?"
             -- Edward Hersey

"A serious writer may be a hawk or a buzzard or even
    a popinjay, but a solemn writer is always a bloody owl."
             -- Ernest Hemingway

"I'm not very keen for doves or hawks.  I think we need
    more owls."
             -- Senator George Aiken (R., Vermont)
                in January 1966 during discussion in
                Congress about warfare in Vietnam.

## The Heart of an Ox

One of the sights you hardly ever see any more is a team of oxen straining against a yoke and oxbows to pull a heavily loaded wagon. Weighing almost a thousand pounds each, these oxen were light reddish-brown, with spots of white here and there. Their brass-tipped horns, long and rounded, shone like a scooped-out halo around their heads. And there on the high wagon seat sat the driver, cracking his whip and frequently shouting: "Giddap, boys! Giddap! Lay to, lay to, boys! The sun is still high, and we've got to make it."

In the olden days oxen had many things to do: pulling a creaky wagon loaded with oak logs to the sawmill, assisting in the harvesting and threshing of wheat, ploughing the soddy and red land, laying by the tall corn, and--if no horses or mules were available--pulling a coffin to a funeral service. Day after day, year after year, this tortuous pattern was enacted in the valleys and on the sunlit hills--a slow and patient course that was the mainstay of the primitive economy.

The ox that has survived in scattered areas is a castrated bull belonging to the genus Bos taurus of the Bovidae, a very large family of hardy ruminants or cud-chewing mammals with two stomachs. The ox is a member of the suborder Bovinae, represented by cattle, bison, buffaloes, and the giant ox of the Americas. His horns are hollow, rounded or angulated; his hoofs are cloven; his muzzle is broad, moist, and naked; his face has no glands; his hair is short, fine, and silky; and his long tail is tufted with long strands of coarse hair.

This creature, traditionally called dumb, has been a significant part of the social structure for at least eight thousand years. The Egyptians, Assyrians, Babylonians, Greeks, and Romans gave him legal protection and used him in rituals and sacrifices. Their architects placed him high in their temples and other important structures.  The Hebrews also venerated him and elevated his stricken body on altars in acts of adoration or appeasement.  The Hindus consider him holy and refuse to eat his flesh.  Christians, who have made full use of his labor and nutritious meat, have enshrined him in masterpieces of art and story centered around the birthplace of Jesus.

Likewise in the lore of the people, the heart of the ox is preserved in proverbial expressions and folk names of animals, plants, processes, and devices.  Those who have lived close to the ox have qualified him as awkward, clumsy, dumb, silent, strong, stubborn, and sweaty, or as apathetic, proud, slow, and stupid.

There are colorful plant names such as oxbane, oxberry, oxeye, oxeye daisy, oxheart, oxlip, and oxlip primrose.  Of considerably less appeal are the names of insects such as the oxbot, oxbiter, oxpecker, oxfly, and ox warble.  And a miscellaneous group includes the following: ox balm, oxbile, oxeye molding, oxeyed arch, oxbow lake, Oxford blue (also chrome, gray, and so forth), oxbow, oxgoad, oxhide, ox penny, and oxbow stirrup.

In contrast with this sort of beneficial use, the folk have been dubious about the character of the black ox, probably because of his somber color.  Bearing the yoke or not bearing it, he symbolizes misery and misfortune.  And by some imaginative twist, this animal represents human and supernatural forces beyond man's power to control.  For instance, the saying "The black ox has trod on his feet" signifies poverty, old age, ill-health, and despair.  In the course of time the black ox degenerated into the diabolical and thus was conducive to conjuring evil spirits.  An overtone of this dire force in nature is reflected in these lines of William Butler Yeats:

> "The years like great black oxen tread the world
> And God, the herdsman, goads them on behind."

Except as man has attributed magical and fantastic influence to him, the ox has been a force for good through his creative energy, endurance, and usefulness.

## Derivative Names

ox: castrated bull; loosely, any animal of the bovine family

ox: stupid, slow-thinking person, especially tough, large, awkward one (Sometimes called a "dumb ox")

ox ball: hair from ox's stomach

ox balm: horse balm

oxbane: South African plant, poisonous to cattle

oxberry: fruit of black bryony

ox, Big: train conductor, the "Big O" (railroad use)

ox bile: ox gall

oxbird: dunlin; sandpiper; oxpecker; African weaverbird

oxbiter: cowbird; oxpecker

oxblood: brilliant, deep red color; monochrome glaze in Chinese porcelain

oxbot: botfly or larva of warble fly

oxbow: U-shaped part of ox yoke, passing around and under the neck of the animal; land within oxbow lake

oxbow lake: crescent or bend in meandering stream

oxbow stirrup: large wooden stirrup resembling oxbow

oxboy: boy who cares for oxen

oxbrake (also oxcage): frame in which oxen are shod

oxcart: cart drawn by oxen

oxcheek: cheek of ox, especially cut of meat

oxeye: any of several plants having conspicuous disk and marginal rays such as oxeye daisy

oxeye bean: American woody vine

oxeye camomile: yellow camomile

oxeye daisy: daisylike plant with flowers of yellow rays around a brown disk (see oxeye); black-eyed Susan oxeye molding: similar to casement

oxeyed: having large, calm eyes like those of an ox

oxeyed arch: pointed arch

oxfence: oxer; fox hunting

oxfly: ox warble fly

ox-foot: made of oxen feet

Oxford (originally Oxenford): ford of oxen; city and seat of Oxford University

oxford: type of laced shoe

Oxford blue: reddish blue

Oxford chrome: yellow ochre

Oxford gray: neutral with medium brilliance

oxgang: herd of bovate

oxgoad: goad for driving oxen

oxharrow: large, primitive harrow requiring great strength to pull

oxheart: large cherry shaped like a heart; kind of cabbage

oxhide: measure of land (confusion of it with hide or skin)

oxhorn: horn of an ox

oxhouse: stable for oxen

oxlip: plant of primrose family, having clusters of pale-yellow flowers

oxlip primrose: hybrid primrose

oxpecker: any of African starlings that feed on parasitic larvae found on the hides of oxen; beefeater bird

ox penny: tax on oxen

ox-pop: butcher

oxtail: tail of ox, especially when skinned and used to make soup

oxtongue: any of several related plants with rough, tongue-shaped leaves

Ox

ox warble: warble fly or oxfly

## Proverbs and Proverbial Phrases

Awkward as an ox.

Big as an ox.

Bow-backed as an ox yoke.

Bovine as an ox.

Clumsy as an ox.

Crazy about "licker" as a steer is about pond water.

Dumb as an ox.   (See probable relationship to taciturn.)

Heart like an ox.

Lazy as an ox.

Like an ox in the ditch.

Slow as an ox.

Strong as an ox.

Strong as an ox and almost as smart.

Strong as an ox, and ignorant as strong.

Stubborn as an ox.

Stupid as an ox.

Sweating like an ox.

To drive the wrong ox.

Whoever leads an ox to water must first wet his own feet. (Chinese)

Don't wait until the ox gets into the ditch to pull the reins.

To go through the ox-house to bed:  to be cuckolded.

The black ox has (hath) trod on his foot:  he knows what poverty, old age, ill-health, and misfortune are.

Take heed of an ox before, of a horse behind, of a monk on all sides.

If the ox falls, whet your knife: (many will help to kill him).

An ox is taken by the horns, and a man by the tongue.

It makes a difference whose ox is gored.

The ox when weariest treads surest.

He has an ox on his tongue (that is, keeps silent).

An ox when he is loose licks himself at pleasure.

Don't beat the ox for not giving milk (Russian).

He must plough with such oxen as he has.

I haven't seen you since Buck was a calf.

### Superstitions and Motifs

#### From Brown Collection

To make oxen move, twist their tails or bite off one's ear. VII, 7673

To prevent fruit tree from withering, dig hole about it and pour in ox, calf, or cow's blood. VII, 8417

If one wishes to hurt an enemy, let him make a circle at midnight (and be sure not to step out of it) and repeat:

> The black ox hath trod
> Live morf see evas dog
> Appear, thoth!

And a spirit will appear who, upon the master's bidding, will work all manner of harm to one's enemy short of death. His crops will fail, his stock will die, luck will not be with him. One must never repeat this charm unnecessarily or step out of the circle during the incantation, or feel remorse for his enemy afterwards. If these rules are transgressed, the devil will come to take the "spell-binder" himself. VII, 5778

#### From Motif-Index

The ox curses man. J1905.3

The ass who has worked with an ox thinks himself equal. J952.4

Why the ox has no hair on his lip. A2342.2

## Quotations--Literary and Otherwise

"I didn't know hit from Beltashazur's off ox." -- Joel C. Harris

"Who drives fat oxen should himself be fat." -- James Boswell, Life of Johnson

"Better is a dinner of herbs where love is than a fatted ox and hatred with it." -- Proverbs, XV, 17

"The ox knoweth his owner, and the ass his master's crib." -- Isaiah, I, 3

"The years like great black oxen tread the world
And God, the herdsman, goads them on behind."--William Butler Yeats, The Countess Cathleen

Bats in Belfries

"Now air is hush'd, save where the weak-eyed bat,
With short shrill shriek, flits by on leathern wing."
-- William Collins, Ode to Evening

Have you got any bats? If you live in the East, you may be blessed with happiness and prosperity. If you reside in the West, that's a different matter. It all depends upon your personal state of mind. For the time being, let us scan the evidence that mankind has been accumulating about the bat over the centuries.

The bat, of which there are several hundred species including thirty-five or more in North America, belongs to the genus Chiroptera, meaning "wing-handed." It is a mouse-like mammal whose forelimbs are modified to form wings. The bones of the outspreading hand and arm are covered by a delicate, nearly hairless, leathery membrane possessing the essential dynamics of flight. The bat is the only animal so equipped.

Contrary to popular opinion, the bat has highly sensitive vision. When its eyes are sealed, it is able to avoid striking objects because of its well-developed sense of hearing. The head of this non-walking bird is bald and somewhat bowed, and its body is protected by a woolly covering. In this country it is usually black or brownish-black. Some of the fruit-bats are yellow, some of the South American species are white, and some, such as Blanville's bat, are bright orange.

Bats vary from approximately one foot to five feet in wingspread. They make their homes in caves, belfries, and other deserted or "haunted" places. They live chiefly on insects that they catch during their flight; however, the fruit-bats, also called foxbats or flying foxes, depend upon fruit for their sustenance. These flying foxes, the largest of the bats, are deliciously edible, but they are considered a nuisance among the fruit growers in the tropics and Australia. Bats are gregarious and nocturnal, and where winters are severe they migrate or hibernate. In most areas, they are very useful predators.

Used alone or with other words, bat is suggestive of the sordid and questionable. If you are a bat, you are an ugly girl or gossipy old woman; if you are a bat carrier, you are aiding the police in raiding bat houses or brothels; if you are batting around, you are an idler or loafer; if you are a bat-fowler, you hunt bats at night with glaring lights or you may swindle the simpletons; if you go on a bat, you are wild and soused; if you attend an Indian bat dance, you may be celebrating the secret power of the bats. A batty sportsman or flyer has a packsaddle or a jockey's whip, or drops gliderlike bombs on the enemy.

Because of its gloomy appearance and nightly activities, as well as its living by day in dark places, the bat is feared and avoided. Long associated with witch's brew and the underworld, it is, furthermore, symbolic of the dark madhouses that once imprisoned the insane. The folk also state that the bat is blind, an erroneous conclusion traceable to its staring in the daytime. They vow that its speed is excessive, and that there is nothing faster as it comes out of a brush heap, or hell, or the State of Georgia. If you are so qualified, you are batty or bats and, besides, you have bats in your belfry. Moreover, if you are a lousy bat, you are a devil, or a witch, or a ghost.

The folk also state that bats are omens of baldheadedness if they hit you on the head; if one of them bites your hand, it will rot off; if it strikes your head, you will always have headaches; if it flies over your head at sundown, you will have lice; if it flies into your house, you may expect a death. On the other hand, its blood is a preventive of baldheadedness; its gall will cure sore eyes; and if it cries or attempts to enter a building, it is foretelling rain.

Bats, Bats, Bats!

### Derivative Names
bat: gliderlike bomb, automatically guided to target

bat: any of certain moths or butterflies of the West Indies

bat: unattractive, ugly girl

bat: pace (British)

bat: packsaddle

bat: prostitute, especially at night

bat: souse, habitual tippler, carouser

bat: wild, gay drinking bout or spree

bat: watchman (rare)

bat: jockey's whip

bat: gossipy or mean old woman

bat around: to loaf or idle

bat bug: hairy bug related to ectoparasites on bats

bat carrier: police informer

bat dance: among Papago Indians a ceremonial dance commemorating secret messages delivered by bats

bat ear: an ear (of the dog or other animal) having resemblance to that of bat

batfish: any of several fish resembling bat

bat fly: one that is an ectoparasite on bats

bat for: defend a person or principle

bat-fowl: to swindle or victimize a simpleton

bat-fowl: to catch birds nocturnally by means of a glaring or blinding light

bat-fowler: one who bat-fowls or goes bat-fowling

bat house: brothel

bats: foolish, crazy, nuts

batswing burner: gas burner having narrow slit in domed-shape top

batswing coral: Australian tree, having spongy wood

# Bat

bat tick:   member of wingless, degraded Diptera, parasites on bats

bat tree:   evergreen magnolia

batty:   mad, crazy, queer

bloodsucking bat:   South American species (vampyrus spectrum) deriving its name from bloodsucking ghost or vampire that quit the body of a dead person to suck the blood of the living, usually at night

fox-bat (also fruit bat and flying fox):   largest of bats, found in tropical areas and Australia; very destructive of fruits; edible

## Proverbs and Proverbial Phrases

Blind as a bat.

Crazy as a bat.

Crazy as a bat out of hell (also Hades).

Fast as a bat out of hell.

Passed like a bat out of Georgia.

Passed like a bat out of a brush heap.

Ugly as a bat.

Bat the breeze:   to chatter or talk excessively.

Have bats in the belfry:   to be crazy or mad, eccentric.

Go on a bat:   to go on a wild spree.

## Superstitions and Motifs

Singing "Bat, bat, come under my hat" brings good luck unless the bat brings bedbugs.

From Brown Collection

If a bat bites you, your ears and nose will change places.   VI, 510

If a bat happens to light on or hit one on the head, that person will soon become baldheaded.   VI, 844

The blood of a bat was an excellent preventive of baldness in the good old days.  VI, 845

For eye troubles, use the gall of a bat.  VI, 1366

If a bat bites your hand, the hand will decay.  VI, 1565

If a bat strikes you on the head, you will suffer with headaches the remainder of your life.  VI, 1577

If a bat flies over your head after sundown, you will have lice. VI, 1771

When bats fly into a house, a death is looked for.  VII, 5184

When bats cry or attempt to fly into buildings, you may expect rain.  VII, 6656

Bats are regarded as omens of bad luck.  VII, 7183

From Motif-Index

Why bats cry as they fly.  A2426.1.6

Why bat is bald.  A2317.8

Friendship exists between bats and owls.  A2493.2

Bat wars against birds and quadrupeds.  B261.1

Bat in the house is a sign of a ghost.  E436.3

Bat appears as a witch.  G211.2.10

## King of the Birds--The Eagle

For over two thousand years the eagle has been a symbol of both man's highest aspirations and of man's meanest ambitions. This pre-eminent bird has shaped and nurtured the policies and culture of empire after empire. To demonstrate their greatness, the Romans, associating the eagle with Jove and lightning, held aloft the eagle's image on pikes and banners. Later, the empires of Austria-Hungary, Russia, Germany, and France adopted the eagle as the emblem of their power and influence--the first two emphasized their superiority by using double-headed eagles.

In 1782 the United States of America adopted the eagle as its national emblem. A streaming banner bore the legend "E Pluribus Unum" between two uplifted wings, supported by two strong claws clutching a bundle of sticks (fasces) and olive twigs. In various arrangements, these symbols have appeared on shields, flags, banners, stamps, seals, uniforms, insignia, coins, paper currency, doorknockers, trademarks, and other objects. This image of pride, hope, and victory is boldly written into our social, economic, and artistic history. It is also a part of our religious outlook, for we have coupled with it another legend, "In God We Trust." As thus depicted and glorified, its magic influence has been felt by many an American citizen.

The choice of the eagle was protested against almost from the beginning. Benjamin Franklin felt that the turkey would be a much better representative of the nation than the "poor" and "lousy" eagle, known generally as a sharper and robber. Also opposed to the eagle was the great naturalist John J. Audubon, who did not wish to glorify a bird with so many ignoble qualities. The founding fathers, however, had their way, and we have been stuck with the eagle image ever since. Judging by the spirit of these times, the majority of our people will continue to embrace this bird no matter if he does let out an occasional scream.

The eagle (*Aquila* of the sub-family *Aquilinae* of the principal family *Falconidae*, excluding vultures), now becoming rare, is a large, diurnal bird of prey. It soars higher than all other birds, is supposed to be able to stare at the sun without injury to the eyes, and builds its nest on the crags of very high mountains. It has a wingspread of seven to eight feet, and is three feet from head to tail. The upper side of its bill is sharply curved downward, and its claws are also sharp and curved. It avoids carrion and lives as a carnivore on fish, rabbits, serpents, lambs, antelopes, and other small animals. Contrary to legend, it does not abduct and eat small children. Its life span is long, close to a hundred years, and it mates for life. Despite the fact that the female lays two to four eggs yearly--and may make use of the eaglestone as a nest egg to stimulate or facilitate egg-laying--there has not been any population explosion among the eagles.

The chief species are the sea eagle, the harpy eagle, the monkey eagle (the largest, inhabiting the Philippines and related to the harpy), the golden eagle, and the bald eagle. Because of the imperial prominence of the last two, some additional statements are appropriate.

The golden eagle (*Aquila chrysaetus*), known also as the mountain eagle, is observed in Asia, Europe, and North Africa, and in North America from Labrador to the interior of Alaska and southward to central Mexico. It has dark brown plumage, with a cowl of golden or tawny feathers about the neck. Its tail feathers are gray and purple.

The bald or American eagle (*Haliaetus leucocephalus*) inhabits the United States from Maine to Alaska and southward to northern Mexico. It is baldheaded, its plumage is dark brown, and its neck and tail are white-feathered. Its belly (underside) is usually unfeathered. It is not as attractive and stately as the golden eagle, but it is a mighty bird in these parts.

Aside from the nationalistic uses of the eagle, its name is perpetuated in the names of other creatures and objects noted for strength and swiftness. An eagle is an expert fighter pilot as well

Eagle

as two strokes under par in golfing. An eagle-boat is a submarine chaser, an eagle dance is a rapidly moving Indian celebration, and an eagle-eye is a keen-sighted detective or locomotive engineer. Eagle-hawks, eagle-gulls, eagle-kites, eagle-owls and eagle vultures are also fast and ferocious in attacking their prey. The eagle fern, the eagle flower, and the spread-eagle orchid are colorful plants. And then there are those big-clawed cultivators and spread-eagle lecterns.

In proverbial expressions, the eagle-eyed belong to a superior breed that never stoops to eat insects--they are keen, far-seeing, soaring, strong, grasping, and imperious in pursuit of big game. In their aspirations to be great, they are spread-eagled and intent upon flying the eagle with bombast and protestations of might. They indulge in big shows of inferior quality; they prefer the empty purple patches to the logical argument; and, from the days of William the Conqueror, they have been creating family trees or promoting patriotic causes while the commoner shoots it out to save the day. The folk also say that if the eagle dies after a hundred years, the despicable crow is sure to pick out his glassy eyes.

Don't blame the eagle for all this mischief. Allowing for his reported excesses in rapacity and discord, he has an abundance of what most people want--bigness, strength, keenness of vision, marvelous and graceful soaring power, fearlessness, fortitude, majesty, and splendor. Sovereignty and victory are his. As he sits in his eyrie on a sunlit crag, he is truly a most regal figure.

## Derivative Names

eagle: former gold coin of U.S.A., worth $10 (double, $20; half, $5; quarter, $2.50)

eagle: two strokes less than par (of over three) on a hole in golfing

eagle: insigne used as emblem on a flag, stamp, money, etc.; emblem worn by colonel in U.S. Army

eagle: expert fighter pilot

eagle-beak: large-nosed person

eagle bird:  roulette, third zero

eagle boat:  submarine chaser

eagle claw:  American cultivator

eagle dance:  American Indian ritual dance, especially for rain or peace

eagled:  punished by being spread-eagled (nautical)

eagle day:  payday

eagle-eye:  one who watches like an eagle; locomotive engineer; detective on the watch for shoplifters and similar persons

eagle-eyed (also eagle eye):  able to see far and clearly

eagle fern:  brake

eagle flower:  any flower of genus Impatiens

eagle gull:  black-backed gull

eagle hawk:  large crested South American hawk

eagle-hawking:  plucking wool from dead sheep (Australia)

eagle-kite:  Brahminy kite

eagle lectern:  podium or stand supported by emblem of eagle

eagle owl:  big owl in Europe and Asia, allied to great horned owl of North America but greater in size

eagle ray:  fish of order Raiae

eagle scout:  highest rank in the Boy Scouts

eagless:  female eagle

eagle-stone:  mineral nodule of clay ironstone about size of walnut; the ancients believed that eagles took these stones (as nest eggs) to their nests to facilitate egg-laying

eaglet:  young eagle

eagle vulture:  large West African bird between hawks and vultures

eaglewood:  agalloch

spread eagle:  indulgence in bombastic language; figure in heraldic arms; characteristic of being spread-eagle person

# Eagle

spread-eagle orchid: tropical American orchid having spreading petals

## Proverbs and Proverbial Phrases

Bald as an eagle.

Wheresoever the carcase [sic] is, there will the eagles (ravens) be gathered together.

Like an eagle among the crows.

The carrion which the eagle has left feeds the crow.

When the eagle is dead, the crows pick out his eyes.

Eagles do not breed doves.

Eagles catch no flies.

To fly the eagle (to orate at length, proudly and sometimes ridiculously). Cf. he spreads himself like an eagle.

Keen as an eagle.

Eyes like an eagle.

He held the silver dollar till the eagle screamed.

Soared like an eagle.

Strong as an eagle.

Swift as an eagle.

## Superstitions and Motifs

### From Brown Collection

For eye troubles a favorite remedy is the gall of an eagle. VI, 1367

For rattlesnake bites the gall of an eagle is a dependable remedy. VI, 2135

An eagle stone, taken from a bird (eagle) while still alive, and worn around the neck, will keep a husband or a wife faithful. VI, 4870

### From Motif-Index

Eagle as an omen of victory.  B147.2.1.2.  Cf. B147.2.2.5, as ill-omen.

Fight between eagle and fish.  B264.2

Eagle carries off condemned child.  B522.4

Giant as an eagle.  F531.1.1.8.3

Reincarnation as an eagle.  E613.3.1

Eagle warns shepherds that wolf is eating sheep.  J715.1

### Quotation

"I wish the bald eagle had not been chosen as the representative of our country; he is a bird of bad moral character; like those among men who live by sharping and robbing, he is generally poor, and often lousy."

-- Benjamin Franklin, Letter to Sarah Bache, Jan. 26, 1784

## Wolf! Wolf! Wolf!

Nowadays there are many devilish ways of arousing horror; but some years ago a sure means of stimulating it, especially among young children, was the reading of "Little Red Riding Hood." The wolf in that story, as you may recall, disposed of an old grandmother, donned her clothes, crawled into her bed, and waited for Red Riding Hood to appear. He almost got her too, but thank goodness the trusty woodsman turned up in time.

The wolf has seldom deviated from being the scoundrel that he is. His murderous exploits were probably known to Noah, but there is no record that he and his mate were selected for the free ocean voyage. Aesop characterized him as a sheep killer. But it fell to the Romans to dignify this creature--they turned the wolf into a milk station for Romulus and Remus, thereby establishing the lupine ascent of the Roman Empire.

This wolf of legend and fact is of the genus Canis lupus of the big family Canidae. As a carnivore of the Northern Hemisphere only, he inhabits a wide area ranging from the Far East, across Asia and Europe, thence to Greenland and the high mountains and Great Plains of North America, and southward to Mexico. The most widely known among us is the gray or timber wolf (sometimes designated Canis occidentalis), observed in the West and reported as declining in numbers. In this area the prairie wolf (coyote), though far less frequent in tale or legend, is very numerous. Breeds in the East are called Indian, Japanese, and so forth.

The various species differ in size, length, coloration, and thickness of fur. Excepting the large domesticated dogs, they are the biggest of the dog family. They are gaunt and long-legged and have wide heads, long noses, pointed muzzles, thick tails, and erect ears. They are flesh-eaters, particularly of sheep, antelopes, poultry, other smaller animals; occasionally they eat larger ones that have been injured. In summer they hide away in trees and clefts of rocks; in winter they run in packs and hunt a variety of game. According to some reports, wolves when exceedingly hungry have attacked travelers on the highways and have carried off children in Siberia and elsewhere. They are savage predators, lacking the courage and loyalty of their cousins the dogs.

To understand the wolf and his character, consult the people who have been hurt by his terrifying acts. Fearing and hating him, they would like to see him dropped in his tracks. They say that he is a tricky glutton, a clever trader with devils and saints, a figure in pompous heraldry, a destructive larva of beetles and moths, a dissonance in several musical instruments, a male or female homosexual, and a philanderer that uses a shrill wolf-whistle to entice a victim. He is bloodthirsty, cruel, greedy, hungry, lank, sly, and villainous. His arrogance is phenomenal, but he will slink away from tight places.

The wolf must be credited with stimulating a sizable number of English words. Take note of a few inoffensive uses: plants--wolfberry, wolf's-claw, wolf fruit, wolf grape, wolf's moss, wolf's peach, and wolf willow; animals--wolfhound, wolf-moth, and wolfkin; persons--wolf cub (a rank in Boy Scouts), wolfer, and wolf society. By way of contrast, there are the murderous types such as the wolf-tree that crowds out younger trees, the very poisonous wolf's-bane, the wolf eel, the wolf herring, and the wolf-spider. In the category of scientific application, consider the wolf pack, used to designate an aerial unit for combat or a flotilla of submarines in pursuit of big game at sea.

Furthermore, say the folk, if you ever see a wolf you may be struck dumb or behold a woman eager to be seduced. If you have a wolf in your breast, you are putting on a pretended show of agony to avoid an arrest for illegal begging. If you have a wolf by the ears, you are in one hell of a fix. If you have a wolf in the stomach, you are poverty-stricken and famished. If you want to keep the wolf from your door, you must get a paying job and lay up treasures on this earth.

The wolf is a greedy killer that attacks first cautiously, then desperately. Reputed to be a challenger of horses, lions, witches, and devils, he usually confines his diet to the products of lesser breeds. His primary concern is lamb chops and mutton, in the fold if necessary. His conscience can never be elevated by a sermon on brotherly love. And should he be brought to bay while devouring a sheep or goose, he will plead benefit of clergy by piously quoting passages from St. Paul, Thomas Aquinas, Chaucer, and Martin Luther. "The wolf may lose his teeth, but never his nature." His strategy is based upon one principle: salvation comes only through a full stomach.

To insure your safety and that of the sheep, the guards must always be up. The eagle that has his own belly to cram may warn you that the wolf is ravaging the countryside, but that is not enough. The shepherd that goes to sleep commits the first blunder. To trust a wolf is stupid. And the lamb or the mutton-head that can be induced to bring him food is ready to be plucked. Isaiah's prophecy of the wolf and the kid lying down together may yet come to pass--in the meantime, the lamb had better count the headstones of his relatives in the cemetery. If this lonely tour does not arouse his belief in highway safety, he should once more read the warning of old Aesop: "The Lamb that belonged to the Sheep, whose skin the Wolf was wearing, began to follow the Wolf in Sheep's clothing."

It is clear that something must be done to control this representative of the tooth and claw. At the outset, as a matter of mercy, hold a dialog with the wolf about the virtues of domestication. If this communication does not subdue him--and it will not in all probability--then load him onto an Atlas and shoot him at the moon on a one-way ticket. Or use him for cancer research along with kidnapped dogs. If these procedures leave much to be desired, then incarcerate him, drug him, castrate him or give his mate some pills, or hybridize him. If these good intentions fail, then club, beat, trap, or shoot him. That's what the British did and rid England of him forever.

Once you have put him out of the way, you might try compensating for your losses by extracting his teeth to hang over your doors for good luck, or for easing your child in teething, or for preventing hydrophobia. But remember, if you allow him to live, he may eat your grandmother, nab your granddaughter, or waylay you in high places.

## Derivative Names

wolf: to eat ravenously

wolf: fierce, greedy person

wolf: figure in heraldry

wolf: destructive larva of various beetles and moths

wolf: dissonance in some musical instruments such as piano, violin, etc.

wolf: male homosexual seducer; sexually depraved youth pursuing women; female pursuing men; philanderer with wolfish or predatory qualities

wolf: dire poverty

wolf: clever trader

wolfberry: western U.S. shrub having white berries

wolf child: legendary child raised by wolves

wolf cub: a cub scout

wolf dog (also wolfhound): hybrid of dog and wolf; big Irish dog used in hunting wolves; any of several large breeds formerly used in hunting wolves

wolfer: one who hunts wolves

wolf eel: long, slender wolf-fish, a savage sea fish having powerful teeth

wolfish: fierce, ravenous, lupine, and showing wolfishness

wolf fruit: South American grandiflorum

wolf grape: bittersweet; chicken grape

wolf herring: any of various large, long fish

wolf-hole: lair of wolf; in warfare, a concealed trap or pit

wolfkin: small wolf

# Wolf

wolf-moth: whitish-brown moth

wolf pack: flotilla of submarines; aerial unit

wolf-robe: wolfskin robe or rug

wolf snake: any of several types of snakes, usually harmless

wolf society: dancing group of northwest Pacific Indians

wolf-spider: hairy spider

wolf-tooth: small premolar tooth of the horse

wolf tree: a tree that in growing crowds out others

wolf whistle: drawn-out whistle expressing admiration of another; an invitation to a sexually attractive woman; call to get attention of the opposite sex

wolf willow: buffalo berry

wolf's-bane (also wolfsbane): poisonous plant with yellow flowers; kind of aconite or monkshood; May 24 birthday flower symbolic of misanthropy

wolf's-claw: common club moss

wolf's-fist: puffball

wolf's-head: interjection used in hunting wolves and in pursuing outlaws; outlaw

wolf's-milk: any one of the spurges, acrid and juicy

wolf's moss: yellow lichen

wolf's peach: tomato

## Proverbs and Proverbial Phrases

Bloodthirsty as a wolf.

He cries wolf! wolf! (He gives a false alarm. See Aesop.)

Cunning as a wolf.

To have (hold) a wolf by the ears. (To be in a desperate situation.)

To have a wolf in the stomach. (To be famished.)

To keep the wolf from the door. (To lay up provisions and so forth for any emergency. Cf. Enough to keep the wolf away.)

To see a wolf. (To be struck dumb.)

To see a wolf. (To see a woman eager to be seduced.)

To have a wolf in the breast. (To impose complaints upon others, such as those by beggar women who are supposed to have gnawing pains in the breast.)

Gaunt as a wolf.

Hungry as a wolf.

Sly as a wolf in sheep's clothing. Cf. A wolf in sheep's (lamb's) clothing.

Like sheep among wolves.

The wolves rend the sheep when the shepherds fail.

The wolf often eats the sheep that has been warned.

By little and little the wolf eateth the sheep.

Like setting the wolf to keep the sheep.

The wolf knows what the ill beast thinks.

Vicious as a wolf.

Who hath a wolf for his mate needs a dog for his man.

The wolf does something every week that keeps him from going to church on Sunday.

The wolf may lose his teeth, but never his nature.

The wolf must die in his own skin.

The wolf and the fox are both privateers.

When the wolf comes in at the door, love flies out at the window.

## Superstitions and Motifs

One can become a werewolf by crossing under three chairs backwards and saying a voodoo dialect at 12 p.m. The werewolf lives on blood which he sucks from his prey, mostly pregnant women, and can be caught by sprinkling grains of salt on its outer cover or by laying ninety-nine grains of rice or corn on its path.  Clark, 997

The wolf's tooth is a talisman to assist children in teething.

From Brown Collection

Against hydrophobia wear a dog's (tooth) and a wolf's tooth. VI, 1694

The hanging of a wolf's head on the door has the same power as the horseshoe.  VII, 5807

From Motif-Index

The wolf bites off the devil's heel.   G303. 4. 5. 7

Enmity exists between the lion and wolf.   A2494. 7. 2

The eagle warns the sheep that wolf is eating sheep.   J715. 1

The wolf is a devil in the form of a witch.   G303. 3. 3. 2. 1

The wolf poses as the grandmother and kills the child.   K201

The wolf persuades the lamb to bring him food:  the lamb is to be the food.   K815. 11

The wolf loses interest in the sermon when he sees a flock of sheep.   U125

The wolf is the devil's craftiest enemy.   G303. 25. 1

The wolf eats the devil.   G303. 17. 3. 3

The wolf excuses his killing the goose by referring to the saints.   K2055. 1

The wolf does not mind dust from the flock of sheep.   J352. 1

The wolf boasts of having eaten horses.   J2351. 4

Quotations--Literary and Otherwise

"As the saying is, I have got a wolf by the ears."--Terence, Phormio

"The wolf also shall dwell with the lamb, and the leopard shall lie down with the kid." -- Isaiah, XI, 6

"The Assyrian came down like the wolf on the fold..." --Byron, The Destruction of Sennacherib

"He's mad that trusts in the tameness of a wolf, a horse's health,
a boy's love, or a whore's oath." -- Shakespeare, King Lear

"Now this is the Law of the Jungle--as old and as true as the sky;
And the Wolf that shall keep it may prosper, but the Wolf
that shall break it must die." --Kipling, The Law of the
Jungle.

"The boy called out 'Wolf, Wolf!' and the villagers came out to
help him. He tried the trick the next day, and they came
to help. Later a wolf came, but the boy got no help." --
Aesop, The Shepherd's Boy

"The Lamb that belonged to the Sheep, whose skin the Wolf was
wearing, began to follow the Wolf in the Sheep's clothing."
-- Aesop

## The Rabbit's Foot

The rabbit arouses a great variety of human emotions, provoking every kind of expression from belly laughter to frustration and disgust, as illustrated in many popular games, jingles, and tales. With trickery and finesse he plays his game, apparently without malice toward those that harry him. If pursued by dogs and armed men, he darts about in a zigzag manner; long before the hunters are aware of his maneuvers he manages to get in behind them. Some say he is a devil, a demon, a witch, a ghost, and a perennial glutton who takes more than his due share of the world's food. He can be a delightful pet, but you must remember that he is excessively prolific and he also has power in his punch. His foot is reputed to be a charm that opens many a door to good fortune.

No doubt the rabbit understands how and why he practices his varied behavior. For centuries he has guarded his own security--he and his children have kept their eyes open, their ears erect, their stomachs crammed, and their feet ready to leap at a moment's notice toward the nearest hole or thicket. Under stress and strain, this hungry predator has sharpened his manners and made the best of what he has.

He is known by many names. Folks affectionately call him a bunny, a name also for the squirrel. Once, but rarely now, they said that he was a cony (Hyrax syriacus), as noted in Psalms 104:18 in the King James Version of 1611; however, in the Revised Standard Version of 1952, the Hebrew word is translated as a badger, a rodent-like and hoofed relative of the wombat or bandicoot. The rabbit should not be confused with the hare (Lepus europaeus of the family Leporidae), which originated in Europe and the Mediterranean basin and now is found in most parts of the world. The species closely related to the hare are the blue or mountain hare (Lepus timidus or hibernicus in Ireland); the polar, snowshoe, or arctic hare (Lepus arcticus); and the misnamed jackrabbit (Lepus macrolagus or compestris). In contrast to the rabbit, the hare (both gray and brown) does not burrow, and its young are covered with some hair and are able to see at birth. The adult hare is larger than the mature rabbit, has an overall length of about twenty-five inches, a cleft upper lip, long hind legs, long and erect ears, and a bushy and cocked tail.

The rabbit (Oryctolagus cuniculus) belongs to the same family as the hare. It originated in Europe and North Africa and now is very common in North America, New Zealand, and Australia. The best-known of the more than 50 species in this nation is the gray or wood rabbit, generally called a cottontail (Sylvilagus floridanus) and popularized in the works of Joel Chandler Harris. Other domesticated types are the misnamed Belgian hare, the long-eared rabbit, the small Dutch rabbit, and the long-furred Angora rabbit, including the highly valuable albino (Lepus americanus).

The rabbit produces young that are blind and almost helpless when born. When mature they weigh about three pounds, have an overall length of about eighteen inches, and may live for seven or eight years. Rabbits, like hares, begin mating when they are six months old, have four to eight harelipped youngsters about a month after conception, and have as many as eight broods a year. The population rise is astronomical, and it is no wonder that the folk say about some people: "They multiply like rabbits." Both rabbits and hares live on tender grasses and vegetables, especially lettuce and cabbage. In some areas they are a pesky lot, yet they produce palatable meat and valuable skins for industry and commerce, such as felt for hats and upholstery. You may be wearing a rabbit stole under a fancier name, and your college diploma may be inscribed on a rabbit skin.

This multiplicity of names for one animal is reflected in numerous compounds. To illustrate, a bunny and a cony refer to dupes; a bunny and a rabbit-pie are prostitutes that are hustled along by rabbit-pie shifters or policemen; a bunnymouth, a bunny rabbit, and a rabbit's mouth are snapdragons; bunny-grub and rabbit food are vegetables used in salads; a bunny cat and a rabbit cat are Abyssinian cats; a cony and a rabbit bandicoot are badgers; to bunny and to rabbit and pork are to talk too much; and to run the rabbit is to convey liquor from a public-house, whereas to swallow a hare is to become very drunk.

There are rabbit fleas, lice, mites, and ticks; also rabbit fish, hawks, rats, and squirrels. The cony is a figure in heraldry and the hare is immortalized in the constellation Lepus. A live rabbit is a free-wheeling male member of a club. The most frequent compounding is found in the names of plants: harebell, rabbit flower, rabbiteye blueberry, hare's-bane, rabbit-foot fern, rabbit thorn, and rabbit tobacco.

Information of this kind is of little consequence to the ordinary folk, in whose expressions the hare and the rabbit are one and the same. A rabbit, or hare, is a leaping trickster that uses his wits; he is not the losing sort as implied in Aesop's fable. Though he may limp across the frozen fields, he is usually fleet of foot. He is also timid, jumpy, flighty, and freakish; but on most occasions he is a respectable gentleman in the presence of those who hound him. Call him a dupe or simpleton, a madman in March, a laggard in competition with the tortoise, and most of the time you are wrong. Characterize him as rabbity--hare-brained, hare-eared, hare-eyed, hare-footed, or even harelipped--accuse him of hare-sleeping--and you will be complimenting him.

If you expect to bag a windfall of rabbits in the wood, you must start long before breakfast. Merely kissing or licking his hind feet will avail you nothing; so take charge of him from head to tail--then you've got him. And, for goodness' sake, do not look him in the face if you are pregnant. You might have a harelipped baby.

To keep in step with the superstitious lore, always carry a rabbit's foot, preferably from one caught in a Negro graveyard, as a trusty and remedial talisman. To doubly assure yourself of high fortune, carry a forefoot in your pocket or around your neck. The forefoot is also useful to ward off asthma, spells, rheumatism, and other complaints. Many an old wife has said that this foot is a reliable aid in reducing the pains of childbirth or teething. It is also stated that it will counteract the curses of witches, demons, and ghosts. It will assure you, for a certainty, of getting a new silk dress, of speeding up a simmering romance, or inducing a hesitant lover to send you a love token. It will tell you about the number of years before your marriage, and it may specify the date of your death and where you will be buried.

Oh, the magic in a rabbit's foot!

## Derivative Names

bunny: rabbit or squirrel; Welsh rabbit

bunny: pet name

bunny: dupe or dolt; habitually perplexed person

bunny: Bismarck brown

bunny: female pudend; female prostitute to lesbians; male prostitute to male homosexuals

bunny: to talk or chat excessively

bunny cat: Abyssinian cat; bobtail cat

bunny-grub (also bunny's meat): green vegetables

bunny hop: short leap

bunny hug: dance popular about 1910

bunnymouth: snapdragon

bunny rabbit: snapdragon

coney (cony): European rabbit, the hyrax or badger

coney: dupe or simpleton

coney: figure in heraldry

coney: any of several fish such as burbot

cony-catch: to cheat, deceive, or trick

cony-catcher: deceiver or cheater

cony-dog: one who assists in cony-catching

# Rabbit

hare: to run fast

hare: constellation Lepus

hare: passenger without ticket (British)

hare and hounds: game in which players as hares are followed by players as hounds

harebell: perennial herb with blue flowers; wood hyacinth

harebottle: knapweed

hare-brained (also harebrain): foolish, flighty, giddy

harebur: burdock

hare ears: showing fear and suspicion

hare-eyed: having eyes timidly alert

hare-finder: leader in rabbit-hunting expedition

harefoot: long, narrow foot; rabbit-foot clover

hare foot: showing agility and speed

harefooted: fleet-footed

harehearted: timorous

harehound: one used to hunt hares

hare kangaroo: small Australian kangaroo resembling hare

harelip: congenital fissure in upper lip; being harelipped

harelipped bat: large tropical American fish-eating bat

harelip sucker: cutlip

hare-sleep: feigned sleep

hare tracks: showing fleetness or swiftness

hare's-bane: wolf's bane

hare's-meat: wood-sorrel

hare's-parsley: European herb

rabbit: a cheap fur

rabbit: broccoli-brown color

rabbit: contemptible person; a novice

rabbit: new-born babe

rabbit: salad, composed of greens

rabbit: sort of wooden drinking vessel

rabbit and pork: to talk or chat

rabbit ball: baseball

rabbit bandicoot: bandicoot or badger with long ears

rabbitberry: buffalo berry

rabbit brush (also rabbit bush or rabbitweed): common shrub in western United States; used by jackrabbits for hiding

rabbit cat: Abyssinian cat. Cf. bunny cat.

rabbit-eared: like a rabbit's ears

rabbit-ear faucet: self-closing faucet

rabbit-ear mite: one attacking ears of rabbits

rabbit ears: showing sensitivity to criticism; portable TV antenna

rabbiteye blueberry: type grown in United States for canning

rabbit fever: tularemia

rabbit fish: any of several kinds resembling rabbit

rabbit flea: one of several types attacking rabbits

rabbit flower (also rabbit-ear): toad-flax; purple foxglove

rabbit food (also rabbit's food): vegetable salad; any kind of greens. Cf. bunny-grub.

rabbit-foot: to move quickly; to escape from prison

rabbit-foot grass: European clover or rabbit's foot, a weedy grass

rabbit hawk: red-tailed hawk

rabbit hutch: coop in which rabbits are bred

rabbit louse: common louse on rabbits

rabbit-meat: red archangel

rabbit moth: moth affecting southern oranges

rabbitmouth: rabbitmouth sucker. Cf. harelip sucker.

rabbit-mouthed: hare-lipped

rabbit-o: seller of rabbits on streets

rabbit pea: catgut

rabbit-pie: harlot

rappit-pie shifter: policeman

rabbit punch (also rabbit's punch, and rabbiter): sharp blow to back of head

rabbit rat: small rodent or bandicoot

rabbitroot: wild sarsaparilla

rabbitry: group of hutches for rabbits

rabbits: contraband or smuggled goods; customs officer

rabbit's-ear cabbage: Canadian weed

rabbit's foot (also rabbit foot): hind leg of rabbit used as talisman for good luck

rabbit's foot clover: rabbit-foot clover. Cf. rabbit-foot grass.

rabbit's-foot fern: serpent fern

rabbit's mouth: snapdragon. Cf. bunnymouth and bunny rabbit.

rabbit-skin: parchment for certificate or diploma

rabbit squirrel: large South American rodent

rabbit stick or club: boomerang

rabbit-sucker: young spendthrift

rabbit-tail grass: hare's-tail grass

rabbit thorn: rough and thorny shrub

rabbit tick: common tick

rabbit tobacco: balsamweed

rabbit vine: groundnut

rabbit warren: place to keep rabbits; crowded tenement house

rabbit, Welsh (also Welsh rarebit): melted cheese and toast

rabbitweed: stiff woody herb

rabbitwood: shrub parasitic on hemlocks

rabbity: like or resembling rabbit

## Proverbs and Proverbial Phrases

Crazy as a March hare.

Cute as a bunny.

Funny as a bunny.

Harried as a rabbit.

Jumps like a rabbit.

Like sending carrots by a rabbit.

Mad as a March hare. (Very old; source: John Heywood, Pro-verbes, II, V; related to time when rabbits mate) Cf. Crazy as a March hare.

Multiply like rabbits.

Quicker than a rabbit to his hole.

Runs like a rabbit.

Swift as a hare.

Timid as a hare.

Make a hare of: to make ridiculous.

Make rabbits: to follow a hobby.

Buy the rabbit or rabbits: to have worst of bargain.

Run the rabbit: to convey liquor from a public-house.

Get one's rabbit-skin: to get college bachelor's degree. Cf. sheepskin.

Swallow a hare: to get very drunk.

# Rabbit

Seek a hare in a hen's nest: to try to do the impossible.

Go rabbit-hunting or cony-catching with a dead ferret: unsuitable or useless means.

Kiss the hare's foot: to be late. Cf. Get the hare's foot to lick: to get little or nothing.

He that will have a hare for breakfast must hunt overnight.

It's rabbits out of the woods: windfall or sheer profit.

He hath devoured a hare: something has made him melancholy.

Set the hare's head against the goose giblets: stingy or unfair exchange.

Like a fat and lean rabbit: responding promptly to food after being lean for twenty-four hours.

Run with the hare and hunt with the hounds: to play a double game. Cf. To hold with the hare and run with the hound: to be erratic and freakish. --John Heywood, Proverbes.

Hares may pull dead lions by the ears.

Who will change a rabbit for a rat?

The hare always returns to her form.

## Superstitions and Motifs

From Brown Collection

It is bad luck for a hare to cross the path on which you are traveling. VI, 3849. Cf. Bad luck to have rabbit cross your path. 3850. Cf. It is good luck for a rabbit to cross your path. 3846

Rabbits fatten on frost, etc. VII, 7427

A rabbit can be caught in a newly-made box if made of old planks and allowed to stand a year. VII, 7177f

Hunt rabbits after first white frost. They are then fat from eating persimmons and frost. VII, 7894

When it has snowed, it is a good time to go rabbit hunting. VII, 8564

If a fisherman meets a hare on his way fishing, he turns back, knowing that his luck is lost for the day. VII, 7809

The right forefoot of a hare (rabbit) is good to ward off disease.
VI, 743. Cf. 744, 746-49

Carrying a rabbit's foot caught in a Negro graveyard on Saturday night gives good luck. VII, 5795

A rabbit's foot worn around neck will prevent asthma. VI, 819

To bring the child, tie asafoetida around mother's neck and put a rabbit's foot under her head. VI, 27

If a pregnant woman sees a rabbit, the child will have a harelip. VI, 110

Put rabbit tobacco in a corncob pipe and smoke it. Blow the smoke into the ear and it will cure earache. VI, 1327

To make people break out with measles, make rabbit pill teas. VI, 1808

The right forefoot of a rabbit is used to ward off rheumatism. VI, 1985

Rabbit feet worn around your neck will keep off spells. VII, 5571

Put a rabbit bone around a baby's neck when he is teething. VI, 367

A young rabbit's brains rubbed on a baby's gums will ease them in teething. VI, 365f

Tie a rabbit foot around the baby's neck so that cutting teeth will be easy. VI, 368

A red-haired Negro is a witch. If he gives you a rabbit's foot, you have an all-powerful talisman against a witch, and also for good luck. VII, 5589

To break charms from witch rabbits or witch cats, turn all your pockets inside out. VII, 5659

If you carry a rabbit foot in your pocket, you cannot be bewitched. VII, 5676

A rabbit's foot in one's pocket will keep away ghosts. VII, 5730

If cold chills run down your spine, a rabbit is then running over your grave. VII, 5239. Cf. 5240

If you carry a rabbit's foot in your pocket, you can get a new silk dress. VI, 3163

# Rabbit

To break love tokens, send the gift back to the giver and wear a rabbit's foot, namely, the left hind foot of a graveyard rabbit. VI, 4262

If a rabbit runs across path in front of you a certain number of times, that will be the number of years until you get married. VI, 4638

On the first day of the month say 'Rabbit! rabbit! rabbit!' and the first thing you know, you will get a present from someone you like very much. VII, 7178

From Motif-Index

Frightened rabbit puts head into charred tree; hence black ears. A2212.1

Why rabbit has long ears. A2325.1

Hare sleeps with open eyes as defense. A2461.1

Hare instructs sons to use their eyes to advantage. J61

Laughs cause harelip. A2211.2

Why hare has short tail. A2378.4.1

Why rabbit continually moves mouth. A2476.1

Coyote and hare are enemies. A 2494.6.2

Hare escapes lion by going into brushwood. K521.10

Hare flatters other animals and bites off their ears. K1018

The sleeping hare and tortoise race one another. K11.3

Race won by deception when rabbit disguises himself as his little son. K11.6

Rabbit is punished in the briar patch. K581.2

Hare demands equal rights for all animals. J975

The man in the moon is a rabbit. A751.2

Man in the moon is more timid than the hare. J881.1

A witch transforms herself to a hare so as to suck cows. D655.2

A demon appears in form of the hare. F401.3.6

## Quotations--Literary and Otherwise

"When the Hare awoke from his nap, he saw the Tortoise just near the winning post. Plodding wins the race." --Aesop, <u>The Hare and the Tortoise.</u>

"The hare limp'd trembling through the frozen grass..."-- John Keats, <u>The Eve of St. Agnes</u>

"W'en ole man Rabbit say 'scoot,' dey scooted, en w'en old Miss Rabbit say 'scat,' dey scatted." -- Joel Chandler Harris, <u>Legends of the Old Plantation</u>

### A Folk Song

### Old Molly Hare (Mr. Rabbit)

'Ole Molly Hare, what you doin' there?'
'Runnin' through the cotton patch hard as I can tear.'

'Bru'r Rabbit, Bru'r Rabbit, what makes your ears so long?'
'Cause, by God, they're put on wrong.'

'Bru'r Rabbit, Bru'r Rabbit, what makes you look so shy?'
'Cause, my Lord, I don't want to die.'

'Bru'r Rabbit, Bru'r Rabbit, what makes you look so thin?'
'Cause, by God, I'm burning the wind.'

'Bru'r Rabbit, Bru'r Rabbit, what makes your tail so white?'
'Cause, by God, I'm going out of sight.'
-- Brown Collection, III, 211-212

## Goosey Goosey-Gander

Since far back in ancient history, the goose has made a fool of himself. Regardless of what the folk have said about him, he has kept his goosiness and has taught his goslings to uphold the sound and unchangeable principles of their fathers. The ordinary man has enjoyed goose on his dinner table and at the same time has found much fun and self-knowledge in observing the peculiar manners of the breed. The sportsman has also added to the lore about the goose, noting the splendor of the V-shaped flight of geese and the unerring succession of command whenever the leader of the formation drops out. The patriot, too, has expressed at length his regards for the goose as a mighty bulwark of the state. Doubtless you recall that the Gauls in 390 B.C. were poised to scale the walls of Rome. But the frightened geese rose to the occasion by setting up a cackling and clamoring that warned the Roman citizens, who mounted their attack and routed the invaders. Thus it was that the goose, somewhat in the tradition of the wolf that suckled Romulus and Remus, came into his own--his squawking made him an empire builder.

The goose (_Anser_ of the sub-family _Anserinae_ of the _Anatidae_) is classified into some forty groups throughout the world, including about ten in Canada and the United States. The largest species is the Chinese goose (_Cygnopsis cygnoides_), said to be the originator of several orders in the Far East. The second important type is the Branta, embracing the black geese and the following related kinds: the barnacle goose (_Branta leucopsis_), supposedly named for the barnacle tree whose fruit turned into barnacles or fish, and now extensively observed in areas from northeast Greenland to Spitzbergen and on to Siberia; and the Branta-goose (_Branta bernicla_), breeding in circumpolar regions and inclusive of the Canada goose (_Branta canadensis_). The folk know best the greying or grey-lag goose (Anser anser), which is related to the bean goose (Anser fabalis) and the pink-footed goose (Anser brachyrbychus)--all of them being seen from Lapland to Spain, from Scotland to China, and from the Aleutian Islands southward to Mexico. The commonest American members of the group are the white-fronted goose (Anser gambeli), the emperor goose (Anser canagica), and the popular white or snow goose (Anser hyperboreus).

Geese are web-footed, are larger than ducks but smaller than swans, and live primarily on vegetables and grain. Excepting the domesticated breeds, they migrate during the seasons, and are noted for their curious honking while in their V-shaped flight. However, they spend most of their time on land, where they pair off with their mates, moult after the breeding periods, and engage in a distinct partnership in the raising of their young. As long as they live--some for as long as fifty years--they demonstrate a deep sense of community.

The goose--often characterized as conceited, foolish, and silly--is far better than his reputation. Aside from his commendable qualities of imagination, wakefulness, and love for his own breed, he is an important factor in the domestic economies of the world, providing meat, eggs, quills, and feathers. Weighing up to twenty pounds, his body yields a percentage of fat and protein higher than that of beef.

The goose's contribution to the word horde of the English-speaking nations is particularly apparent in areas where the domesticated goose is widely dispersed. The lore about the goose, the gander, and the gosling is extensive. For instance, without repeating a number of colorful examples stated later, you might note the following expressions: to goose, to go whoring; to goose-cackle, to chatter; goose drownder, downpour of rain; goose file, single or Indian file; goosebill, sort of forceps; gooseneck and ball, andiron; gooseneck lamp, one shaped like a goose's neck; goose-share, cleavers; goose's gazette, lying story or silly-season tale; goose-shearer, beggar; and goose-step, a stiff-legged marching step.

If you wish to understand the innards of the goose you must consider the sayings of the folk, who think they know what a goose is. To them, "What's sauce for the goose is sauce for the gander." Furthermore, "Goose and gander and gosling are three sounds for one thing." Indeed, a gone gander, a gone goose, and a gone gosling are one and the same--all of them have had a knock-out blow and are no longer capable of effective action. In short, their goose has been cooked, especially if they have crashed a revival conducted by a fox that has escaped the hangman's noose.

Moreover, the gosling, silly as he may be, shows some meritorious qualities when he proudly leads the geese to the ponds or green pastures and when he finally flies alone across some mighty river. Feeling the independence of manhood, he returns from his venture to compete in the goosiness of his elders. The folk say that he is a dolt, a country bumpkin, a plain goose-cap, or a flighty girl. And if this goose is a gander, with all the prerogatives and shortcomings of married men, he can sometimes find a safe retreat in a gander-party. Wandering and waddling, he is a gander-mooner throughout the gander-month, while his mate broods on her nest and hopes that a Sunday thunderstorm will not spoil her eggs. To be a gander is to be at the end of a line of gluttons. By way of realizing how he may be ignored, you should recall that a group of dwarfs agreed to receive a goose as a gift, but under no circumstances would they accept a gander. And if you wish to show your contempt for him, pick out the seed of one of your warts, insert it into a grain of corn, and feed it to the gander. He will get your wart and score again in foolishness.

The folk, who have closely watched geese in the air, about the barnyards, on the ponds, and in the green pastures, have been very outspoken and unrestrained in their expressions about them. They have observed them during the breeding seasons. When mulberries are ripe, they also note that their rumps are red just as is the bear's in polkberry time. As the geese hop here and there while cramming themselves in the green fields, they color the vegetation in unforgettable hues known to the common people as goose-green and gosling-green.

This detailed lore, suggestive as it is, may afflict you with goose flesh, goose pimples, or goose bumps, normally produced by sudden cold or fear. You may also be goosed, irritated or frenzied with laughter. In fact, you may feel worse than a team that has been goosed or goose-egged by a superior opponent and has scored only a conspicuous zero. Or you may become a silly goose, like the tailor that confused his goose (smoothing iron) with the andiron in the same fireplace.

As you continue your meditations and investigations, you must be "sound on the goose," that is, you are expected to bear true allegiance to your principles. You are warned, however, not to be fooled by venturing out on a wild-goose chase. All the odds are against you, and you are bound to appear goosed or made ridiculous. You are also reminded, in Aesop's story, that there is no profit in killing the golden goose. And if you are pressured to steal a goose, be generous enough to donate the best of it to the needy instead of doling out a few tough giblets that you do not like. Such tightfisted goosiness is sure to call forth the sarcastic remark: "Go! Shoe the goose."

Let it not be said that you did not hang your goose high, both literally and figuratively. Once you have plucked him and raised his body out of reach of the fox, all will be rosy for you and your household. You will never have any excuse for grumbling, provided that your goose has sufficient fat to baste itself. Everybody, including the tailor, will rejoice and wax strong in health and prosperity.

When the goose comes out of the oven, be sure to make full use of all the resources, especially the abundant supply of fat. For a cold or sore throat, rub in some goose oil around the throat, on the chest, and about the ribs. A mixture of goose grease and molasses is an excellent remedy for the croup. A combination of alcohol, olive oil, and goose oil is effective in reducing the pains of rheumatism. And goose manure, when stewed with sweetgum leaves and hog lard, is a first-class ointment for burns. Moreover, vigorous applications of goose oil, alone or mixed, will make your body supple and tingle with unusual vitality. Incidentally, if your crops are suffering from a drought, watch the movements of a goose--they may foretell the coming of an early rain.

# Goose

## Derivative Names

gander: male goose; dunce or stupid person

gander: married man

gander: to ramble or wander, waddle like a goose

gander: to look over another's shoulder at his mail; to be a rubberneck or "take a gander"

ganderess: goose girl

gander-faced: silly-faced, proletarian

gander-goose: male orchis

gander-grass: plant supposed to be <u>Orchis masculus</u>

gander-month (also gander-moon): month after childbirth

gander-mooner: husband during the gander-month

gander-party: party for men only

gander pull: game in the southeastern U.S.A. of pulling off head of gander while riding past it

gander teeth: sensitive brier in southern U.S.A.

gander's wool: feathers of gander

goose: both male and female of goose, more specifically female of geese

goose: tailor's smoothing iron, shaped like a goose's neck

goose: to outwit someone or take advantage of his lack of alertness; to ruin oneself

goose (also goose-egg): to prevent an opponent in sports from scoring

goose: to condemn by hissing; to poke finger at or threaten

goose: to give no tip to a waitress

goose: to go wenching or whoring

goose: to feed gas in spurts into an engine

goose barnacle: barnacle that attaches itself to bottom of a ship and thus legend that geese so originated (See goose tree.)

goosebeak: dolphin

goosebeak whale: small and rare whale

gooseberry: to gather gooseberries

gooseberry: small and sour berry somewhat like currant but larger; thorny or spiny bush. See goose-gob

gooseberry-eyed: having dull-gray eyes

goosebill: sort of forceps

goosebird: Hudsonian godwit

goosebone: bone from goose

gooseboy: keeper of geese

goose bumps: goose pimples. See gooseflesh

goose-bumpy: frightened, having goose bumps

goose-cackle: chatter

goose call: call of geese

goose-cap (also goosecap): dolt or simpleton; flighty girl

goose chase: wild-goose chase

goose club: club formed to raffle for geese

goose corn: coarse rush

goosedrownder: downpour of rain

goose-egg: cipher, naught, zero, complete shutout in a game

goose file: single or Indian file

goosefish: the angler

gooseflesh (also goose pimples, gooseskin): roughness of skin caused by fear or cold weather

gooseflower (also goose plant): tropical vine

goosefoot: group of plants such as spinach, beets, etc. with coarse leaves shaped like the foot of a goose

goosefoot family: Chenopodiacea

goosefoot maple: striped maple

goosegirl: girl that keeps geese

goose-gob (also goose-gog): gooseberry

goosegrass (also gooseweed): any of various herbs and grasses, especially catchweed bedstraw

goose gray: lama gray

goose grease: rendered fat

goose-green: yellowish-green color

goose gull: great black-backed gull

goose-hawk: goshawk

gooseherd: tender of geese

goosehouse: place in which to keep geese

goose influenza: fatal pulmonary inflammation

goose mildew: mildew affecting gooseberries

goose-month: month following childbirth; same as gander-month

goosemouth: deformed mouth of horse, with upper lip overhanging lower lip

gooseneck: anything long and curved like goose's neck

gooseneck and ball: andiron

gooseneck lamp: one with base shaped like a goose's neck

gooseneck pediment: two balanced, double-curved members of a scroll or rosette

gooseneck slicker: tool to cut weeds

gooseneck trailer: front part of trailer shaped like a goose's neck

goose pen: pen for geese

goose-persuader: tailor

goose plum: American wild plum

goose quill: quill from goose, used for writing; symbol of authorship gooser:  knock-out blow

goose rump:  rump set low like that of a goose

goose-rumped:  having rump like that of a goose

goosery:  silliness

goose's gazette:  lying story; silly-season tale

goose-share:  cleavers

goose-shearer:  beggar

gooseskin:  skin of goose; having gooseflesh

goose-step:  march in goose-step; step with legs stiff and unbent

goose tansy:  silverweed

goose teal:  pygmy goose

goose tongue:  sneezewort

goose tree:  fabulous tree bearing fruits that became barnacles or fish

goose turd:  cigarette

goose-turd green:  light yellow-green

goose walk:  move in game of checkers

goosewing:  studding sail; lower corner of a foresail or square mainsail; to make goosewinged

goosey (also goosy):  stupid or foolish; nervous or jumpy; having a goose-flesh feeling

goosey-gander:  gander

goosish:  to be like a goose

goosiness:  state of being goosey

gosling:  young goose; silly person

gosling:  a tree

gosling:  catkin or ament; pasqueflower

gosling-green (also gosling weed):  pale, yellowish green

Goose

## Proverbs and Proverbial Phrases

Goose and gander and gosling are three sounds for one thing.

A gone gander. (Wornout or incapacitated.) Cf. A gone goose and gone gosling.

Gray as a gander.

Red as a gander's foot.

To be a gander-mooner: male gone to wander while goose is sitting.

To see how the gander hops.

He that has a goose will get a goose.

Like a goose's ass in mulberry time.

It is a sorry goose that will not baste herself.

It is a blind (silly) goose that comes to the fox's sermon. Cf. wolf.

Not able to say "boo" to a goose: bashful or timid.

Say "boo" to a goose: be not altogether lacking in courage.

To find fault with a fat goose: to grumble without cause.

Full as a goose.

To give someone the goose: to goose or surprise someone; to speed up something

It's a gone goose with him: wornout or left in the lurch. Cf. A gone gander or gosling.

His goose is cooked: chances spoiled or everything lost.

A goose cannot graze after him: nothing left to eat.

There is no goose so grey in the lake that cannot find a gander for her make (mate).

A man ought to know a goose from a gridiron.

A tailor, be he ever so poor, is always sure to have a goose at his fire.

The goose hangs (or honks) high: all prospects are good and favorable. Cf. Everything in the garden is lovely, and the goose hangs high (that is, the plucked goose is hanging high and out of reach of the fox).

Get the goose: to be hissed.

Hot as a hen laying a goose egg.

Don't kill the goose that laid the golden eggs. Cf. "Thinking to get at once the gold the Goose could give, he killed it and opened it only to find nothing." --Aesop, The Goose With the Golden Eggs

Loose as a goose.

Young (or old) is the goose that will eat no oats.

What's sauce for the goose is sauce for the gander.

A setting goose never gets fat.

Go! Shoe the goose: a sarcastic retort.

Silly as a goose.

Slick as goose grease.

Don't smother the goose with the featherbed.

To be sound on the goose: to hold on to true principles; to be loyal to a political party.

Squirts like a goose.

To steal a goose and give giblets in alms: to amass wealth and give little to charity. Cf. Set the hare's head against the goose giblets.

Every man thinks his own geese are swans. Cf. A crow thinks her young are white.

A wild goose never laid a tame egg.

To go on a wild goose chase: to pursue foolishly the unattainable.

To be a gone gosling: wornout or done for.

Goslings lead the geese to grass (or water): the young lead the old.

A gosling flew over the Rhine and came back a goose: growth and wisdom take time.

Goose

## Superstitions and Motifs

### From Brown Collection

Old people say that the juice of goose grass is an excellent blood purifier. VI, 893

Goose manure stewed with sweetgum leaves and hog lard, strained and made into an ointment, is good for burns. VI, 977

Rub chest, palms and soles of the feet with goose grease to cure colds. VI, 1126

Administer a mixture of goose grease and molasses to cure the croup. VI, 1254

If it thunders on Sunday, goose eggs will not hatch. VII, 7504

When a goose flies east, and walks west, there will be rain. VII, 6695

Alcohol, goose grease, and olive oil are good for rheumatism. VI, 2029

If you eat goose on New Year's Day, you will be rich. VI, 3358

To cure sore throat, rub in goose oil and tie up with a stocking or flannel. VI, 2192

Goose grease applied externally will make you supple. VI, 644. Cf. 1834

To get rid of wart: Pick the seed out of a wart, put it in a grain of corn and give it to a gander. VI, 2511

### From Motif-Index

Cackling geese spread alarm. B521.3.2

A captured goose warns the tortoise. B143.1.6

Goose is mistaken for a tailor. J1762.1

The devil is a goose. G303.3.3.8

The dwarfs accept the goose as a gift, but not the gander. F451.3.6.4

A witch uses goose wings as oars. G241.4.1

A fox that is about to be hanged asks to be allowed to see the geese. J864.2.

A goose that laid the golden egg.   D876.   Cf. B102.1.3

A hawk flies away with geese on a line.   X1267.1

A man is carried through the air by a goose.   X1258.1

## Monkey See, Monkey Do

How can you ever forget your first sight of a monkey? You were thrilled, and puzzled too, by his antics in a cage by the roadside, in a zoo, at a fair, or on a street corner where he was the agile handyman of an Italian organ grinder. A busy little scamp, he did his daily workout--sometimes in utter nakedness, sometimes sporting a tight and many-colored jacket--eating peanuts and bananas, hanging by his tail and cutting all sorts of capers.

The sprightly monkey belongs to an order of mammals called primates, which also includes man, the apes, tarsiers, and lemurs, all of whom have certain similarities in bone structure, posture, brain capacity, locomotion, family life, and so forth. In this group of relatives the monkey is the one that most resembles man.

Monkeys are smaller than most other primates and differ in important respects from the anthropoid apes (gibbon, chimpanzee, orangutan, and gorilla). The New World monkey is distinctly flat-faced, more rounded in the head and less calloused in the buttocks than the Old World species. He is found in Central and South America, the tropics being his most favored habitat. Equipped with a prehensile tail, and four hands with nimble thumbs and fingers, he thrives best as an arboreal creature in the wilds of nature. Generally he has more intelligence than is acknowledged, for he has acute and well-developed senses of seeing and hearing; in addition, he has speech signals that are expressed emotionally in shrieks to vent his anger or to sound an alarm for the benefit of his fellows.

Monkeys have an integrated family life. They pair off for romancing and reproduction, and are reputed to hold a deep love for one another and for their children. Blessed also by an appreciation of communal ties, they like to travel in groups for enjoyment and common safety. They have clean habits and usually live on fruits, nuts, and insects; sometimes they devour eggs, young birds, and reptiles. In the view of human observers, their principal characteristics are flattery, mimicry, imitativeness, lasciviousness, maliciousness, petty thievery, and ugliness.

The monkey's name serves as the base of several score of English words. His smallness and agility, his comic nature, have provided names for some unusual concepts. Despite the belief that his presence on a seagoing vessel is an omen of storms, his name appears in a number of nautical terms: monkey-boat, monkey bridge, monkey deck, monkey-gaff, monkey island, monkey ladder, monkey poop, monkey rail, monkey spar, and monkey tail. Plants and trees are his namesakes: monkey-bread, monkey flower, monkey nut, monkey pod, monkey-puzzle, monkey's dinner-bell, and monkey vine. In the business world we find: monkey (British note for 500 pounds), monkey bag, monkey board, monkey cage, monkey-flag, monkey house, and monkey wrench. Then there are these miscellaneous phrases, somewhat barbed in some instances: monkey meat, tough or inferior beef; monkey's allowance, more kicks than pennies; monkey's parade, a procession of young couples down a lane in quest of new acquaintance; monkey wire, telephone wire; monkey time, Daylight Saving Time; Monkey Ward, Montgomery Ward; and monkey oboe, a medical officer.

The foregoing illustrations are a bit spineless as far as the real monkey is concerned. This kindred fellow is a clown and sometimes a fool, whether alone or in the traditional barrel full of his own breed. The folk say that he is tricky and arrogant when he covers himself with a sheet and scares the daylights out of his owner, or when he dons the purple and gold of the nobleman to impress the commoner, or when he cheats the fox out of the bananas, or when thoroughly safe from harm he thumbs his nose at the gorilla.

With no dampers on his monkey business, he trifles, meddles, deceives, and cuts all kinds of monkeyshines. If he is a lover trying to show his virility, he puts on a special sequence of monkey-tricks. If he is a boot-camp soldier, he wades through mud holes or pumps his limbs in calisthenic drill to indicate that he is disciplined and, incidentally, to impress a none-too-well-informed second lieutenant. If he is inclined to monkey around with buzz saws or hydrogen bombs, he is indeed in a zone of danger.

Man feels compelled to bedeck himself with gaudy neckties and monkey jackets, to wave flags as tokens of national glory, or to parade here and there before a host of other monkeys, in much the same manner of the monkey punk who buzzes around the guests of a hotel. The small monks, the children, are not far behind--they have learned all the antics of their elders and even more. It is excellent training for the youngsters, especially for the girls who are rosily budding and laying monkey-traps for the supposedly untutored guy that has some hidden tricks of his own.

The Americans and British have seen this sort of monkeyish behavior and have noted it in their folklore. The latter have commented at length about the social and economic aspects of being a free-wheeling fool, often in a Puritanical or moralistic vein. For instance, if your house is mortgaged something has got you by the tail--you have a monkey on the house or you have one with a long tail. If you are addicted to drugs, you have a monkey on your back. If you are sucking the monkey and using numerous monkey chasers (that is, swigging the bottle excessively), you are as jerky, unstable, and ludicrous as a monkey on or up a stick.

It is fair enough to probe into comparative manners of monkeys and men, along with a suggestion of how they can get redemption from their immemorial and mutual damnation. By all odds the monkey, despite the limitations of his slow evolution, has been doing no more than being himself. On the other hand, this creature called homo sapiens has something that he has inherited, but he does not know how to manipulate it to the best advantage. In form and spirit, in knowledge and skills, man has untapped resources to make our good earth a plentiful home for all. He knows how to dream and sing, shape words and colors and stones into things of joy, and elevate the commonplace into the peace of the blessed. He can feel deeply, but the monkey is on his back--jittering and jerking and despoiling himself and the earth about him. He rapes, he ravishes, he flattens cities with bombs, he poisons the air with gasses, he uproots the protecting forests, he plows deep into the rich soil and sends it away in clouds, he contaminates his water-- in brief, he is hell-bent on ruining the resources of nature and mankind.

In consideration of countless warnings and protests--and in desperation of not finding a better way--let man return to the zoo and renew his relationship with the monkey. Let him banish forever the fears and prejudices of his upbringing. Let him in all humility engage the monkey in a give-and-take dialogue on the unfinished agenda. And together let them resolve for all time that they are kindred souls seeking to recover their lost opportunities for mutual advancement. Let them roar with belly laughter with and at each other.

## Derivative Names

monk: short for monkey (munkey); high-ranking judge; term applied to Chinese by Irish neighbors

monkey (also monkey with): to play, fool, trifle, meddle, or act in grotesque manner

monkey: dupe; person acting like monkey; victim; one dressed to look like a monkey

monkey: small, active, and mischievous child; silly or frivolous one

monkey: device used as iron block or ram in pile driving

monkey: one given to narcotics addiction

monkey: British note for 500 pounds

monkey act: entertaining or sensational action

monkey apple: pond apple

monkey bag: small bag for money, etc.

monkey-ball: fruit of the plane tree

monkey bass: piassava

monkey bear: koala in Australia

# Monkey

monkey belt: cord to which monkey is tied

monkey-bite: amorous bite on the shoulder

monkey block: nautical term for small block with swivel

monkey board: footboard at rear of vehicle used by conductor or footman

monkey-boat: small boat used in docks

monkey-bread: a tree, the baobab; also its gourd-like fruit, eaten by monkeys

monkey bridge: narrow platform above deck of vessel

monkey business: foolish and mischievous action, often unethical

monkey-cage: barred room from which convicts converse with visitors

monkey cap: small pillbox

monkey-chaser: drink composed of gin, sugar, water, and ice

monkey clothes: tuxedo or formal evening clothes. Cf. monkey jacket

monkey coconut (also monkey's coconut): kind of coconut; coquito

monkey-cup: East Indian pitcherplant

monkey-couch: position or seat in American saddle

monkey deck or forecastle: anchor deck

monkey-dodger: sheep-station hand

monkey drill (also monkey-motions): physical drill or calisthenics

monkey engine: engine for lifting monkey device in pile driving

monkey-faced: having face like a monkey

monkey-faced owl: barn owl

monkey fist (also monkey's fist): large knot weighting a heaving line

monkey-flag: flag, insigne, or standard of armed services; or of business, social, or political organizations

monkflower (also monkey flower): one of several curious orchids, such as members of figwort family; toadflax

monkey flush: three cards of same suit in poker

monkey foresail: square foresail on a sloop

monkeyfy: to make one look like a monkey

monkey-gaff: a light gaff on mizzenmast of vessel to display signals

monkey-god: a god in form of monkey

monkey grass: coarse fiber from Brazilian palm

monkey hammer (also monkey press): drop hammer

monkeyhood: state of being a monkey

monkey-house (also monkey wagon): caboose of railway train

monkeyish: being like a monkey

monkey island: uppermost tier of a big ship's bridge

monkey jack: pick used in pulling stumps

monkey jacket (also monkey suit and monkey-coat): short and tight jacket, worn by sailors and others

monkey jar or jug: goglet

monkey ladder: light ship's ladder

monkey line: line used in lowering a boat

monkey link: repair link in automobile chain

monkey meat: inferior, tough beef

monkey-monk: the intensive of monkey

monkey nut: peanut; fruit of European basswood

monkey oboe: medical officer

monkey orange: African shrub

monkey pie: cocoanut cream pie

monkey pod: rain tree of Hawaii

monkey-poop: half deck of flush-decked ship

monkeypot: urn-shaped fruit of various trees of Brazil and Guiana; also tree bearing this fruit

monkey-pump: drinking straw in glass of liquor

monkey punk: bellhop or porter in uniform

monkey-puzzle: large, urn-shaped Chilean tree, having hard, yellowish-white wood and edible seeds

monkey rail: second and lighter rail on a ship

monkey-rigged: having reduced spars

monkey-rope: Liana; safety rope on a ship

monkey rum: distilled syrup of sugar cane or sorghum cane

monkeyry: place where monkeys live

monkey's allowance: more kicks than pennies, or more rough treatment than gifts of money

monkey's dinner-bell: capsule of sandbox tree

monkey's hand: ass's-foot

monkey's instep: the cat's meow (rare)

monkey's money: payment in kind, especially labor, goods, etc.

monkey's parade: a length of road where young couples go to strike up acquaintance

monkey shaft: small trial shaft in a mine

monkey-shine(s): mischievous trick, antics, clownish joke

monkey skin: being brown, reddish, or red-yellowish in hue

monkey spar: small mast or yard

monkey stick: cane or walking stick

monkey strap: strap on side of the pommel of a saddle

monkey suit: uniform or suit of clothes, usually disparaging. See monkey jacket

monkey tail (also monkey's-tail): short round bar or hand-spike used in training naval guns; piece of rope

monkey-tail valve: starting valve of marine engine

monkey tie: gaudy necktie

monkey time: Daylight Saving Time

monkey-traps: female finery

monkey-tricks: sexual liberties

monkey vine: tropical morning-glory

Monkey Ward: a Montgomery Ward store

monkey way: airway in a mine

monkey wheel: gin block

monkey wire: telephone wires between towns

monkeywood: quira

monkey wrench: wrench with a movable jaw that can be adjusted to fit various sizes of nuts; same as monkey spanner

monkfish: angler fish

## Proverbs and Proverbial Phrases

Agile as a monkey.

Comic as a monkey.

We had more fun than a barrel (box) of monkeys. Cf. Funny as a barrel full of monkeys.

Funnier than monkeys.

Hot as monkeys.

Looks like a monkey.

Monkey around (with a buzz saw): to handle something dangerous.

Sit like a monkey on a gridiron: said of ungraceful bicyclist or horseman

Like a monkey on a wheel: bicyclist.

Make a monkey of: to make look ridiculous.

Have a monkey on one's back: to be addicted to drugs.

Get the monkey off (one's back): to break the drug habit.

# Monkey

Take the monkey off one's back: to be calm.

Suck the monkey (or tap the admiral): to drink liquor.

Have a monkey with a long tail: mortgage. Cf. Have a monkey on the house.

Monkey see, monkey do: avoid doing something that sets a bad example for others.

Cut a monkey-shine: to perform monkey-like tricks, jokes, or antics.

Like a monkey on (up) a stick: a man with jerky movements. Cf. A monkey up one's back.

Hold on by somebody's monkey-tail: to take somebody's word for a story (used in naval circles).

Like a monkey with a tin tool: to be self-satisfied or impudent.

Tricky as a monkey.

Ugly as a monkey.

Well, I'll be a monkey's uncle.

Get one's monkey up: to anger someone

Useless as monkey's grease.

## Superstititions and Motifs

### From Brown Collection

If you carry monkeys on an ocean trip, you will have storms. VII, 6923. Cf. 6989 (wind)

Monkeys are attracted sexually by human females. VII, 7182

### From Motif-Index

A monkey is mistaken for a nobleman. J1762.6

A monkey cheats a fox out of bananas. K171.9

A monkey when safe in a tree insults a gorilla. W121.2.6

Enmity exists between monkey and leopard. A2494.2.7

A pet monkey in a sheet frightens his owner. K1682.1

A monkey lures a tiger into a tree and sets it afire.   K812.3

Why the monkey's buttocks are red.   A2362.1

How the monkey got its tail.   A2378.1.8

What causes the monkey's manner of walking.   A2441.1.1

### Monkey Sitting on a Rail

Monkey sitting on a rail,
Picking his teeth with the end of his tail;
Mulberry leaves, calico sleeves,
Old school teachers are hard to please.
           -- Brown Collection, I, 178

### The Monkey Married the Baboon's Sister

The monkey married the baboon's sister,
Smacked his mouth and then he kissed her,
Kissed her so hard he raised a blister,
And she set up a yell.

What do you think the bride was dressed in?
A blue gauze veil and a green glass breastpin,
White kid gloves; she was interestin';
Oh, she cut a swell.
           -- Brown Collection, III, 220

## Bear in Mind!

At zoos, parks, circuses, and on television, bears entertain us with their antics--dancing, riding bicycles, tumbling and performing on bars, and doing other stunts. Somewhat slow and stumbling in movement, they show a fairly high degree of trainability and discipline under patient trainers, to say nothing about their gentleness when treated with consideration.

Such talent and civility, however, have not always been associated with the bear. Years ago the bear that came over the mountain to see what he could see left a much different impression. He appeared to be something of a bugbear, created by God to keep naughty and wandering children under the constant scrutiny of their parents. When night came, fear of the bear kept the kids indoors. On wintry evenings, imaginative mothers and grandmothers regaled their offspring with hair-raising yarns about bears eating children. No youngster dared take a chance with a hungry grizzly that might come roaring down the mountain after his long hibernation. If he could chase preachers out on limbs, what might he do to a tender adolescent?

Parents in those days were convinced that a folktale, be it ever so devoid of reality, was a dependable means of propping up moral standards. But this horrendous discipline, like an old wagon, eventually creaked to a stop. Youth, egged on by psychologists and humane storytellers, began prowling about the countryside after dark to see what they could see. Seeing no bearish monsters, these adolescents questioned all tall and fabulous bear tales as they did the belief in Santa Claus and in infants being brought in the saddlebags of doctors.

What can be believed is that bears, which are decreasing in number year by year, are strong and heavy mammals of the family <u>Ursidae</u>, residing chiefly in the Northern Hemisphere. A few related species are found in the tropics, Africa, and Australia.

The most widely known species is the brown bear (Ursus arctos), existing chiefly in Europe and Asia and frequently referred to as Bruin in children's stories. It has a length of about eight feet and weighs up to 1,000 pounds; it is largely carnivorous. A close relative is the American black bear (Euarctos americanus), residing in the forests of North America. Because of similarities in body and fur, it is sometimes classified as a brown bear. It is a vegetarian, but under the pressure of hunger will devour pigs and sheep. Timid and inoffensive if unmolested, it is playful and trainable, like the brown bear. A somewhat larger species is the polar bear (Thalarctos maritimus), residing in the north polar regions, weighing up to 1,600 pounds, and having a creamy-white fur and stiff bristles. As a non-hibernating carnivore, it lives on fish, walruses, and dead animals; its flesh is not edible. Another huge species is the grizzly bear (Ursus horribilis), sparsely distributed in the mountains of western North America, weighing about 1,000 pounds, and having a length of almost nine feet. It is carnivorous, very strong, and extremely ferocious. Its fur is brownish-yellow, and its flesh is uneatable. A close competitor in strength and ferocity is the Kodiak bear (Ursus gyas or middendorffi), residing chiefly in Alaska. Its fur is dark brown or yellowish brown and it lives on fish.

The species of less note are the Himalayan black bear (Ursus torquatus), a carnivore with a white horseshoe-mark on its chest; the Malay bear (Ursus malayanus), living chiefly on honey; the spectacled bear (Ursus ornatus), ranging in the Andes; and the sloth bear (Ursus libiatus), a shaggy-haired creature lacking one pair of incisors that lives in India and is often called the honey bear. The cave bear, according to the fossils discovered, was much larger than any living species.

Bears have massive and strong bodies, long and coarse hair, small ears but a keen sense of hearing, plantigrade feet with five large toes and non-tractable claws suitable for climbing. Their movements are slow and clumsy, but they can run fast for short distances. They can be carnivorous, vegetarian, or omnivorous.

In some areas they are highly destructive of crops. They stay with their cubs and do not run in packs. Most of them, if let alone, are good-natured and friendly. They usually give birth to two cubs at a time, sometimes one, three, or four.

We owe to these bears several score of useful words. Among the plants we find bearbane, bearberry, bear bush, bear grass, bear huckleberry, bear's-bed, bear's-ear, bear's-garlic, bear's-wort, bear tongue, bearwood, etc. In the animal kingdom are bear animalcule, ant-bear, bearcat, bear caterpillar, woolly bear, and bear-pig. Our language would be poorer without such terms as bear market, bear dance, Big Bear and Little Bear for the northern constellations, The Bear (Russia), and the Bear State (Arkansas).

The bear is particularly hungry after his long winter hibernation. During the warm weather he grows fat on a variety of food. A favorite snack, the pokeberry, turns his rump a splendid red. If he is a marauder among the farmer's beehives, the honey sweetens his disposition as well as his size. But if you have a mind to molest him, he will resent your meddling. He can be cross, grizzly, gruff, rough, and savage. A she-bear with her cubs, if provoked, is vicious; a soreheaded bear can be worse. So don't fool yourself by quoting that old saw: "He's like the bear going to the fair; he's making tracks but he ain't going nowhere." You will have a bear by the tail if you try to skin him alive and sell his fur.

The folk have also noted that there are both four-legged and two-legged bearcats. But the panda and the Asiatic civet called a bearcat are poor specimens when compared with the human bearcat, a humdinger and go-getter. He is aggressive and virile; he is also important and significant in the eyes of his fellows. In business, or politics, or romance he has nerve and verve; he operates with finesse and assurance. Whenever feasible, he kisses babies and does a lot of bear hugging of both men and women.

Bearbaiting, the most notorious relationship between bears and people, lasted some seven hundred years in England, before it was abolished by Parliament in 1835. Patronized by many thousands and egged on by the rabble in the bear gardens, the sport was extremely bloody and horrible. Brown bears (some of them blind) were chained by the hind legs or necks, tied to stakes in the center of the arena, and worried by snarling dogs. The whole demonstration was marked by tooth-and-claw savagery. The louder the bears roared, tossed, and screamed, the greater the delight for the spectators.

There were numerous protests against this spectacle from sensitive people aware of its brutality. About 1500 the scholarly Erasmus noted that there were numerous bear-gardens in his time. A century later Shakespeare referred to the attacks made by dogs on helpless bears in Macbeth and King Lear. In King Lear Gloucester says: "I am tied to the stake, and I must run the course." In 1663 Samuel Butler in the first canto of Hudibras described and satirized at length this bloodletting. A few years later John Evelyn, in his Diary (June 16, 1670), recorded his contempt for the sport along with his indictment of bull-baiting, cock-fighting, and dog-fighting. In like manner Richard Steele opposed all of these pastimes in the Tatler. The Puritans were constant opponents of bearbaiting, but their motives were open to question. In his History of England, T. B. Macaulay wrote that the Puritans were against the spectacle "...not because it gave pain to the bear, but because it gave pleasure to the spectators."

What value does a bear have anyway? Brown and black bears provide tender and succulent steaks, and their furs make excellent clothes, rugs, mountings, and other attractive things. Rendered bear fat was once used as a hair-dressing preparation. In some sections of our nation the folk vow that a bear's tooth rolled vigorously in the mouth will stop a toothache, that a child can speed up its teething by chomping on a bear's tooth, that early hibernation by bears indicates the coming of a hard winter. In some parts of Russia bears are considered sacred.

To the adolescent with a superstitious bent, a rousing bear tale is a warning about dire things to come, especially that one about the bear that abducted a girl and made her his wife. Recount those stories about bears transformed into ghosts, goblins,

Bear

and even preachers, and you may decrease nocturnal larking and other delicious enterprises. Baloney? Just ask some crone, and she'll put you straight about the power of a bear.

## Derivative Names

ant-bear: tropical American anteater, with powerful claws, tapering long snout, coat marked with bands of shaggy black hair; aardvark

bar: dialectal for bear

bear: koala in Australia

bear: gruff or surly person

bear: first-rate person or thing; humdinger or bearcat

bear: beast, an ugly girl

bear: one who trades in anticipation of lower prices on stock market

bear: Cub Scout of third rank, at least nine years old

bear: one of two northern groups of stars--Little Bear and Big Bear

bear: caterpillar of the tiger moth

Bear, The: Russia, where bear is regarded as friend of man

bear: portable press or device used in punching iron plates

bear: heavy block covered with matting and used in scrubbing decks of ships

bear animalcule: water bear that resembles ant-bear and woolly bear

bearbaiting: cruel and spectacular sport of setting dogs on chained bears

bearbaiter: one who baits bears

bearbane (bear's-bane): wolfsbane

bearberry (bear whortleberry): trailing evergreen plant, with tonic astringent foliage and red berries; deciduous holly

bearbine: European species Convolvulus; American herb

bearbrush: western U.S. shrub

bear bush (bear's-bush): inkberry

bearcat: Asiatic variety of civet, with prehensile tail; panda; a strong and vigorous fighter

bearcat: aggressive and powerful person; spirited or passionate young woman

bear caterpillar: woolly bear

bear clover (bear mate): mountain misery

bear corn: American hellebore

bear dance: rhythmic animal dance among American Indians, often performed for curative purposes

Bear Flag: white flag used in California in 1846 when state revolted against Mexico

bear garden: place for baiting bears and for other rough pastimes

bear grape (bear's grape): bearberry

bear grass: southern and western U.S. species of Yucca, with grasslike foliage

bearherd (bearward): man who tends bears

bearhound: hound for hunting bears

bear huckleberry: common low huckleberry

bear hug: rough, tight embrace

bearish: like a bear; rough and surly; tending toward a decline in prices

bear-leader: one who leads a trained bear; one who takes charge of a young man on his travelling

bearlet: little bear

bear market: declining market favorable for bears (short-sellers)

bear moss (bear's-thread): haircap moss

bear-mouse: meadow-mouse

bear oak: shrubby evergreen oak

# Bear

bear-paw: snowshoe for rugged terrain

bear-pig: the balisaur

bear pit: place in zoo where bears are kept

bear-play: rough and noisy behavior

bear plum: bearberry

Bear River: river in Utah, Wyoming, and Idaho

bear's-bed: soft, cushionlike tuft or mat of haircap mosses

bear's-breech: thistlelike shrub with spiny or lobed leaves, bear-skeiters

bear's-ear: the auricula or primrose

bear's-foot: fetid or stinking hellebore

bear's-garlic: ramson

bear's-grease: rendered fat of bear, once used on human hair

bear's-head: edible fungus that grows on trees

bearskin: skin or fur of bear

bear's-moss: Adam's needle Yucca

bears-paw: shell of large East Indian bivalve

bear's-paw root: male fern

bear's-tail: perennial herb of Asia Minor, with yellowish-violet flowers

Bear State: Arkansas

bear's-weed: yarba santa

bear's-wort (bearwort): spicknel; bear's-breech

bear tongue: Clintonia, species of scapose herbs of lily-of-the-valley family

bear-trap dam: movable dam used to deepen shallow streams

bear wallow: declivity or sink in ground, possibly made by bears

bearwood: cascara buckthorn

## Proverbs and Proverbial Phrases

Big as a bear.

Chubby as a bear.

Civil as tamed bears.

Crabbed as a wounded bear.

Crazy as a wild bear.

Cross as a bear with cubs.

Cross (savage) as a she-bear with a sore head.  Cf. Wicked as a she-bear with a sore head.

Fights like a she-bear for her cubs.

Fat as a bear (in December).

Though the bear be gentle, do not bite him on the nose.

Go like a bear to the stake.

Grizzly as a bear.

Handsomely as a bear picketh mussels.

Hearty as a bear.

Huge like a bear.

Hungry as a bear (after his winter's nap).

Like a bear to a honey-pot.  Cf. Like a bear swallowing honey.

An old bear is slow in learning to dance.

Plain as a bar up a gum tree.

Plain as a bear's track.

Play the bear: to behave rudely and roughly.

Pore (poor) as a bear that's wintered up in the balsams.

Red as a bear's ass in pokeberry time.

Rough as a bear.  Cf. Rough as a Russian bear.

Safe as a bar in a hollow tree in winter.

Bear

Safe as a skinned bear.

Sleepy (dormant) as a bear.

He speaks bear-garden: rudely and uncivilly as the rabble at a bearbaiting.

Strong as a bear.

Sullen (surly) as a bear.

Make sure of the bear before you sell his skin. (Aesop)

The bear wants a tail and cannot be a lion.

Ugly as a bear.

Warm as a bear.

Have a bear by the tail.

He must have iron nails that scratcheth with a bear.

To be a bear for punishment: to endure rough treatment.

### Superstitions and Motifs

From Brown Collection

There was a pregnant woman who became frightened by a bear's skin, and when her baby was born it had a place of skin like a bear's skin on its leg. I, 104

Indians use a bear's tooth attached to scissors to cure the toothache. I, 2344

Use a bear tooth as a teething ring for teething babies. Take teeth from native black bears. I, 355. Cf. entry I, 354

From Funk & Wagnalls Standard Dictionary of Folklore

Bear's gall is applied to an aching tooth as a cure.

In India bears are believed to be powerful against diseases.

Early hibernation by bears portends hard winter.

Louisiana Negroes say that to dream of fighting a bear portends persecution, and to dream of a running bear means happiness.

Bears are sacred and as such are celebrated with appropriate rites.

## From Motif-Index

Bear boasts of having eaten horses.  J2351.4

Bear abducts girl and makes her his wife.  B601.1.1

Bear thought to be a dog.  J1753

Bear fishes through ice with tail.  A2216.1

Bear in human form.  B651.7

Bear keeps human wife captive in a cave.  R45.3.1

Bear on a haywagon thought to be a preacher.  J1762.2

Bear throws hens to the fox.  K1022.3

The fox persuades the bear to lie in the hay, and then sets it afire.  K1075

Ghost in form of bear sneezes.  E552

Man sets dogs on bear that rescued him.  W154.25

A tame bear rings the church bells.  X412

A strong man is son of bear who has stolen his mother.  F611.1.1

A witch transforms man to bear.  G263.1.1

### Quotations--Literary and Otherwise

> If I were a bear
> And a big bear, too,
> I shouldn't much care
> If it froze or snew.
> -- Alan Alexander Milne, Furry Bear

The Puritans hated bearbaiting, not because it gave pain to the bear, but because it gave pleasure to the spectators.
-- T. B. Macauley, History of England

> They have tied me to a stake, I cannot fly,
> But bear-like I must fight the course.
> -- Shakespeare, Macbeth

> What man dare, I dare:
> Approach thou like the rugged Russian bear.
> -- Macbeth

Bear

Make ye no truce with Adam-zad--the bear that walks like a man.
>	-- Rudyard Kipling, The Truce of the Bear

How to catch a polar bear:  Go to the Arctic, cut a hole four feet in diameter, and place garden peas around the edge of the hole.  When the bear comes to take a pea, knock him in the ice hole.

### The Preacher and the Bear

1  A preacher went out huntin'
   One nice bright Sunday morn.
   It was against religion,
   But he took his gun along.

2  He killed some nice fat quail
   And a great big molly har',
   And on the way home he met
   A great big grizzly b'ar.

3  'O Lord, if you can't help me,
   . . . . . . . . . . . . . .
   . . . . . . . . . . . . . .
   For the Lord's sake don't help that bear!'

4  Parson went up the 'simmon tree,
   Bear went out a limb;
   Preacher said, 'If he stays there
   I don't give a dim'.'
>	-- Brown Collection, III, 511

## Baa, Baa, Black Sheep

The sheep has both a joyous and a pathetic appeal that shows itself in our speech, sayings, games and rhymes, superstitions, songs, and fine arts. This useful creature is expressive of some of the highest aspirations of the human race. It is embedded in the ethics and worship of countless millions of believing people and is thus found in their rituals, liturgies, hymnologies, feasts and festivals, and in aspects of their artistry and customs. Portrayed as singularly meek and sacred, its utter helplessness in times of trouble calls forth pity and acclaim from those who also have lost their way.

This prized animal belongs to the genus Ovis of the family Bovidae, a group of ruminants or cud-chewing mammals somewhat related to goats. The domesticated species (Ovis aries) came under the control of man some seven thousand years ago. Valued for their milk and meat products, their hides and fleeces, they mature by the end of their second year and are bred preferably at three years of age.

The wild species of sheep are supposed to have descended from the argali of Central Asia, the Altai mountains, and Mongolia. Another early type was the blue sheep, the bharal, residing in Tibet and bearing a close likeness to the goat. Other kinds of wild sheep have been observed in Asia, North Africa, and North America, which has several varieties including the bighorn. These species resemble goats and have been classified as intermediates between goats and sheep. Their wool is coarse, their bodies are large and agile, they usually possess protruding, curved horns. They are not as smelly as goats because of the secretion glands between their toes. These high spirited, adventurous, and self-reliant animals prefer the high places or crags for grazing. Domesticated sheep have softer wool, usually have no horns, and choose to live on plateaus and slopes.

Over the past two centuries the domesticated species have been improved by extensive and profitable crossbreeding. The base for this breeding has been the Spanish Merino, distinguished by its white face and legs, fine wool, and excellent flesh. Large flocks of this breed have been established in the United States, Australia, New Zealand, South America, France, and Germany. The Merino was introduced into France in 1786 to produce the Rambouillet, which has a larger body, a longer fleece, and a better grade of lamb or mutton. In 1840 the Rambouillet was brought to the United States, and it is very popular there and in Canada. Next best-known of the domesticated sheep are the English breeds: Cheviot, Corriedale, Cotswold, Dorset Horn, Hampshire Down, Leicester, Lincoln, Oxford Down, Romney, Shropshire, Southdown, and Suffolk. Some of these English species are also popular in Australia and in some areas of the United States.

The widespread dispersion of sheep and the large consumption of their products throughout the English-speaking nations have led to extensive related concepts and words. Plant names include lambkill or sheepkill, lamb-mint or sheepmint, lamb's-toe or sheep foot, mutton corn, mutton grass, ram's-head, ramtil, sheepberry, sheep fescue, sheep grass, sheepnose, sheep's-bane, sheep's-gowan, and sheep sorrel. In the animal kingdom we find the muttonbird, muttonfish, ramshorn, sheep blowfly, sheep crab, sheep ked, wether, wooler, and woolly bear. Useful devices include the mutton-ham, battering ram, hydraulic ram, ramjet, ramrod, ram schooner, ram's horn, sheepcote, sheep leg, sheepsfoot roller, sheep's-head clock, sheep vault, woolpack, and woolsponge. Our diet is enriched by ewe's-cheese, lamb chops, lamb's wool, mutton chops, and shepherd's pie. (See the list at end of sketch for explanations of these and other words.)

The folk look upon domesticated sheep as docile, trusting, harmless, innocent creatures, rather meek and inoffensive. Unlike goats, sheep do not take the bark off trees and shrubs; they generally confine themselves to grass and fodder, and chew their cuds without a whimper. They do not prey upon other animals, though they themselves are preyed upon by dogs, coyotes, foxes, and wolves. But these predators are apt to get the worst of it when they attack a virile ram. This strong male has maimed many unarmed owners and has killed some butchers. Just the opposite of the castrated wether sheep, he has stamina and courage, and is reckless on any rampage. He tolerates no other ram in his flock and a bloody battle ensues should a rival enter his green pastures. The winner becomes the undisputed master of the flock, which he jealously guards and disciplines.

The folk say that the ram is a real devil, or a goblin, or a witch. They also consider him a sign of good luck and fertility. In some areas of the world he is a blessed symbol of the sun and in others a sacred object.

Regardless of the aggressiveness of the ram, sheep and particularly their young have been glorified and woven into the structure and teachings of Judaism, Christianity, Mohammedanism, Hinduism, and other religions. For example, the Hebrews specified that sacrificial offerings be white as wool, from the first of the flock, and without blemish. Christians exalted the lamb and identified it with the Lamb of God, the Redeemer, and the Messiah. Hindus believe that the lamb is divine and representative of God. The Greeks proclaimed sheep as sacred to the goddess Hera, and the Romans portrayed the ram as a symbol of the two-faced Janus. Throughout Greece and Rome the ram's head was a decorative element in shrines and temples.

The sheep is significant in the arts as well. The lamb's head is carved on many a gravestone. Pictures portray a lamb nestling in the arms of a beaming child, a lamb beside Jesus, a sheep being broiled by a Muslim in honor of a stranger, or a faithful herdsman rounding up his flock for the night. In literature there is much imagery associated with the good shepherd, accompanied by his shepherd dog or collie, as he ministers to his flock in fair weather and bad. William Blake in <u>Songs of Innocence</u> describes the association of lambs and children as an exchange of innocence for innocence.

Nevertheless, the sheep has been subject to the folk's laughter, derision, and satire. If you make yourself a lamb in this naughty world, you are apt to be eaten by the wolves. Try to practice gentility and meekness and the folk will taunt you as a lamb, or a mutton-head, or a sheepshead, or a ram head because you have not the wisdom of a serpent.

Turn on your oppressors with a few tricks of your own. Put your approval on a ewe-mutton that plays the harlot with longing and amorous glances at helpless victims. As a sheepbiter, carry on your petty thievery and philandering while the husbands are out of town. Be yourself--a plain Old Sheep Guts. Be the wolf in sheep's clothing and climb over the walls into the sheepfold. Be as crooked as a ram's horn. Anger everybody by getting into their wool. Make them wool-blind when you jerk the wool over their eyes. Send them out to gather wool, only to come back shorn. Be as confident as those two simpletons that went out to get some milk--one milked the ram and the other held the pail. Pay no attention to that old saying--He was mean enough to steal the wool off the Lamb of God.

In addition to warm wool, lanolin, tallow, glue, soap, etc., the folk that live with sheep get extra dividends in times of sickness or distress. For instance, you may get rid of lameness by drinking nanny tea, a concoction of sheep manure or pellets dissolved in very hot sugar water. To cure an earache, stuff your ear with wool. For fever or chills, tie wool from a black or black-spotted sheep around your waist. Use a wedding ring that has been rubbed over wool to rub away a sty. If you have cancer, make applications of sheep sorrel. If you find a coin in a sheep's track, you may have some great luck like winning a sweepstake. According to much precise observation, sheep give a prediction of rain whenever they bleat loud and long; they can also indicate a coming storm by their friskiness.

### Derivative Names

ewe: female sheep

ewe hog(g) (ewe hogget): young female sheep between weaning and first shearing time

ewe lamb: a beloved or prized possession, such as an only child

ewe-mutton: elderly harlot or amateur prostitute

ewe-necked: low in neck in front of shoulders; badly arched as said of horses

ewe's-cheese: cheese from ewe's milk

lamb: young sheep; also young of other animals such as antelope

lamb: meat of young sheep; fur

lamb: gentle or innocent person, particularly child; term of endearment, also lambie, lambie-pie, lambkin, lambling

lamb: simpleton, one easily outwitted or tricked; one who speculates amateurishly on stock markets

lamb, in: pregnancy in sheep

lamb chop: cut from rib of lamb for broiling, etc.

lambing paralysis: disease during pregnancy

lambing sickness: milk fever of sheep

lambkill: North American poisonous shrub, called killkid and sheep-laurel

lamblike (lambish): having qualities of lamb

lamb mint: spearmint, peppermint

Lamb of God, the Lamb: Jesus, the Paschal Lamb (John I, 29)

lamb's cress: bitter cress

lambsdown: heavy fabric of mixed cotton and wool

lamb's ears: perennial hedge nettle

lambskin: skin of lamb

lamb's-lettuce: corn salad

lamb's-quarters: common weedy goosefoot; any of several oraches

lamb's-succory: small European herbaceous annual plant or herb

lamb's-toe: bird's-foot trefoil

# Sheep

lamb's tongue: hoary plantain, dogtooth violet, lamb's-quarters; a molding and fillet work on board

lamb's-wool: wool from lambs; cloth made from; drink made of ale with sugar, nutmeg, and roasted apples

lamb's-wool sponge: wool sponge

mutton: a sheep (rare); flesh of mature sheep

muttonbird: any of several Australian sea birds

mutton chop: cut from the rib of a mature sheep for broiling; patch of whiskers on each side of human face, shaped somewhat like a chop

mutton corn: ripe sweet corn or roasting ears

muttonfish (mutton snapper): any of several types of fish, said to taste like mutton

muttonfist: large, brawny fist or hand

mutton grass (mutton bluegrass): bluegrass

mutton-ham: small sail shaped like a leg of mutton

mutton-head: stupid person, blockhead, or mutton-top

mutton-leg: woman's dress sleeve, resembling leg of mutton

mutton quad: code word in printing to distinguish em quad

muttony: like mutton in taste

ram (buck): uncastrated male sheep

ram (ram cat): tom-cat

ram: battering ram

ram: pump to raise water; hydraulic ram

ram: to strike against; to stuff; to force into gun as with ramrod

ram: demerit; accomplice of a crook

ram: weight serving as a pile driver

ram: device on vessel with beak or spur projecting from bow

Ram: sign of Zodiac, Aries; constellation Aries

ram: Janus, the horned Roman god

Ram: generalized Hindu term for god or divinity

ram bam: wham bam; same as ramstam, reckless, stubborn or headstrong action

rambunctious: disorderly, unruly, boisterous in manner; being on a rampage; source related to rum or ram

ram head: stupid person (obsolete); a cuckold

ramjet: type of jet engine

rammer: person or thing that rams

rammish: having quality of ram, rammy

ramrod: rod used in loading a gun; cleaning rod of gun

ram schooner: vessel with pole masts but no top masts

ram's-head (ram's-head lady's slipper): orchid of northern North America

ram's head: carved or sculptured decoration in Greek and Roman art

ram's horn: box with holes for washing fish

ramshorn: snail

ramshorn crab: small Australian spider crab

ramtil: annual herb producing oily seeds

sheep: male or female of the species; skin

sheep: docile woman

sheepberry: large shrub with white flowers and blue-black berries

sheepbine: field bindweed

sheepbiter: one who practices petty theft; a philanderer

sheep-biting louse: sheep louse

sheep blowfly: any of several blowflies attacking sheep

sheepbot (botfly or sheep gadfly): botfly larva parasitizing sheep; sheep nasal fly

# Sheep

sheep bur: any of several burs clinging to sheep, etc.

sheepcote (sheepcot): sheepfold or sheephouse

sheep crab: large rough spider crab

sheepcrook: shepherd's crook or sheephook

sheep-dip: chemical used to protect sheep from vermin, etc.

sheep dog: dog trained to care for and protect sheep

sheep eater: one of band of Shoshone Indians near Yellowstone Park

sheepfaced (sheepish): bashful, shy, awkward

sheep fescue (sheep's fescue): hardy European fescue grass

sheep flake: rack or cage for carrying fodder to sheep

sheep fly: any of several flies with larva feeding on flesh of sheep in arid regions; sheep maggot

sheepfoot: bird's-foot trefoil

sheepgate: gate for passage of sheep; pasturage for sheep

sheep grass: Bermuda grass

old sheepguts: term of contempt

sheepshead (sheephead): foolish person; sheep's head prepared for food; large, massive fish having resemblance to sheep

sheepheaded: silly or stupid

sheep ked (sheep tick): blood-sucking insect, parasitic wingless fly

sheepkill: sheep laurel, poisonous to sheep; North American dwarf shrub similar to mountain laurel

sheep-kneed: having knees like those of sheep

sheep leg: old-style pistol

sheep-lice: hound's tongue

sheeplike: like sheep--meek, docile, or stupid

sheep loco: locoweed, poisonous to sheep and other animals; sheep-pod, one of locoweeds sheep measles: infestation of muscles of sheep by dog tapeworm

sheepmint: field balm

sheepnose: any of several varieties of apples with long ends

sheepnut: Jojoba

sheep plant: New Zealand plant resembling sheep at distance

sheep poison: California lupine; wood sorrel

sheep pox: virus disease of sheep and goats

sheep rack: rack for feeding sheep

sheep run: sheepwalk, a pasture or range for sheep

sheep's-bane: marsh pennywort

sheep's-bit: European herb

sheep's-scab: mange on sheep

sheep's eye: sly, longing, amorous glance

sheep's-foot: meter bar used as hammer and as lever by printers

sheepsfoot roller: machine with spikes to roll earth or pavement

sheepshank: shank of sheep; something thin or weak; knot for shortening a rope

sheep's-gowan: white clover

sheep's-head clock: lantern clock

sheep, lost: hardened sinner beyond redemption

sheepshearer: one who shears sheep; sheepshears, broad-bladed device used in shearing sheep

sheepshearing: act of shearing sheep; time of shearing and of feast at time

sheep-sick: heavily infested with parasitic worm eggs

sheepskin: skin of sheep; parchment made from this skin; a diploma

sheep sorrel: weed with fleshy, acid-tasting leaves

# Sheep

sheep's-parsley: wild chervil; annual weedy herb

sheepsplit: split of a sheepskin

sheepswool: wool sponge

sheep tansy: fiddle-neck

sheep vault: gymnastic vault

sheep wagon: enclosed covered wagon for transporting sheep

sheep wash: place where sheep are washed

sheepweed: soapwart, Indian mallow, butterwort

shepherd: keeper of sheep; shepherd dog; collie; clergyman

shepherder: person caring for herds or flocks of sheep; shepherd, sheepman, or sheepmaster

shepherd's pie: meat pie with a mashed-potato crust

wether: castrated male sheep or goat; in basic sense "a year-old animal"

wool: soft, curly or crisp hair of sheep; woolen yarn; cloth made of wool; material similar to such as rock wool; short for wool sponge

wool: to beat or thrash severely

woolball: hairball of sheep

wool-blind: having wool grown over eyes

wool-clip: annual production of wool

wool comber: one that combs wool

wool-dyed: wool dyed before spinning; dyed-in-the-wool

woolens (woollens): cloth or clothing made of wool

wooler: animal bred for wool

wool fat (wool grease): lanolin

woolfell: skin of wool-bearing sheep or other animals

woolgathering: gathering of tufts of wool left on bushes, etc.

woolgrower: one raising sheep or other wool-bearing animals

woolies (woollies): old-fashioned underwear; also the willies

woolly: resembling wool; covered with wool; article of clothing; Western wool-bearing animal; like atmosphere of early West

woolly bear: caterpillar or larva of any of various moths (Note: Many words with woolly prefixed.)

woolly-head: sheep; derogatory for Negro

woolpack: package of wool for transportation; British package of wool weighing 240 pounds; cumulus cloud with fleecy appearance

woolsack: bag for wool; stuffed seat for member of British House of Lords

wool sponge (wool): soft-fibered, durable commercial sponge

wool stapler: dealer in wool; one who sorts wool

## Proverbs and Proverbial Phrases

An old ewe dressed lamb fashion (woman dressed like a young girl).

A lamb in the house and a lion in the field.

An ill sign when a fox licks a lamb.

Gentle as a lamb. (Also harmless, innocent, like a, went in (or out) like, meek, mild, quiet, tame as a lamb.)

God tempers the wind for the shorn lamb.

Skin the lamb: to swindle.

Soon goeth the young lamb's skin to the market.

Like lambs you do nothing but suck and wag your tail.

The lamb where it's tipped and the ewe where she's clipped (proverbial rule regarding tithes).

Make yourself a lamb and the wolves will eat you. Cf. The life of the wolf is the death of the lamb.

Dead as mutton.

To return to our muttons.

Butts like a ram.

# Sheep

Crooked as a ram's horn.

It is possible for a ram to kill a butcher.

Awkward as a flock of sheep after shearing time.

On the sheep's back (being dependent on wool).

Every family has a black sheep.

Every time a sheep bleats it loses a mouthful.

Like trying to sleep by counting sheep jumping over a wall.

Make sheep eyes. Cf. To cast sheep eyes (to look shyly or bashfully; to look at tenderly and humbly).

Good pastures make fat sheep.

Gentle as sheep. (Also docile, innocent.)

Go at it like a flock of sheep in salting time.

Now I have a sheep and a cow, everybody bids me "Good morrow."

Let every sheep hang by his (its) own shank.

Good to be hanged for a sheep as a lamb. Cf. May as well die an old sheep as a lamb.

Two heads are better than one even if one is only a sheep's head. Cf. Two heads are better than one.

Keep sheep by moonlight (to hang in chains).

Sheep in lamb's clothing. Cf. Wolf in sheep's clothing.

If one sheep leap over the dyke (ditch) the rest will follow. Cf. One sheep follows another.

I can lick you on a sheepskin (on a small area). Note: In western North Carolina once a custom to sleep on a small sheepskin placed on ground in a log cabin.

Naked as a shorn sheep.

Many go out for wool and come home shorn.

One scabby sheep will infect (mar) a whole flock. Cf. One bad sheep spoils the flock.

You can shear a sheep many times, but you can skin him only once.

It's a foolish sheep that makes the wolf a confessor.  Cf. A sheep among wolves (a victim among rogues).

The wolf often eats sheep that have been told.  Cf. He that makes himself a sheep is eaten by the wolves.

The death of wolves is the safety of the flock.  Cf. The death of the wolf is the health of the sheep.

All wool and a yard wide (genuine and admirable).

To be in your wool (to anger or annoy; also to be ready for shearing).

More squeak than wool (more noise than substance).  Cf. Much cry and little wool.

Dyed in the wool: colored or imbued thoroughly, as a dyed-in-the-wool Tory.

Better give the wool than the sheep.

Keep your wool on!  Cf. Keep your shirt on!

Pull (draw) the wool over your eyes (to trick or deceive).

A wool-seller knows a wool-buyer (rogues know one another).

Mean enough to steal the wool off the Lamb of God.

Sins washed as white as wool.

There is no wool so white but a dyer can make it black.

Your wits have gone a wool-gathering (having little prospect of success).

Woolly as a sheep.

## Superstitions and Motifs

Nanny tea, a folk remedy for many ailments, consists of sheep manure in hot water that has sometimes been sweetened with sugar.

Black sheep brings bad luck, and three black sheep means tragedy.  Cf. Black lamb is a sinner, and white lamb is pure and innocent person.

It is good luck to have one black sheep in the flock.

A sheep's tail is a token of sovereignty in Rhodesia.

# Sheep

Counting sheep helps you to fall asleep.

## From Brown Collection

There ain't nuthun [sic] better to cure lameness than sheep manure in hot water, applied externally.  VI, 1767

Sheep sorrel is good for cancer.  VI, 1003

To cure sores, put some sheep sorrel plant into a pewter plate with lard and cook it until it forms a salve.  VI, 2180

Chills and fever: Use wool of black sheep or black-spotted one; fasten it around waist of a sick person and let him walk around a persimmon tree as many times as he has chills. Summarized, VI, 1095

To cure earache, stuff the ear with a piece of wool.  VI, 1333

It is good luck to find a coin in sheep's track.  VI, 3424

There is a lucky stone which can be found in a sheephead (fish). It is a small stone with an "L" inscribed on it.  VII, 5810

To cure a sty, rub a gold wedding ring on something wool and then rub the sty with it.  VI, 2287

A herd of sheep bewitched can be cured by placing a horseshoe in the fire until it becomes red hot.  VII, 7743

If, while going to make a visit, one sees a sheep, the visitor will not be welcomed.  VI, 3899

When sheep or goats bleat loud and long, you may expect rain.  VII, 6673

Before a storm sheep become frisky.  VII, 6924

Sheep must be sheared on the full of the moon.  In May the wool will be lighter.  VII, 7742

## From Motif-Index

Ewe's head grafted to man's head.  E785.1.1

Lamb prefers to be sacrificed in temple rather than be eaten by wolf.  J216.2

Devil cannot change into a lamb.  G303.3.6.3

Escaped lamb delivers himself to shepherd rather than to the slaughterer.  J217.1

Only lamb punished of all the animals. U11.1.1.1

Sheep licking her lamb is envied by the wolf. J1909.5

Lamb used to get lawyer's audience. J1653

Wolf persuades lamb to bring him drink. K815.11

Wolf unjustly accuses the lamb and eats him. U31

Devil appears as a ram. G303.3.3.1.7

Dragon appears as a modified ram. B11.2.1.9

Wolf poses as a ram. K828.3

Alliance of sheep and dog. B267.2

Black sheep thought to be devil. J1785.7

Devil stands in church door and writes down names of his own people on a sheep's skin. G303.24.1.4

A wolf is sold as a sheep. K132

Purple wether. B731.9

Good shepherd shears his sheep, but does not skin them.

### Quotations--Literary and Otherwise

My son, God will provide himself a lamb for a burnt offering. -- Genesis, XXII, 8

Your lamb shall be without blemish. -- Exodus, XII, 5

To obey is better than sacrifice, and to hearken than the fat of rams. -- 1 Samuel, XV, 22

The poor man had nothing save one little ewe lamb. -- 2 Samuel, XII, 3

We are the people of his pasture and the sheep of his land. -- Psalms, XCV, 7

The mountains skipped like rams, and the little hills like lambs. -- Psalms, CXIV, 4

The wolf also shall dwell with the lamb, and the leopard shall lie down with the kid. -- Isaiah, XI, 6

All we like sheep have gone astray. -- Isaiah LIII, 6

# Sheep

He is brought as a lamb to the slaughter. -- Isaiah LIII, 7

And before him shall be gathered all nations; and he shall separate them one from another as a shepherd divideth his sheep from the goats. -- Matthew, XXV, 32

The Lamb that belonged to the Sheep, whose skin the Wolf was wearing, began to follow the Wolf in the Sheep's clothing.
    -- Aesop, The Wolf in Sheep's Clothing

This noble ensample to his sheep he yaf,
That first he wroughte and afterward he taughte.
    -- Chaucer, "Prologue" of The Canterbury Tales

He casts a sheep's eye at the wench. -- Cervantes, Don Quixote

A great cry, but little wool. -- Ibid

My thoughts ran a wool-gathering; and I did like the countryman, who looked for his ass while he was mounted on his back.
    -- Ibid

When the lion fawns upon the lamb,
The lamb will never cease to follow him.
    -- Shakespeare, King Henry VI

We were as twinned lambs did frisk in the sun,
And bleat the one at the other: what we changed
Was innocence for innocence.
    -- Shakespeare, The Winter's Tale

The hungry sheep look up, and are not fed. -- Milton, Lycidas

> And did those feet in ancient time
> Walk upon England's mountains green?
> And was the holy Lamb of God
> On England's pleasant pastures seen?
>     -- Blake, Milton

> Little Lamb, who made thee?
> Dost thou know who made thee?
> Gave thee life, and bid thee feed
> By the stream and o'er the mead;
> Gave thee clothing of delight,
> Softest clothing, woolly, bright.
>     -- Blake, Songs of Innocence

And silent was the flock in woolly fold. -- Keats, "The Eve of St. Agnes"

... the freedom of speech may be taken away, and dumb and silent we may be led, like sheep to the slaughter. -- G. Washington, address on March 15, 1783

Little Bo-Peep has lost her sheep,
  And can't tell where to find them;
Leave them alone, and they'll come home,
  Wagging their tails behind them.


Mary had a little lamb,
  Its fleece was white as snow,
And everywhere that Mary went
  The lamb was sure to go;
He followed her to school one day,
  That was against the rule;
It made the children laugh and play
  To see a lamb at school.

Riddle: What did the ram say when he fell over the cliff? -- I didn't see that U turn.

Baa, baa, black sheep,
Have you any wool?
  Yes, sir, yes, sir,
  Three bags full:
  One for my master,
  One for my dame,
  And one for the little boy
  Who lives down the lane.

Baa, baa, black sheep,
Where yo' little lam'?
Way down yonder in de valley,
Buzzards an' de butterflies
  pickin' out its eyes,
Po' little thing cryin' "Mammy!"
    -- Brown Collection, I, 183

We're poor little lambs who've lost our way,
  Baa! Baa! Baa!
We're little black sheep who've gone astray,
  Baa-aa-aa!
Gentlemen-rankers out on a spree,
Damned from here to Eternity,
God ha' mercy on such as we,
  Baa! Yah! Baa!
    -- Kipling, "Gentlemen-Rankers" (refrain)

## Cattle on a Thousand Hills

This sketch is not to certify the existence of purple cows nor to confirm that a cow jumped over the moon. However, cows and their intimate relatives, the group called cattle, were free and independent enterprisers on many a hill long ages before their domestication by man. As far back as 3500 B.C. the Egyptians milked and worked them, as did the Babylonians at a much earlier time. And goodness knows how much earlier the masses of Asia and Africa had used their products and labor in their simple economies, to say nothing at this juncture about their idolatry of them. In general, those who had bulls, cows, heifers, and steers or oxen had wealth. And if they had all the livestock, which the term cattle once included, they had many chattels and much capital, much like our modern cattle barons who ride their vast ranges in their Cadillacs, jokingly called cattle trains.

Cattle in the modern sense are the most productive and profitable of all domesticated livestock. They surpass all other animals in contributing to the sustenance and delight of the human race.

These popular creatures, classified as Bos of the subfamily Bovinae of the family Bovidae, are ruminants or cud-chewers. In the broadest use, the genus Bos includes the following species: the water buffalo of India and Africa, the buffalo or bison of North America, the yak of Tibet, the gaur and gayal and bantin of the Far East, the domesticated zebu of the Near East and Africa, and all the domesticated varieties of the western world.

Western domesticated cattle, whose pedigree is not certain, are usually grouped as follows: major beef--Aberdeen Angus, Brahman, Durham, Galloway, Hereford, Shorthorn, and Santa Gertrudis; major dairy--Ayeshire, Brown Swiss, Guernsey, Holstein-Friesian, and Jersey; minor dairy--Red Danish, Red Sindhi,

French-Canadian, Dutch Belted, and Dexter Kerry; and dual purpose (beef and milk)--Milking Shorthorn, Red Polled, and Devon. Still other breeds have been developed in the British Isles and in numerous areas of the world.

In the United States, where all the domesticated breeds have been imported, the commonest types are the Hereford, Holstein, Shorthorn (for beef), Jersey, Guernsey, Aberdeen Angus, and Holstein-Friesian. In years past these types were to a great extent propagated, fed, and prepared for the markets in the grain and dairy states of the Middle West; but, due to much scientific improvement, they are being raised today in most of the states of the nation. Applied knowledge about nutrition, artificial insemination, and genetic controls has increased both the quantity and quality of cattle and their many products. A good illustration is the crossing of the Brahman with some species to secure higher resistance to heat and insects.

Side by side with this scientific and profitable business is the coinage, by the folk and the scientists, of a long and helpful list of words related to animals, persons or their actions, plants, devices, and numerous miscellaneous terms. For example, in the animal kingdom we have these: beef cattle, beef-fly, bullbat, bull bitch, bullfrog, bull head, bull of the woods, bull snake, bull terrier, cow bunting, cowbird, cowfish, cow-heifer, cowherd, cow horse, cow killer, cow sucker, heiferette, milk adder, milk fish, and bum steer. In the plant kingdom are these: bull bay, bull birch, bull brier, bull grape, bull grass, calfkill, calf lily, calf's-mouth, cattle fly, cowbane, cow bean, cowberry, cow clover, cow grass, cow lily, cow pea, and cow slip. In technological use are these: bull block, bull donkey, bull-tongue, cowbell, cow catcher, bull pen, cattle ranch, and cattle range; and in miscellaneous usage are these: cattle fever, cow pox, milk leg, bulldog edition, bull fiddle, bull's-eye, bull whip, calf (part of lower leg and also a small island), milk shake, and milk-tooth. (See the list of these and other words, with accompanying explanations.)

From earliest times, cattle have been sanctified in the religions of the Far East, the Near East, and the Mediterranean basin. Throughout India cattle are sacred, and thus subject to protection by law or custom. Hindus still have tabus against injuring or killing them, and the most pious reject their meat as unfit for consumption. Furthermore, they glorify the calf as the harbinger of spring, and believe that cattle are reincarnated in other animals or in human beings.

The ancient Hebrews of Palestine held great reverence for the calf (as they did for sheep) in their worship and rituals. The clean and innocent calf became the focus of a cult devoted to the worship of the satanic Golden Calf. It is said that, during the absence of Moses, his brother Aaron had the calf constructed and was instrumental in introducing the idol in other Jewish areas of Canaan, a land of milk and honey according to Ezekiel (XX, 6). This idolatry finally was ended by Hosea and other prophets.

Another aspect of this cult involved the bullock (steer or ox) that was extensively worked and sacrificed not only in Palestine but also in Persia, Egypt, Greece, Rome, and other places. Slaughtered bullocks were placed on high altars or pyres and there burned to appease the wrath of the gods or to secure their aid. Bullocks were sacrificed by sailors in order to forecast the weather.

There was more mercy shown toward the heifer and the cow, who were thought to be the favorites of the deities. Because of their meekness and gentility as well as their necessary roles in regeneration of the herd, they were spared from sacrifices as a general rule. In Keats' "Ode on a Grecian Urn," a brilliantly ornamented heifer accompanies a whole town's population to a wedding.

The bull was once synonymous with the Hebraic Yahweh or Jehovah, a concept probably inherited from neighbors that held allegiance to Baal. In Greece and Rome, and in other nations too, the bull was conspicuous in religion, architecture, and sculpture. He symbolized such deities as Athena, Heracles, Jupiter, Zeus, Minerva, Minotaur (and also the Scandinavian Thor). Roman weddings included the incantation "Where thou art the Bull, I am the Cow." At the end of the nuptial rites the priest proclaimed himself to be the bull, and then he and others deflowered the bride in a wild orgy that lasted several days. This quaint custom stemmed from the recognition of the bull on earth and in the heavens for his fertility and magic strength.  Soothsayers used his blood to predict events, and astrologers placed him in the skies under the name of Taurus.

In contrast with this pious and nationalistic exaltation of cattle, the folk have had a hilarious time in tagging human beings with the attributed characterizations of beeves, little bulls, big bulls, cows, heifers, steers or oxen, even with the qualitities of cow's milk.  The following illustrations indicate this wide variety of fun and contempt.

A beef is a football player--beefy and brawny, half-witted and stolid like an ox.  If one feels himself cheated in a game, he may beef (complain) about the decision.  A beef-eater is well-fed, like the ruddy warders in the Tower of London.  A beef trust is a line of hefty chorus girls.

A bawling calf is the epitome of silliness and gawkiness.  A bull calf is girl-crazy and cow-simple.  The heifer, somewhat reticent and less pushy, has the charm of an attractive young woman, a prize specimen at a show or party.  For the sake of your household, "You'd better watch a frisky heifer."  And one other warning--do not allow a young calf to run over you.  It will be embarrassing, like having to ride a big bull down Main Street on Saturday afternoon.

The cow can be a bugbear or goblin, sometimes a harlot. She can cow the wits out of you, as indicated by your cowering when she protects her calf from your intrusion.  In the main, she is timid and cow-hearted, clumsy and awkward.  In most instances she enjoys being milked, but she does not tolerate having her udders pinched--she will show her manners by spilling you and the milk in several directions.  And if you've got the wrong cow by the tail, you're in for another whack.

And here comes the cow's consort, the bull of bulls, the very image of powerful virility--big, stout, strong, and wild; fiery, bullheaded, bullnecked, and brazen.  Some folk say that he is a ghost, or a reincarnated supernatural spirit that dwells in the bodies of many a human creature.  His name is given to policemen and detectives, to speculators on the stock markets, to the fast-talking and loud orator on a political stump, to a windy dispenser of nonsense in bull sessions, to a roaring foreman or cook in a logging camp, and to noisy invaders of china shops. A bawling and bellowing creature, he is not only bellicose but impulsive and compulsive when challenged by snarling dogs, crimsoned banners, or armed men at bullfights and bullbaitings. He can be especially ornery after he has been penned up for six months. This guy is, indeed, a bulldog and a bulldozer, only rarely a bully boy.

As a final note on these bovine characteristics, consider the role of cow's milk in folklore. If you are labeled a milksop, you are an unmanly man, a mollycoddle, or a sissy; you may be called a milk toast or milquetoast (after Caspar Milquetoast, a comic-strip character). If you have a milk-and-water reputation, you are namby-pamby; if you are milk-livered, you are cowardly.

The folk can tell you just how to manage your cattle. When you milk a cow, do it on the right side. If it is the first milking, do not squirt the milk on the ground--she will certainly go dry. At no time should you step on toads or kill any frogs--your cow will give bloody milk. Watch out for milk snakes, fairies, and vampires--they will suck all your cows dry. Never put your faith in a dwarf--he can bewitch a cow. If a witch casts a spell over your cow, put some milk on a piece of silver to break the spell.

If you are ailing, go thou to the cow--there's magic in her innards. Her milk will heal wounds and draw out infections. To cite a few folk remedies, lard and milk mixed are good for boils; milk that has smoke blown into it can relieve a colicky child; washing in milk eliminates freckles; a poultice of bread and milk draws out poisons; eating figs boiled in milk cures quinsy; warm milk rubbed on the eyes rids them of sores; drinking equal parts of flour and milk mixed stops dysentery; beef oil put into the ear stops an earache; beef gall draws out poisons; an application of raw beef cures a sore throat. Cow manure is excellent for more than fertilizing roses--it stops an aching tooth if applied to the tooth for some time; it draws out poisons when applied as a poultice; and it removes freckles if you fall into a fresh pile and tarry for long enough.

If these remedies do not work, listen to a cow bellowing at noon or night--she may be tolling the bell for you. For a brighter turn of events, take off for a visit with the cattle and other animals on the eve of Old Christmas (January 6). Tradition has it that this night these blessed animals talk and pray and kneel in adoration of the Child in the manger.

## Derivative Names

beef: any adult bovine animal; flesh of adult slaughtered bovine animal; muscular power or brawn; football player; complaint; weight, as of human flesh

beefcake: photograph of scantily clad man

beef cattle: cattle bred and fattened for meat

beef-eater: bluebottle or fleshfly

beef-eater: eater of beef; Englishman; well-fed, red-faced servant; one of the Yeomen of Guard attending British sovereign on state occasions; uniformed warder of the Tower of London

beefed-up: reinforced to increase load capacity, as said of aircraft, etc.

beef fly: any of several species attacking cattle and resembling bees

beefing: kind of apple so called because of its deep-red color; complaining

beefsteak: slice of beef suitable for broiling or frying

beef tea: drink made from beef extract or from boiled strips of beef

beef trust: group of stout actors, ball players, etc.

beef-witted: stupid

beefy: muscular; solid or brawny

bull: uncastrated male of cattle; also male of whale, elephant, seal, walrus, etc.

bull: to be in heat; to serve a heifer or cow

# Cattle

bull: strong or noisy person; one who pushes ahead

bull: foolish talk; buncombe or bunkum; to bluff

bull: ridiculous blunder in speech

bull: bulldog

bull: locomotive

bull: policeman or detective

bull: papal announcement or official document

bull: constellation Taurus

bull: speculator banking on rising prices on stock market

bull (bull board): game resembling quoits

bull one's way: to move forward against opposition

bullbaiting: pastime of tormenting bulls with dogs, etc.

bullbat: nighthawk

bull bay: evergreen magnolia

bull birch: beech in New Zealand

bull bitch: woman who has masculine appearance, features, etc.

bull block: block or die used in reducing size of wire; pulley used in yarding logs

bull brier: kind of vine of greenbrier group

bull cane: thick, vigorous grape cane

bull cook: man who cares for oxen in logging camp

bulldog: heavily built dog with large head and short hair, very muscular and courageous

bulldog: to wrestle a steer or calf by the horns; to lie for gain

bulldog: short-barreled revolver

bulldog edition: early edition of a morning newspaper

bulldogged: obstinate or tenacious

bulldogger: one who bulldogs cattle

bulldoggish: like a bulldog

bull donkey: large donkey engine, fitted with drum and cable, for hauling logs

bulldoze: to frighten by violence or threats; to bully

bulldozer: machine used as scooper or pusher in grading

buller: cow or heifer in constant heat

bull fiddle: double-bass viol

bullfight: organized fight between man and bull

bull-fighter: empty railroad freight car

bullfinch: European songbird, with short beak and handsome plumage

bullfrog: large American frog with loud croaking voice

bull grape: muscadine

bull grass: prairie cordgrass

bullhead (bullpout): any of several American water catfishes; stubborn or stupid person

bullheaded: stupidly stubborn or obstinate

bullish: said of rising stock market

bull moose: male moose

Bull Moose: member of Progressive political party formed in 1912 by Theodore Roosevelt

bullnecked: having thick neck

bull nose: contagious disease of pigs

bullock: steer or ox

bull of the woods: logging-camp foreman or boss; trucking company foreman; an important person; an alligator

bull-party: party for men only

bull pen: place for prisoners; place where ball pitchers warm up; center arena of prize fight; bull ring with enclosed arena for bullfights bull redfish: channel bass

bullroarer: public speaker with loud voice; noise-making toy consisting of small slat of wood fastened to a thong

bull session (bull-fest): informal and usually lengthy discussion, often of little consequence

bull's eye: term applied to many circular objects, particularly the boss (bulla, Lat. for bubble) or protuberance on sheet of blown glass; boss used by Romans on doors, swords, belts, and boxes; often applied to heart-shaped box, usually of gold and containing an amulet; later used on papal bulls or documents

bull's-eye: thick circular skylight; central mark of target; shot that hits mark; direct hit; successful act; convex lens to concentrate light; lantern with such lens; hard, round candy

bull's-eye squall: fair-weather squall off South Africa

bull snake: gopher snake

bull-strong: strong enough to hold a bull, as said of fences

bull terrier: strong, active dog, a cross between bulldog and terrier

bull-tongue: to plow with a bull-tongue and heavy plow, usually with one shovel

bullweed: knapweed

bullwhip: rawhide whip

bull's wool: stolen clothes

bull work: hard work

bully (bullyrag): to frighten, abuse, tease

bully: complimentary expression meaning fine or first-rate

bully: protector of prostitute

bully (bully beef): canned or pickled beef

bullyboy: jovial fellow

bullytree: one of several American trees bearing gum

calf: young, male or female, of cattle; also of elephant, walrus, seal, whale, etc.

calf: small island near a larger one; mass of ice breaking from iceberg; fleshy part of leg below a person's knee

calf: meek, harmless, and occasionally brainless person; silly and gawky person

Calf, The Golden: molten image made by Aaron in absence of Moses (Exodus XXXII); an idol set up by Jeroboam I at Bethel; worship of this calf condemned by Hosea as an act of apostasy

calfbound: bound in calfskin

calfkill: plant whose foliage is poisonous to cattle, etc.

calf love: puppy love

calf's-foot jelly: gelatin or jelly made from calf's foot

calfskin: skin from calf; leather made from

calf's-mouth: snapdragon

calf ward: enclosure for calves

calfy: in calf

cattle: cows, bulls, and steers or oxen; low worthless people; term once used to include sheep, horses, swine--all indicative of property or wealth and from which chattel and capital were derived

cattle baron: wealthy owner of ranges and cattle

cattle country: area where raising cattle is principal occupation

cattle fever: Texas fever

cattle fly: horn fly

cattle grid: cattle guard or a ditch over which ties or rails are laid to prevent crossing by cattle

cattlehide: leather

cattle louse: louse infesting cattle

cattleman: one who raises or cares for cattle

cattle ranch: area for raising cattle, also containing houses, machinery, etc.

cattle range: unsettled area where cattle are grazed

# Cattle

cattle tick: tick infesting cattle

cattle trail: way along which herds are driven

cattle train: Cadillac automobile

cow: female of bovine family; also of other animals such as elephant, etc.

cow: milk, cream, butter, or beef. Cf. armored cow, canned cow, tin cow, etc.

cow: to frighten, scare, or bully

cow: goblin or bugbear

cow: woman; harlot

cowbane: poisonous plant of carrot family

cow bean: cowpea

cowbell: bell hung from neck of cow

cowberry: shrub with white or pink flowers; plant of rose family; fruit of either

cowbind: vine with large, fleshy roots

cowbird: cow blackbird, often seen near cattle

cowboy: ranch hand on horseback; reckless automobile driver

cowboy coffee: black coffee without sugar

cowboy job: amateur holdup

cow bunting: cowbird

cow calf: heifer

cow camp: headquarters of cowboys

cowcatcher: metal frame on front of locomotive to remove obstructions from tracks

cow clover: zigzag clover

cow college: small and little-known agricultural college

cow corn: pod corn

cow cress: field cress

cowcumber (dialect): cucumber

cower: to crouch in fear or shame

cowfish: any of the marine mammals such as sea cow

cowgirl: woman who works on ranch or in rodeo

cowgrass: red clover

cowhage: tropical vine of pea family

cow hand (cowman): person who works on ranch

cow-hearted: fearful or cowardly

cow-heifer: young cow before it develops a full set of teeth

cowherd: one who cares for and drives cattle

cowhide (cowskin): hide of cow used for leather; strong leather whip; to whip or flog; baseball

cow-hocked: having cow hocks

cow horse: cow pony, used in herding cattle

cow juice: milk

cow killer: wasp resembling ant, supposed to sting cattle

cowlick: small tuft of hair that will not lie flat

cow lily: marsh marigold

cow parsley: wild chervil, plant with many-lobed leaves

cow parsnip: any herb of the parsley family

cowpea: plant with long pods, used as food for cattle, etc.; seed of plant

cow pilot: tropical fish

cowpoke (cow puncher): cowboy

cowpox: disease affecting cow's udders

cow salve: butter

cow shark: large European and West Indian shark

cowshed: shelter for cows

# Cattle

cow-simple: girl-crazy

cowslip: wild plant; marsh marigold; English primrose

cow soapwort: cowherb

cow sorrel: sheep sorrel

cow's-tail (cow tail): frayed end of a line

cowsucker: snake that is supposed to milk cows

Cow, Purple: a suppositious cow

cowtongue: yellow clintonia

cow-tree (milk tree): native of Venezuela, with sticky latex, sweet and pleasant

cowy: suggestive of cow

heifer: young cow that has not had a calf; the hide of

heifer: woman or girl, especially pretty and attractive

heifer dust: snuff

heiferette: large heavy heifer almost size of cow

milk: opaque, whitish liquid from mammary glands of female mammals; sap of certain plants; any of certain emulsions

milk adder (milk snake): small, harmless snake

milk-and-water: weak and vacillating; namby-pamby

milkcan: to knock out someone like a row of milkcans, etc.

milker: one who or that which milks; a cow that is milked

milk fever: fever attending secretion of milk after third day; similar disease of milk cows

milkfish: large, toothless silvery fish, allied to herring

milkiness: quality or state of milk

milking machine: automatic milker

milk leg: painful white swelling of leg occurring in connection with childbirth; chronic swelling of horse's leg

milk-livered: cowardly, timorous

milk of human kindness:  natural feeling of sympathy and generosity

milk of magnesia:  milky, white medicine used as laxative or antacid

milkmaid:  dairy maid

milkman:  dairyman; one who delivers milk

milk punch:  punch made with spirits, milk, sugar, etc.

milk run:  routine military aerial mission

milk shake:  drink made of chilled, flavored milk with ice cream

milkshed:  large farm area supplying milk to a city

milk-sickness:  disease caused by drinking milk or eating product of cow fed on poisonous plants

milksop:  sissy or effeminate man

milk sugar:  sugar contained in milk; lactose

milk toast:  milquetoast, any shy, timid or extremely gentle person

milk-tooth:  tooth of first dentition

milkvetch:  plant supposed to increase the secretion of milk by goats eating it

milkweed:  one of several plants having milky juice

milk-white:  bluish-white

milkwort:  any of several plants with varicolored showy flowers, so called from notion that it increases secretion of milk in nursing women

milky:  like milk; yielding milk; very mild or spiritless; containing young or spawn

Milky Way:  luminous band encircling the heavens; composed of distant stars that are inseparably visible

ox:  see list of words in the sketch on the ox

steer:  young ox, usually two to four years old; bullock, castrated bull

steer, bum:  inferior animal; false clue or wrong advice

# Cattle

## Proverbs and Proverbial Phrases

Awkward (clumsy) as a bull in a china shop.

Bawls (bellows, charges, grins, roars) like a bull.

Big (mad, stout, strong, stubborn, wild) as a bull.

Big as a bull-beef (stout and hearty).

Blowing like a mad bull.

Bull one's way (to force strongly against opposition).

Cows have more respect for the ugliest bull than for the handsomest ox.

He that bulls the cow must keep the calf.

Cock-and-bull story.

Get the bull's feather (to be cuckolded).

Hit the bull'seye.

No farther than I can sling a bull by the tail.

He couldn't hit a bull with a bale of hay.

Take the bull by the horns (to deal boldly with harsh facts).

He doesn't know a bull from a bull's foot.

Like a bull at a (five-barred) gate (acting furiously).

Like a red rag to a bull.

Mad as a shorthorn bull in fly time.

Ornery as a bull that has not serviced a cow in six months.

Shoot the bull (to talk nonsense at a bull session).

Bawls (bleats) like a calf.

If you want to catch the calf, give a nubbin to the cow. Cf. Salt the cow to catch the calf.

Frisky as a calf on a forty-acre lot.

I'd rather be a sedate calf than a frisky cow.

The greatest calf is not the sweetest veal.

That calf never heard a church bell. Cf. Born and died between Sundays.

Kill the fatted calf (to have an elaborate feast, etc.).

Licking the calf (to do something over again).

Like (looks or sounds like) a dying calf (with white of eyes showing). Cf. Sounds like a calf in a hail storm.

Looks (acts) like he was run over by a calf.

Calf love, half love;
Old love, cold love.

The calf, the goose, the bee: the world is ruled by these three.

Awkward (big, clumsy) as a cow.

Close your barndoor before the cows get out.

Comely as a cow in a cage.

Now I have a cow and a sheep, everyone bids me "Good morrow."

Crooked as a cow's hind leg.

Cursed cows have short horns.

Cows off yonder have long horns. Cf. Foreign cows wear long horns.

Dark as the inside of a cow (a cow's belly).

Feed the cow that gives the most milk.

Happy as a cow eating clover.

Like the cow that gives a good pail of milk, and then kicks it over.

The cow licks no strange calf.

Like cow, like calf. Cf. Like father, like son. Etc.

Looks like his cow has died.

Many a good cow has a bad calf.

The old cow thinks she never was a calf.

Like a cow's tail, always behind. Cf. Grows down like a cow's tail. Like a cow's tail, straight up and down (fair in action).

# Cattle

Let him who owns the cow take her by the tail. Cf. Got the wrong cow by the tail.

Every cow needs a tail in fly time.

The cow knows not what her tail is worth till she has lost it.

Till the cows come home (indefinite time).

Wouldn't trust him as far as I could throw a cow (bull or horse) by the tail.

Useless as a dry cow.

Not worth a low country cow tick.

Handsome as a prize heifer.

You'd better watch a frisky heifer.

Don't cry over spilt milk. Cf. Don't cry over spilt milk; tears only make it salty for the cat.

Milk says to wine, "Welcome, friend."

Their milk sod (boiled) over.

God gives the milk, not the pail.

Tender as veal.

## Superstitions and Motifs

From Brown Collection

Boil a bar of lard in one pint of milk so that only one-half teaspoon of liquid is left. Drink this liquid to cure boils. VI, 925. Cf. 955

Exactly at midnight of Old Christmas (January 6) all cattle and horses everywhere stand up and then lie down on the other side. VII, 6012. Cf. On Christmas Eve, at midnight, the cattle all get on their knees and low. 6013

Blow tobacco smoke into a saucer of milk and then feed the milk to the baby for colic. VI, 293

Use nightshade and cream for cow itch. VI, 1223

A cowlick is a lucky sign. VI, 484

If a cow bellows after dark, someone is dying. VII, 5195.

Cf. If a cow lows at noon, you will hear of a death before night. VII, 5191

If a cow steps on a toad, she will give bloody milk. VII, 7525.
Cf. If you kill frogs, your cow will give bloody milk. VII, 7524

To see a shadow of a coffin in a glass of milk is a sign of death. VII, 5081

One-half cup of flour and one-half cup of milk is a cure for dysentery. VI, 1309

To cure earache, put beef foot oil in your ear. VI, 1329

Wash your face in hot cow's milk to cure freckles. VI, 1488

Freckles are carried away by washing them in the milk of milkweed. VI, 1501

To cure freckles, fall face down in warm cow manure and lie there for a while. VI, 1492

Cow manure is used to prevent infection. VI, 1738

For infections of various sorts, apply a warm poultice of bread and milk. This draws out the poison. VI, 1743

The first time a cow is milked, pour the milk on her back. This makes her give lots of milk. VII, 7522

Milking a cow on the left side is bad luck. VII, 7523

It is bad luck to milk a cow's milk on the ground. It will make her go dry. VII, 7527

For a nontalking child, let the child drink water from a cowbell. Talking will immediately follow. VI, 342

To draw poison out of a wound, apply beef gall. VI, 2747

Figs boiled in milk, and swallowed whole, will cure the quinsy. VI, 1956

Sex of calves: Build cowper gaps (gates) facing north to bring bull calves and...south...for heifer calves. VII, 7618-19

To clear skin, drink milk in which you have boiled buckshot. VI, 2110

To cure snake bite, boil some new milk with a shoestring in it, and then drink it. VI, 2129

# Cattle

Rub sore eyes with warm milk. VI, 1361

If you put a piece of raw beef on the throat, it will cure the sore throat. VI, 2189

A good cure for toothache is cow manure. VI, 2345

To remove a wart rub a piece of meat on the wart and bury the meat under a rock in running water. VI, 2462

The juice of milk thistles will cure warts. VI, 2528

If cattle keep their heads to leeward, it indicates bad weather. VII, 6175

If the cows low at night, it is a sign of rain. VII, 6688

Cattle refusing to go to pasture in the morning is a token of rain. VII, 6665

Cattle will move north in the afternoon if the wind is going to change. VII, 6984

If cattle flock to their home in the summer, it is a sign of a bad thunderstorm. VII, 7006

You will not take whooping cough if you drink the milk which a black cat has drunk of. VI, 2710

To cure whooping cough, give the patient some milk stolen from a neighbor's cow. VI, 2711

Whichever way the Milky Way is pointed at night, the wind will be the next day. VII, 6955

Horses, cows, and pigs running, kicking, and being especially playful is a sign of wind. VII, 6988

To keep witches away, let some drops of milk fall on a piece of silver. VII, 5650

Boil sweet milk on the fire, and stir it with a fork, if you want to drive the witches away. VII, 5649

From Clark Collection

If you put a fork into milk, it will make the cow kick. 1325

Thunder makes milk sour. 1324

Your cow will die if you kill a daddy longlegs. 1292

Killing a frog will cause your calf to die. 1284

Jerusalem crickets cause death to cows if they are eaten with hay. (Mexican source) 1293

Milk and fish if you eat them together will poison you. 289. Cf. Brown Collection, VI, 2819

Cows, pigs, and other animals find their young (in the ground and dig them up). 1298

Milk snakes suck milk from cows. 1322-23

From Motif-Index

Bull with a man's head. B23.2

Bull is brazen-footed and firebreathing. B19

Devil as white bull. G303.3.3.1.4

Divinely reincarnated as bull. E611.2.1

Ghost as fiery bull. E421.3.4

Lifting bull over fence. J2199.3

Riding through streets on bull as punishment. Q473.1

Brahmin unwittingly kills calf. N361.1

God assumes form of calf. D133.4.1

Golden calf entered by Satan. G303.18.4

Worship of golden calf. V1.11.1

Man transformed to calf. D133.4

Tabu to kill sacred calf. C92.1.2. Cf. Tabu to kill sacred cow. C221.1.1.1.3

Cow follows saints. B159.3

Cow punished for calf's misdeeds. J1863

Cow's reincarnation as calf. E611.2

Vampire milks cow dry. E251.3.2

Why cow eats green grass, gives white milk and yellow butter. J1291.1.1

Why cow has no upper teeth. A2345.7.1

# Cattle

Milk for bath as poison antidote. D1515.3

Milk gushes from cows in deity's presence. H45.2

Tasting of milk and honey. F1094

A bath in magic milk rejuvenates. D1338.4

Witch snared by setting out milk. G274.1

Dwarfs bewitch cow to give no milk. F451.3.3.5

Fairies milk cows. F271.1

Magic milk heals wounds. D1503.7.1

Milky Way as milk from breast of a woman. A778.5

## Riddles

What is it that runs all over the pasture in the daytime and sits in the cupboard at night?--Milk.  Brown Collection, I, 293

Wanders often over the meadow, with a nice little tongue but cannot speak, goes to water but cannot drink. -- Cowbell. Brown Collection, I, 291

It goes all over the hills, but doesn't eat,
It goes to the creek, but doesn't drink. -- Cowbell.
    -- Coffin and Cohen, Folklore in America, 168

## Quotations--Literary and Otherwise

If ye had not plowed with my heifer, ye had not found out my riddle. -- Judges, XIV, 14

Bring hither the fatted calf, and kill it. -- St. Luke, XV, 23

Kiss till the cows come home. -- Beaumont and Fletcher, Scornful Lady

A cow is a very good animal in a field; but we turn her out of a garden. -- Boswell, Life of Johnson

Who are those coming to the sacrifice?
    To what green altar, O mysterious priest,
Lead'st thou that heifer lowing at the skies,
    And all her silken flanks with garlands drest?
            -- Keats, "Ode on a Grecian Urn"

Hey diddle diddle
The cat and the fiddle,
The cow jumped over the moon;
The little dog laughed
To see such sport,
And the dish ran away with the spoon.
   -- Mother Goose Rhyme

I never saw a Purple Cow,
  I never hope to see one;
But I can tell you, anyhow,
  I'd rather see than be one.
   -- Gelett Burgess, "The Purple Cow"

Chickens on and off the Roost

For untold centuries chickens did their best in behalf of the economy, with no guidelines, no quotas, no compulsions except their natural inclinations. Those were the good old days of outdoor plumbing, pigsties, sudden attacks by hawks and foxes, and going to bed with the chickens. When a hen laid out her limit of a dozen or two of eggs--in spots of her own choosing--she brooded over them for twenty-two days, turned them over regularly, hatched those that were fertile, and strutted forth with her biddies into the world.

Nowadays, however, the production of chickens is a far cackle from that leisurely process. Modern birds have no choice; they lay, or they get the axe. With few exceptions, the poultry business is streamlined from the egg cell to the market--by astute farmers, businessmen, scientists, and other eggheads, who take no chances with setting hens, wild animals, poor feeding, deficits, and outrageous crowing. These smart guys know their genetics and breed accordingly; they house their flocks in sanitary and comfortable buildings; they speed up egg laying with electricity and other stimulants; they understand the balancing of rations; they prescribe medicines and operate like surgeons; they have eggs rolling down carriers for inspection, grading, and packaging; they incubate them in temperature-controlled hatcheries; and they say to the hen, "Produce or perish!"

Chickens were imported into the Western World from Persia or India, where they were once venerated. Cocks were sacred to the sun god Apollo in Athens and other areas. Christians erected weathercocks on church steeples to remind their members not to be sleeping Peters. Chickens were thrown into the laps of Slav brides after weddings as symbols of fertility and connubial bliss.

Hens and roosters are classified as poultry (from O. F.

poulet), which also includes turkeys, ducks, geese, guinea fowl, pigeons, and pheasants. Chicken production is one of the most profitable enterprises in the United States and many other nations, the quantities of eggs and carcasses running into the billions every year. Among the more than a hundred breeds, the following are the most noteworthy:

<u>American Breeds</u>: Plymouth Rock, Wyandotte, Java, Dominique, Rhode Island Red, Rhode Island White, Buckeye, Chantecler, Jersey Giant, Lamona, Delaware, New Hampshire, Holland.

<u>Asiatic Breeds</u>: Brahma, Cochin, Lanshan.

<u>Mediterranean Breeds:</u> Leghorn, Minorca, Catalana, Ancona, Spanish, Blue Andalusian, Buttercup.

<u>English Breeds</u>: Dorking, Red Cap, Cornish, Orpington, Sussex, Australorp.

<u>Continental Breeds:</u> Hamburg, Campine, Lakenvelder.

If you wish to know how influential chickens have been, go to the unabridged dictionaries to verify the long list of words coined about people, their activities, animals, plants, devices and contraptions, diseases, and so forth. For example, you will note such animals as chickenbill, chicken flea, chicken lobster, chicken snake, chicken terrapin, cockatoo, cockatrice, cockchafer, cocker spaniel, cock of the wood, cock sparrow, hen fish, and henhawk; such plants as capon's-feather, capon's-grass, chickenberry, chicken grape, chickenpea, chickweed, eggplant, henbane, hen pepper; such devices as cock feather, cockhorse, and cockloft; and miscellaneous terms such as chicken gumbo, eggnog, egg orchard, cock-ale, cockaleekie, chicken pull, henfeathering, henwife, egg trot, cock-beaded, chicken skin, Cockaigne, cock-and-bull story, chicken bronchitis, chicken cholera, and chicken flu.

The warmth and zest of hens and roosters has been expressed by the folk in their speech, proverbs, and superstitions. For instance, a small chick, held in the hands or against the cheeks of a child, is an innocent and downy partner as compared with the stiff-and-feathered world of adults. It is called a biddy, a chickabiddy, or a cockollybird, especially in nursery rhymes and games.

# Chicken

When this young thing begins to put on feathers, the jibes and snares mount into a brush war. Call him a young chicken and he'll resent your implying that he knows nothing about practical matters. Or stir up the vanity of some girl this side of thirty by calling her a cute chicken. Or take a pot shot at some old sister with the expression, "You ain't no chicken!" She'll never forgive you. Or yell to some nervous Nellie, "Chicken!" Occasionally he will knock you into a cocked hat, but the chances are that he will chicken out for higher timber. In substance, this sneaking coward is chicken-hearted or chicken-livered. Or he may be chicken-pecked and harrassed to near death by a cockerel that has achieved honors in cockiness.

A hen is a fussy and queer old woman, a wife that mans a frigate, the iron-handed ruler of the roost that instigates hen parties to gather gossip and scatter news about the latest methods of henpecking. Sometimes this old bird is as techy as a rooster with a sore head, or as busy as a wet hen with a single chick, or as chaotic as one with her head lopped off. If she has a daughter in a henpen (college dormitory), she can strut and crow like any rooster. This old gal, indeed, puts no faith in the old saying about whistling girls and crowing hens. Come what may, she will fly the coop whenever she pleases.

While this hen is smirking about her inside job, she peers forth from the loft with reserved adoration toward her lover putting on his act in the barnyard. There he is--that creature of song and story, the cockiest and crowingest--the proverbial Chanticleer, chanting and crowing as he stands tiptoe in the morning sun. He may be hen-hearted, but he is telling nobody! He is Sir Cockalorum, the Cock of the Walk, even though he may be a bantamweight from Java. He is lean and muscular; he steams with manhood from ivory toes to flaming comb. He looks awry at fat and foolish capons. Like a true son of Mars, he is saucy, pert, impudent, plucky and spunky, quarrelsome, and obviously superior as he struts and swaggers.

He may be called on to defend the honor of his breed in a cockfighting arena. In this deadly contest, armed with sharp spurs, natural or attached, he may fight until his eyes are closed and half or more of his comb nipped away. As the cockmaster can tell you, this game rooster, unless eliminated by his better, will rise to crow again.

This same Sir Cockalorum, moreover, has often been futile and devilish. He has laid many a cock's egg (one without a yolk), as illustrated by the disastrous stock market crash of 1929. He fathered the word cockney, literally a cock's egg, referring to the Londoner that crows in a strange dialect. He is also credited with hatching out the serpent's egg that became the cockatrice or basilisk, whose very glance could kill you on the spot.

With a straight face, the folk vow that all this palaver is true about chickens and people who do their damnedest in in-fighting, out-fighting, boasting, strutting, threatening, and wiretapping. They argue over which end of an egg is easier to crack; they snarl at those who have nothing but chicken feed; they jibe at Army colonels for nurturing chickens on their knees and shoulders.

As for the eggs catapulted by these birds, the thankful folk call them henfruit, chicken-fruit, henapples, cackleberries, or chicken-berries. Generally they are yellow-yolked, but if the hens have been fed special ingredients they can be red-yolked or green-yolked. You can't get them without cackling, you have no idea how many will hatch, you can't shave one, you don't need a hatchet to open one, and you will never enjoy dancing over a pile of them. Furthermore, if you are an egg-sucker, you adore being flattered; if you are an egg-blonde, no barber can restore your hair; and if you are an egghead, take in stride the jibes of the proud illiterates, or settle down in a university or Washington. And if you are prone to be reckless, put every last one of your eggs into one basket, but watch that basket.

As the folks say, after a chicken is in the pantry and an egg is in the cooler, use them for other purposes than delicious eating. For instance, if young people desire to be attractive, they should swallow handfuls of gizzards. If they are concerned about ridding themselves of freckles, they should bathe their faces in vinegar that has stood in eggshells over night. If they are worked up over the

# Chicken

prospects of lovers and marriages, encourage them to pull wishbones apart to determine who gets the longer piece and the wish, or have them grab the first person who walks under a pulleybone over a door. If, however, a bachelor bites a spinster without permission, egg her on to cover the place bitten with chicken manure and his teeth will fall out.

There are many medical uses of a hen or rooster: for bleeding, apply a freshly killed and cut-open chicken to the wound or sore; for smallpox, grease the child with chicken fat and place him naked in a henhouse; for colic, make the child eat an egg laid on Friday; for fever, bind a cut-open black chicken to the bottom of the victim's foot. To obtain prosperity, dream often about eggs. To keep away hawks, burn chicken feathers in the chimneys. To dispose of a wart, take blood from it and smear it on a grain of corn and give it to a rooster--he'll get the wart. To predict the weather, watch the hens dusting themselves in the soil, or pay attention to their singing in the rain, or note the drooping of their wings. And for foretelling the future, use the blood of a chicken.

Go thou also to the chickens for hints about the coming of visitors and for numerous cures for boils, sore mouth, indigestion, vomiting, sties, hoarseness, measles, mumps, pimples, shingles, pneumonia, arthritis, and all sorts of bites, serpent or otherwise. All the remedies can be found at your favorite grocery store. If perchance your sins are as red as a cockscomb, forget not the weather vane on the high steeple--it calls thee to worship!

### Derivative Names

Bantam (banty): small-size or dwarf breed of fowl; small person who is fond of fighting, saucy, plucky, and quarrelsome; probably so named after Bantam, a small village in West Java. Cf. cockalorum.

bantamize: to make like a bantam

bantamweight: boxer who weighs 118 pounds or less

biddy: hen or chicken, often associated with the young and sometimes disparagingly; young woman such as spring chicken; young and inexperienced person

biddy: female Irish servant; any maid or housekeeper; gossipy woman; toothless old ewe

capon: castrated rooster, especially when fattened for table; effeminate or homosexual man

caponize: to castrate a cock to increase growth and quality of flesh

capon's-feather: common columbine

capon's-grass: rattail fescue

capon's-tail (capon's-tail grass): capon's-feather

Chanticleer (Chantecler): literally a clear crower; cock's name appearing in many old stories

chick: small chicken or other bird; young person; term of endearment

chick: cant or bunk; insignia of U.S. Army colonel or U.S. Navy captain

chickabiddy: child's term of endearment for chicken or biddy

chick bronchitis: infectious bronchitis in poultry

chicken: young of domestic fowl; fowl of any age or sex; flesh of fowl; child or inexperienced person; young woman of loose morals; to chicken out (be a coward)

chicken-berries: hen's eggs, chicken-fruit, henapple or henfruit

chickenberry: wintergreen; partridgeberry

chickenbill: the sora; an American coot

chicken body louse: yellowish biting louse on poultry

chicken breast: malformation of the chest

chicken cholera: contagious bacterial disease of fowl, accompanied by diarrhea

chicken colonel: U.S. Army colonel

chicken corn: annual non-saccharine sorghum

chicken-feed (chicken money): small change or pittance

chicken-fighters (chicken fights): children's game; one of several kinds of violets. See cockfight.

# Chicken

chicken flea: common flea or pest in tropical regions

chicken flu: infectious disease of the larynx in poultry

chicken grape: stout, tall-growing grape

chicken gumbo: soup made from chicken and okra

chicken guts: gold trimming on military uniforms

chicken halibut: young halibut

chicken hazard: game with small stakes

chicken-hearted (hen-hearted): faint-hearted, cowardly or timid; also chicken-spirited, chicken-livered

chicken lice: several species affecting birds and poultry

chicken lobster: young lobster

chicken mite: any of several mites in warm regions

chicken, Mother Carey's: any of several small petrels, especially a stormy petrel

chickenpea: plant in Mediterranean regions, having seed in short and hairy pods

chicken-pecked: irritated or harrassed by a domineering child

chicken pepper: small-flowered buttercup

chicken-pox: mild contagious disease of children

chicken pull: game or contest to see who gets longer part of wishbone

chicken skin: fine, thin vellum used for covering fans

chicken snake: harmless American snake; milk snake

chicken, spring: young and inexperienced person

chicken terrapin: small, edible aquatic turtle

chicken tick: argasid tick

chicken-toed: having toes turned in

chicken tortoise (or turtle): medium-sized aquatic turtle

chicken tracks (hen tracks): illegible handwriting

chickweed (chicken's-meat): spreading white-flowered herb of pink family

cock: rooster, the male of domestic fowl, known for swaggering, boasting, or strutting; to strut or swagger

cock: turning or tilting upward as of the eye; small boat called also cockboat; faucet; pile of hay, etc.; hammer on gun; weather cock, gamecock, or woodcock; leader of group or organization; to pull back hammer on gun

cockade: rosette or knot of ribbon worn on hat

cockaded: wearing a cockade while patrolling an area

cock-a-doodle-doo (cock-a-doodle): cock's crow at dawn

cock-a-hoop (cock-a-whoop): boastful or elated as in boisterous speech; setting cock on the hoop and implying unstinted drinking and cheer

Cockaigne (Cockayne): imaginary medieval Utopia with continuous luxury and idleness in cockneyland, as in 13th-century The Land of Cockayne, a satire on monastic life

cock ale: ale fermented with fruits, spices, and the jelly or mincemeat of a boiled cock

cockaleekie: Scottish soup made of cock or other fowl and leeks

cockalorum: little cock, a bantam; a self-important man

cock-and-bull story: extravagant, incredible tale

cock-and-hen: party for men and women

cockapert: impudent

cockateel (cockatiel): small parrot, native of Australia

cockatoo: any of numerous large, noisy Australian parrots

cockatrice: fabulous monster, believed hatched from cock's egg by a serpent, synonymous with basilisk--its glance would kill; a pernicious person

cock-beaded: shaped or decorated like a cock bead in architecture

cockbird: male bird

cock-brained: foolish or scatterbrained

cock bread: stimulative food for fighting cocks

# Chicken

cockchafer: any of certain scarab-like beetles

cockcrow: early morning crowing by cock; dawn; exultation of superiority

cockcrower: one who crows like a cock

cocked and primed: ready for fight or discussion

cocked hat: hat with brim turned up, usually three-cornered and pointed in front and back; cockup; a bowling game. Cf. cocked hat and feather.

cockup: hat or cap turned up in front as in cocked hat; something superior

cocker: cock fighter; short for cocker spaniel; one who cocks hay, etc.; to nurture with fondling, etc.

cockerel: young domestic cock, especially one less than year old

cocker spaniel (cocking dog): small spaniel, so called from hunting woodcocks

cockeye: squinting eye

cockeyed: askew, awry or squinting; crazy or dumb

cock feather (hen feather): feather on arrow; vane at right angle in archery

cockfight: fight between roosters or gamecocks, armed with metal spurs

cockfighting: sport of fighting cocks or chickens

cockhorse: child's rocking horse or hobbyhorse

cockily (cockish, cocky): in cocky or strutting manner, conceited

cockiness: conceit or arrogance

cocking: cockfighting

cockloft: upper loft or attic

cocking main: series of cockfights

cockmaster: gamecock fancier

cockmatch: cockfight

cockney: Londoner with unusual speech; effeminate town dweller;

spoiled child; simpleton; understood as coken-ey, literally cock's eggs

cock of the plains: large grouse or sage cock

cock-of-the-rock: bird nesting in rocks in Amazon valley, about size of pigeon, with orange-colored plumage; males of species hold elaborate dancing parties

cock of the walk: figuratively, the undisputed, overbearing master of a group or situation

cock of the wood: pileated woodpecker

cock penny: a school fee originally, so called from being spent at cockfighting

cockpit: pit for cockfights

cockscomb: fleshy red crest on rooster's head; plant of amaranth family having crested or feathery clusters or red or yellow flowers; a jester's cap

cock's egg: small yolkless egg

cock's-eggs: egg-shaped, white or yellow fruit of herbaceous vine

cock'sfoot: orchard grass; millet

cockshead: herb with spiny pod

cockshut: twilight or close of day (British)

cockshy: cockthrowing as in throwing shot at target or object

cock sorrel: sour dock

cock sparrow: male sparrow; especially a small, pert or sparrow-like man

cockspur: spur on leg of cock

cockstride: cock's stride or cocksureness; short distance

cocksure: perfectly certain

cocksurety: state of being very sure

cockswain: coxswain

cockthrowing: old sport of throwing sticks at a cock tied to a stake and somewhat related to cockshy

Chicken

cockweed: peppergrass

cocky: pert or conceited; term of endearment; small cock

cockyollybird: any small bird; a nursery expression

egg: oval or spheroidal reproductive body produced by birds; to throw eggs at or pelt; to cover or mix with eggs; fellow or chap, especially good or bad egg

egg and dart (or anchor or tongue): egg-shaped ornament, alternating in form with dart or anchor or tongue

egg-boiler: bowler hat in Australia; utensil for boiling eggs

egg-bound: slow-witted

egg cell: reproductive cell produced by female plant or animal

egger: any of various moths whose larvae feed on the foliage of trees; one who eggs on or stimulates to action

egghead: intellectual or highbrow, often in derogatory sense; a bald man; stupid person

eggnog: drink made of eggs, milk, and sugar, often containing whiskey, brandy, or wine

egg orchard: henhouse or chicken farm

eggplant: plant with large and purple-skinned fruit; the fruit of that plant

egg rolling: ancient European folk ceremony of rolling eggs down hill as symbol of the coming of spring; now confined largely to Easter. Cf. coloring and breaking of eggs at Easter.

eggshell: thin and delicate or very brittle material

eggshell blonde: bald person

egg-sucker: one seeking advancement through flattery

egg-trot: gentle trot

eggy: irritated or excited

hen: mature female of common domestic fowl; any female bird; wet hen or fussy old woman

hen-and-chickens: plant that propagates by offshoots, runners, and other ground parts, such as ground ivy henbane: poisonous herb of nightshade family

henbit: low herb of the mint family

hencoop: cage or enclosure for poultry; women's dormitory in college

hen-feathered: having plumage like that of hen

hen-feathering: plumage on a cock, resembling a hen's

hen fish: any of several marine fish

hen-frigate: ship bossed by captain's wife

hen-harrier: harrier or hawk

hen-hawk: one of various hawks preying on poultry, such as American red-tailed buzzard

hen-heart: chicken-hearted fellow

henhouse: house for poultry; Army officers' club; house controlled by a woman

henhussy: man who pries into women's affairs

hennery: place where fowls are kept

hen-party: one for women only

henpeck: to domineer or annoy, as said of women who control husbands

henpecked: said of man controlled by his wife

hen-pen: girls' school, especially a private one

hen pepper: shepherd's-purse

henroost: place where poultry perch

hens and chickens: any one of several herbs. See hen-and-chickens.

henwife: woman who raises poultry

roost: to sit on perch; to lodge for the night; a place to perch

roost cock: cock or rooster

rooster: domestic male fowl, a cock; a cocky, strutting or active person

roosters: common North American blue violet; white adder's-tongue

## Proverbs and Proverbial Phrases

That's your chicken (concern).

Like hen, like chicken.

Downy as a chick.

Chicken!: (coward)

No chicken: elderly person.

Young as a spring chicken.

Where the chicken got the axe.

Runs around like a hen with her head cut off.

He's a gone chicken. Cf. Gone gosling, goose, or coon.

Cross (fussy) as a setting hen.

A setting hen is never fat.

Setting hens don't want fresh eggs.

Mad (wild) as a wet hen. Cf. Wanton (dejected) as a wet hen.

Never sell a hen on a wet day.

Fat as a hen on the forehead.

Fly the coop: escape.

Like seeking a hare in a hen's nest.

Pecked to death by a hen.

Strutting like a bantam-hen.

Techous (irritable) as an old hen.

Busy as Mother Carey's chicken in a storm.

Like a picked chicken in a rain storm.

As quare as a chicken hatched in a thunderstorm.

Busy as a hen with one chicken.

Fussy as a hen with one biddy.  Cf. Proud as a hen with one chick.

Jealous as a hen with young chickens.

It is a poor hen that can't scratch for one chick.

Don't count your chickens before they are hatched.

Sociable as chickens in a coop.

Tender as chickens.

Warm as a chicken in a basket of wool.  Cf. Hot as a hen in a wool basket.

Children and chickens must always be pecking.

As the old cock crows, the young one learns.

Brave as a gamecock.  Cf. Game as a rooster.  Crowed like a game rooster.

Cocky as a bantam rooster.

Crazy as a mad rooster.

A good cock will crow on any dung-heap.

A good rooster crows in any henhouse.

That cock won't fight.

Hard as sneaking past an eager rooster.

Polite as a rooster.

Pounces upon them like a cock at a blackberry (or fly).

Red as a cock's comb.

Spunky as a Dominicker rooster.

Struts like a rooster.

Struts like the cock of the walk.

Don't put all your eggs in one basket.

The man who put his eggs all in one basket should watch that basket.

Better an egg today than a hen tomorrow.

# Chicken

Big as hen's eggs.

Black hens lay white eggs. Cf. Black cows give white milk.

To have both the egg and the hen.

Send not for a hatchet to break open an egg.

Eggs and oaths are easily broken.

He that buys eggs buys many shells.

He that would have eggs must endure the cackling of hens.

Fresh as an hour-old egg.

Like as two fried eggs.

When the eggs come to be fried: that is, when thief brings a frying-pan to fry the stolen eggs.

I have other eggs to fry.

So hard up they have to fry the nest eggs when company comes.

Full as an egg is of meat.

Better half an egg than an empty shell.

Lay an egg: to fail completely, as in putting on a performance or in a business enterprise.

To take eggs for money: that is, something worthless.

They quarrel about an egg and let the hen fly.

It is very hard to shave an egg.

Sure as eggs: that is, undoubtedly or certainly.

He steps like he is walking on eggs.

Like a hen on a hot griddle.

Like a hen on a junebug.

You look like a hen chawing nails.

You look as nice as an old hen and biddies.

Scarce as hen's teeth.

A whistling girl and a crowing hen
Always come to some bad end. Cf. with the following.

> A whistling woman and a crowing hen
> Are fit for neither God nor men.

> A whistling maid and a crowing hen
> Neither fit for God nor men.

> Whistling girls and hens that crow
> Make their way wherever they go.

It is a sad hour when the hen crows louder than the cock.

His writing looks like a hen's scratching.

Chickens come home to roost (a project boomerangs).

Go to bed with the chickens.

Rule the roost.

So weak he can't pull a hen off the roost.

Knocked into a cocked hat (demolished).

## Superstitions and Motifs

It is good luck to open an egg with two yolks, and then get your wish while eating it.

It is bad luck to sell a crowing hen. Coffin and Cohen.

If a person eats a chicken gizzard, he will become beautiful (pretty).

Brown eggs are richer than white eggs.

### From Brown Collection

Swallow a gizzard whole, and you will become handsome. VI, 677-8

If the housewife burns the eggshells before the cake is baked, it will fall. VI, 2784

If you drink water in which eggs have been boiled, you will have cancers. VI, 999

If a child has chicken pox, grease him with chicken grease and put him naked in the chicken house. VI, 1021. Cf. 1023 and 1025

Chicken

If a cow loses her cud, put an egg in her mouth and make her swallow it. It will bring the cud back. VII, 7570

Your chickens will be like the first person that comes on New Year's morning--if fat person, fat chickens; if poor person, skinny chickens. VII, 8474. Cf. If a Negro comes on New Year's day, the chickens will be black that year. Clark Collection, 1232

Chickens crowing after sunset means death. VII, 5251

Feed chickens eggshells, and they will lay. VII, 7453

If hens eat snow, it will stop them from laying. VII, 7452

To draw out fever: Cut a black chicken open while alive and bind to the bottom of the foot. VI, 1415

If you dream of finding eggs, you will be in a fight the next day. VI, 3611

It is unlucky to hold a dying chicken. VII, 7200

Throwing a lucky egg over a house backwards is good luck. VII, 7202

If a rooster crows repeatedly at twelve o'clock, he is crowing for Christmas. VII, 6010. Cf. Roosters crow at midnight on Old Christmas (January 6). Clark Collection, 1055

Eggs laid on Friday will cure colic. VI, 1151

To stop vomiting or to cure dyspepsia, use the inside of a chicken gizzard, dried and powdered. VI, 1314

To cure freckles, peel the shell from an egg and place in vinegar to soak over night. Bathe in the vinegar the following day. VI, 1493

If you see two hens with their heads together, like they are talking, people are talking about you. VI, 3610

Burn chicken feathers to keep hawks away. VII, 7477. Cf. Use of eggshells in the chimney to keep them away. 7479

To cure hiccoughs, tickle the nose with a chicken feather. VI, 1675

The white of an egg, beaten with lemon juice and sugar, will cure hoarseness. VI, 1690

For indigestion: Cook tuata leaves without water and mix with two eggs to make omelet, which patient eats while sipping the juice. VI, 1722. (Summary.)

Marriage: if you eat five chicken gizzards in one day, you can marry anyone you like. VI, 4483. Cf. If two people make a wish and pull the wishbone of a chicken, the one who gets the shorter end gets the wish. VII, 7197. Also cf. Put the pulleybone of a chicken over the door. The first person that passes through that door will be the one you are to marry; and it will happen in ten days. VI, 4493. If you eat an eggshell full of salt before going to bed, you will dream of the one whom you will marry bringing you water. VI, 4313

To cure measles, kill a black hen; after cooking, skim the grease off of the pot and rub it on the body. VI, 1804

Chickens crowing after sunset means hasty news. VI, 4085

To prevent pimples, apply a mixture of sulphur and molasses. To bring to a head, cover with a mild soap or with the inner skin of a raw egg. VI, 1931

For pneumonia, kill a chicken, cut it open, and use the warm organs as a poultice on the chest. VI, 1933

For rheumatism, bind the entrails of chickens to the feet. VI, 1974

If you dream of a nest of eggs, you will be rich. VI, 3363

Setting hen: To break a hen from setting, put an alarm clock in the nest and let it go off. VII, 7430. If there are thunderstorms while eggs are setting, the eggs will not hatch. VII, 7444. Always set a hen on thirteen eggs. Cf. Setting on an odd number of eggs. VII, 7433 and 7432. If you set eggs when the wind is eastward, the chickens will holler themselves to death. VII, 7436. Cf. Set a hen with a south wind. Clark Collection, 1316. If a hen is set in the afternoon, all the chickens will be roosters. VII, 7440. Cf. If you pull a baby chick's tail three times and say magic Italian words while it rearranges its feathers, it is a female. Clark Collection, 1317

For shingles, use the blood of a black chicken. VI, 2099

If a hen crows, there will be sickness in the family. VI, 709

To cure snake bite: put as much salt as the yolk of an egg will dissolve, and bind this to the bite. VI, 2133. Cut a black hen open and bind it to the bite. VI, 2131

Sore mouth: Bake an egg in corn pone for an hour. Mix yolk with tablespoon of hen's oil, ten drops of turpentine, tablespoon

# Chicken

of sulphur, and a half teaspoon of alum or borax. VI, 1824

To keep off spells, keep a "ruffled" chicken in the yard to scratch away the "goofer" or conjure bags. VII, 5570

When a hen cries between the hours of eight and twelve at night, it is a sign that a bachelor has stolen a spinster. VII, 8549

To cure a sty, beat the white of an egg and put it on the eye. Do not let it dry on the eye. VI, 2280

To keep a baby from having serious trouble cutting teeth, rub its gums with the brains of a chicken. VI, 357

Take the red of a roasted egg, crumbled and mixed with alum and sugar, as a cure for thrash. VI, 408

If a rooster crows in the front yard, you will trade horses that day. VI, 7640

If a rooster comes to the door and faces the house, a stranger is coming. VI, 3938. Cf. Preacher. Clark Collection, 688

If two hens start fighting, you will have a stranger as a guest. VI, 3962. Cf. with 3965: If two roosters fight, two men are coming.

Put an egg on your chest to keep from vomiting. VI, 2401

Water that eggs have been washed in will cause warts. VI, 2406

To cure a wart, rub a grain of corn over it; then feed it to a chicken. VI, 2497. Cf. with 2509: Get some blood from a wart, put it on a pea, and feed the pea to a rooster. The wart will disappear.

Weather: A sign of cold weather is the thickening of the feathers on a rooster's legs. VII, 6082. Chickens dusting in the sand foretells bad weather. VII, 6184. When chickens droop their feathers, it is the sign of rain. VII, 6678. Cf. with 6687: When chickens crow after going to roost. The singing of hens during a rain denotes fair weather. VII, 6371. When chickens get on the fence during a rain and pick themselves, it is a sign of clear weather. VII, 6242.

Drink hen manure tea to cure the whooping cough. VI, 2713

It is unwise to keep eggshells because witches go to sea in them. VII, 5621

To cure excessive bleeding, kill a chicken and apply fresh-bleeding meat to the place. VI, 857

Boils: Take the skin from around the egg and put it over the boil to cure it. VI, 919. The white of an egg (beaten) and honey will draw boils to a head. VI, 918

## From Clark Collection

White chickens lay more eggs than brown chickens. 1228 and 1230

It is bad luck to eat a crowing hen except on Friday. 886

If a woman enters your home first on New Year's Day, you cannot raise chickens that year. 647

If someone bites you put chicken manure on the place bitten, and his teeth will rot out. 284

The mumps will go away if you tie fried eggs and sardine oil to the jaw. 225

White chicken manure boiled in water makes a medicine for stomachache. 241

## From Motif-Index

Cock believes his crowing makes sun rise. J2272.1

Cock feigns death to overhear hens. H1556.1.1

Cock persuaded to crow with closed eyes. K721

Cock persuades fox to talk and release him. K561.1

Fox confesses to cock and then eats him. K2027

Fox feigning illness admitted to henhouse and kills hens. K828.2

Fox had rather meet one hen than fifty women. J488

Cock shows browbeaten husband how to rule his wife. T252.2

Cock in Valhalla wakens the gods. A661.1.0.4

Devil disappears when cock crows. G303.17.1.1

Basilisk hatched from cock's egg. B12.1

Swallow advises hen against hatching out serpent's eggs. J622.1.1

Cocks that crow about mistress's adultery killed. J551.1

Mouse teaches her child to fear quiet cats but not noisy cock. J132

Between midnight and cockcrow is best time for unearthing treasure. N555.1

Treasure to be found by man who plows with cock and harrows with hen. N543.2

Blindness cured by chicken dung. F952.6

Magic chicken thigh. D166.1

Numbskull tries to wash black hen white. J1909.6

Why hen has no teeth. A2345.8

Witch in form of a hen. G211.3.1

## Quotations--Literary and Otherwise

Do not count your chickens before they are hatched.--Aesop, "The Milkmaid and Her Pail."

As a hen gathereth her chickens under her wings. -- St. Matthew, XXIII, 37

> Hickety, pickety, my black hen,
> She lays eggs for gentlemen;
> Gentlemen come every day
> To see what my hen doth lay.
> -- Hickety, Pickety

'Tis the part of a wise man to keep himself to-day for to-morrow, and not venture all his eggs in one basket. -- Cervantes, Don Quixote

Going as if he trod upon eggs. -- Robert Burton, Anatomy of Melancholy

What! all my pretty chickens and their dam
At one fell swoop? -- Shakespeare, Macbeth

> They say we are
> Almost as like as eggs.
> -- Shakespeare, The Winter's Tale

I can suck melancholy out of a song as a weasel sucks eggs.
-- Shakespeare, As You Like It

A hen is only an egg's way of making another egg. -- Samuel Butler, Life and Habits

It is computed that eleven thousand persons have, at several times, suffered death, rather than submit to break their eggs at the smaller end. (Conflict between big-endians and small-endians). -- Jonathan Swift, Gulliver's Travels

She's no chicken; she's on the wrong side of thirty, if she be a day. -- Jonathan Swift, Polite Conversation

It's as full of good-nature as an egg's full of meat. -- Richard Brinsley Sheridan, A Trip to Scarborough

Put all your eggs in the one basket and--Watch That Basket. -- Mark Twain, Pudd'nhead Wilson

Hongry rooster don't cackle w'en he fine a wum. -- J.C. Harris, Uncle Remus: Plantation Proverbs

As innocent as a new-laid egg. -- William S. Gilbert, Engaged

An old Spanish saying is that "a kiss without a moustache is like an egg without salt." -- Madison J. Cawein, Nature-Notes

What's the use? Yesterday an egg, tomorrow a feather duster. -- Mark Fenederson, The Dejected Rooster

Wall Street Lays an Egg. (Headline announcing stock market crash of Oct. 1929) -- Sime Silverman

If God grants me the usual length of life, I hope to make France so prosperous that every peasant will have a chicken in the pot on Sunday. -- Henry IV of France (1553-1610), when he was crowned king.

A Chicken in Every Pot. -- Republican slogan of 1932.

### It Pays to Advertise

The codfish lays ten thousand eggs,
   The homely hen lays one.
The codfish never cackles
   To tell you what she's done,
And so we scorn the codfish,
   While the humble hen we prize,
Which only goes to show you
That it pays to advertise.

### Riddles

What is that of which the outside is silver and the inside is gold?
   -- Egg

When I was going over a field of wheat
I picked up something good to eat,
Whether fish, flesh, fowl or bone,
I kept it till it ran alone. -- Egg

Love Me, Love My Dog

Let's hope you are not yet too old to recall the time when you and your daddy tripped homeward with that first pup, perhaps a gift from a friend or a stray mongrel picked up on the road. He may have been spotted or speckled and the prettiest thing that ever curled up in a red wagon. It was not long before he became the center of family interests--every child vied to take turns in feeding or fondling him, or in dressing him or tucking him snugly in bed. He was up early with the children, ready for all sorts of antics and fun. Between acts he liked to rear back on his haunches, tilt his head high, and sniff or grin from ear to ear. He kept every child's attention from breakfast to bedtime--a baby-sitter of the first order.

But as this innocence of puppies and children inevitably passed away, you discovered that adult dogs have peculiarities, engage in knavish trickery, and assume rights not delegated to them. You had to endure their yelping and howling long after midnight while they were chasing a big tomcat, or hunting a rabbit or coon or possum, or fighting a strange and shaggy dog, or snarling at a passing bum, or startling a sad Romeo on his late journey home, or baying at the moon. On occasion, you observed packs of dogs hurrying from all directions in pursuit of a bitch in mating season, or a staggering mailman jumping fences or climbing trees to evade a plunging bulldog, or a milkman desperately pitching biscuits and bones to ward off a frontal attack. And you perhaps also noted a scourge of dogs trampling the flower and vegetable gardens; you saw a similar devastation of green lawns and heard the threats and curses of upright men, who had had enough of this friendly dog business. This havoc taught you that a dog does not care an iota about cucumbers, tomatoes, string beans, irises, snapdragons, and sweet peas. You further learned that no dog can read signs like

Land Posted! or Keep Out! or Trespassers Shot Without Warning!

The reputation of dogs has zigzagged through history with both bright and dark aspects. Dogs were the esteemed companions of the huntress Artemis and the strong-armed Heracles; dogs also served the dark goddess Hecate in her wandering over Hell, the moon, and the earth. At the entrance to Hades sat the three-headed Cerberus, who proudly welcomed the damned; and his boss, the inimitable Satan, was symbolized by a dog biting his own tail. In Roman communities a black dog represented evil spirits. In India dogs were sacrificed to appease the wrath of the gods; here too dogs were transformed into human beings, and vice versa. According to other mythologies, dogs had human heads, persons had dog heads, devils looked like dogs, and witches appeared in their likeness. The early Hebrews and Christians considered dogs unclean and therefore unholy.

In more recent times scientists have projected dogs' names into the skies. The meteorologists have surely gone to the dogs in their use of two interesting words, sundog and foxdog; the astronomers have designated Sirius or Procyon as the Dog Star, Ursa Minor or the Polar Star as the Dog Tail, and the constellation Canis Minor as the Smaller Dog and Canis Major as the Great Dog or Orion's Hound.

The versatile dog, domesticated some six to seven thousand years ago, is a carnivorous mammal of the genus Canis familiaris of the family Canidae, which includes also the wolf, fox, coyote, jackal, and others. Probably originating in Asia or Europe, the dog was once considered the offspring of a cross between the wolf and the jackal, but now it is believed that he had a specific prehistoric ancestor, canine and no more. This has been seemingly confirmed by drawings and pictures or other remains found in caves, near ancient lake sites and in other places of human abode. The Basque area of Spain has been identified, in part, as one of the earliest bases in the propagation of the dog; from this and other regions he was disseminated, with much crossing, throughout the world by explorers and settlers.

Nobody knows how many dogs there are in the world, or the

number of breeds. There are at least 200 registered species, of which about 120 are found in the United States, where they are discussed and celebrated in more than a score of high-class doggy publications. A count a few years ago disclosed that there were 1.2 dogs per family, or one for every eight persons in this land.

Dog business has become big business. There is 50 percent more dog food than baby food sold in this country, and the lucky dogs are catered to with the latest styles and gimmicks. Many dogs enjoy esthetic kennels and wide playgrounds. Haberdashers outfit dogs with jewelled collars, trinkets, necklaces, sweaters, vests, coats, gowns, belts, girdles, leashes that sparkle, breast protruders, cruppers for droopy tails, blinders to prevent romantic side glances, and even the latest mini-skirts. Food processors provide grain and meat products measured for vitamins and calories; veterinarians diagnose ailments, stuff in sulpha drugs and penicillin, and operate in antiseptic fashion; professional dog-walkers exercise them; ship lines arrange special quarters, with piped-in music, and serve prescribed diets. Morticians and chaplains lay them to rest in pet cemeteries with much pomp and ceremony; the funerals include colorful headstones, and the thoughtful pet owners set aside trust funds to guarantee care in perpetuity.

These honors are surely deserved, for some of the pedigreed generations exceed in number and quality the best human lines back to Adam. The following listing classifies the best-known breeds:

<u>Working Dogs</u>: Boxer, Collie, Doberman Pinscher, German Shepherd, Great Dane, Old English Sheepdog, Newfoundland, St. Bernard.

<u>Sporting Dogs</u>: Brittany Spaniel, Chesapeake Bay Retriever, English Setter, German Short-haired Pointer, English Springer Spaniel, Golden Retriever, Irish Setter, Irish Water Spaniel, Labrador Retriever, Weimaraner Pointer.

<u>Sporting Hounds</u>: Afghan Hound, Basset, Beagle, Bloodhound, Coonhound, Dachshund, Foxhound, Greyhound, Irish Wolfhound, Russian Wolfhound or Borzoi, Whippet.

<u>Non-Sporting Dogs</u>: Boston Terrier, Chow Chow, Dalmatian,

English Bulldog, French Poodle, Schipperke.

<u>Terriers</u>: Airedale, Bull Terrier, Cairn Terrier, Fox Terrier (smooth), Manchester Terrier, Miniature Schnauzer, Sealyham Terrier, Skye Terrier.

<u>Toy Dogs</u>: Bedlington Terrier, Chihuahua, Fox Terrier (wire-haired), Pomeranian, Pekingese, and Scotch Terrier.

Thanks to the dogged application of the dictionary compilers, there is a fine assortment of doggy names for plants, animals, devices, persons or their actions, and so forth. For example, in the plant kingdom we have dogbane, dog bent, dogberry, dog button, dog cabbage. Useful devices include the bitch box, bitch lamp, dog iron, dog tag, dog tent. Among miscellaneous terms are dogfight, dogtrot, dogface, dog days, puppy-love, dog Latin, and dog hysteria. (Refer to the list below for brief explanations and many other terms.)

The real nature of the ordinary dog is revealed in the proverbial expressions of the folk. Here you find that all dogs, regardless of their physical structure, are silly, conceited, and cowardly, inferior, mean, and contemptible; wretched and worthless. Even the hound, reputed for clean teeth and excellence in the chase, is a suck-egg or sheep-killing monster, fit to be hanged. However, he is superior to the cur and the bitch, the lowest of dogs. The cur, sometimes a rough-neck mongrel, has the audacity to bite before he barks. His shameless rudeness is notorious. And a bitch, showing all aspects of unrefined bitchery, is a drudge, a prostitute or slut--she complains incessantly and acts erratically, grows hot in season, and trades her wares with finesse in the evenings. Her name is aptly used in bitch box (loud public-address speaker) or bitch goddess (material success), and she must be credited with producing an inexhaustible supply of sons.

Some dogs never bark; others bark all the time, often for good reason. Although much barking is sheer bluff, it can scare the daylights out of tramps, thieves, strange visitors, or plain meddlers. But do not be fooled--a dog's bark is not always worse than his bite. You need not fear a dead dog and you have more than an even chance with a sneaky type. But beware of an old dog, perhaps that one in the manger. Keep a steady eye on a silent dog too. Never venture close to a mad dog, or a bulldog on a rampage, or a sleeping dog that wakes easily. Provoke none of these breeds, and don't try to make headlines by biting one. That would be barking up the wrong tree.

There is not much to a dog's life or a dog's chance, according to the folk. If one of your friends has gone to the dogs, pity him.

Yet the dog can also be your counsellor and physician--the folks say that the dog has the balm of Gilead. For example, if you suffer with asthma, buy yourself a Mexican asthma dog and cuddle up to him--Presto! your trouble is gone. If you have been bitten by a crazy mastiff, you are advised to yank out a few of the dog's hairs and apply them to the wound. If that does not work, wear a dog's and/or wolf's tooth to draw out the poison. If this too is of no avail, try drinking several jiggers of whiskey saturated with turpentine. For snakebite, a sure cure is to put lots of grease on the wound and let a dog lick it. If you have rheumatism, sleep with your dog and he will absorb all the pains and stiffness. Do not have an abscessed tooth pulled during the dog days; you will die from bleeding. And you had better not allow a dog to swallow your child's freshly pulled tooth--a dog tooth will come in its place.

If you really want to get married, eat plenty of dog grease. If you are expecting company, listen to the barking of a dog; it may indicate that your expectations or fears are nearly fulfilled. If you note a dog moving about in an uneasy manner, count on rainy weather. If the dog eats grass, you are going to have more rain. However, if he lies on his back, the weather will soon be clearing. And since dogs can see ghosts and other evil spirits, have special regard for a dog's howling--it means that death is around the corner or that a witch is stalking you. Should a witch appear, make a mixture of the dung and blood of a black dog and smear it on the posts and walls of your dwelling. When the witch smells it, she will disappear into thin air.

Allowing for his limitations and abuses, the dog since prehistoric times has been an affectionate, loyal friend of man. His faithfulness and forgiving spirit are legendary. Despite frequent humiliation, he limps back with tail between his legs to lick the offending hand. As an optimist, he rebounds from scanty feeding and sloven dogholes to serve the thoughtless or indifferent. Oh, yes, he may whimper a bit, but he will not beg one third as much as he is able to give. His cold nose proclaims his good health and eagerness for the chase. His bearing is honest--deep and fresh and warming. And as his master directs with understanding and kindness, he responds with cheerful intelligence.

As pet, watchdog, herder, hunter, pointer, setter, pursuer of criminals, Seeing-Eye guide of the blind, and entertainer on the stage or track, he has no superior. In the field he is all ears and eyes and nose and tail, expertly cocked for duty and game; up the long hills and down the meadows he steers the flocks and herds to green pastures and flowing water holes; in the lonely watches of the night he ever guards the animals as well as the human family; he pours forth his joy upon the master's household; he manifests his sorrow in hours of tragedy and pain, and waits by the fallen body of his beloved. In good times and harsh ones, in life and death, the dog is magnificent in spirit and rare in nobility.

## Derivative Names

bitch: female of dog, fox, or wolf; lewd woman; male harlot; any difficult or unpleasant task; to complain; to bungle or spoil something; queen of any suit in deck of cards; a grasping device

bitch box: public-address loudspeaker

bitch chain: short chain with hook and ring used in logging

bitchery: behavior of or like that of a bitch

bitch goddess: success, especially material or worldly kind

bitchily: like a bitch

bitch kitty: obstinate, disagreeable girl or woman

bitch lamp: makeshift lamp, an oil lamp; slut lamp

bitch party: party of women

bitch session: bull session with much complaining

bitchy: spiteful or arrogant

cur (cur dog): mongrel or inferior dog; worthless, yellow, snarling fellow

dog: worthless man or wretch; outward and ostentatious show or style; inferior woman, usually a prostitute

dog: to hunt or track like a dog; to pester; to jog along at a dog-trot

dog: dogskin used as fur; short for dogfish, prairie dog, etc.; firedog or andiron; frankfurter or hot dog; device with spike or bar of metal with hook or claw at end to hold objects; low-grade stock; low-grade beef animal; inferior or poor-selling item

dog: sundog and foxdog in meteorology; in astronomy, the constellations Canis Minor or Canis Major (Great Dog or Orion's Hound in Southern Sky)

dog ape (dog-faced ape): baboon or allied ape

dogbane (dog's-bane): plant of dogbane family, mostly poisonous plants with milky juice; wolfsbane

dog bent (dog's bent): common grass with slender culms and narrow leaves, used as emetic and eaten by sick dogs

dogberry: fruit of the dogwood Carnus sanguinea

dogberry tree: red osier

dog biscuit: hardtack

dogbit: bitten by dog

dogbody: squared-sterned boat

dogbolt: slim bolt used for holding work during machining

dogbrier: dog rose

dog bur: hound's-tongue

dog button: nux vomica

dog cabbage (dog's cabbage): fleshy southern European herb

Dog

dog camomile: mayweed or dog fennel

dog carrier: ventilated crate on top of vehicle to transport small dogs

dogcart: small, two-wheeled cart pulled by dogs

dog-catcher: one licensed to catch stray dogs

dog-cheap: extremely low in price

dog cockle: any of certain marine mollusks

dog-collar: stiff collar, worn sometimes by ministers; muffler clamp

dog daisy: plant as of some daisies, amyweed or camomile

dog dance: Indian dance that includes the eating of dog meat

dog dandelion: fall dandelion

dog days: hot and uncomfortable weather in July and August

dog disease: distemper

dog-ear (dog's-ear, dog-eared): folded-down corner of page

dog-eye: stare of reproach or supplication

dogface: soldier in U.S. Army

dogfall: a draw in contest such as wrestling

dogfight: close fighting by planes, like the fighting of dogs

dogfish: any of several small sharks

dog flea: flea chiefly noticed on dogs and cats

dog flower: daisy; purple trillium

dog fly: orchard grass

dog food: corned-beef hash

dog fox: male fox; corsae

dogged: stubborn and tenacious

dogger: broad-bowed, two-masted fishing vessel in North Sea

doggerel: low-styled and irregular verse or rhymes, rudely comic and usually poor--uncertain connection with dogs

doggerman:  sailor on a dogger

doggery:  doglike behavior; dogs collectively

doggish:  like a dog, surly; stylish or showy

doggy (doggie):  pet name for dog; like a dog, doggish; pretentious or garishly dressed

doggone:  expletive meaning Darn!

dog grass (dog's grass):  dog bent; couch grass; yard grass

dog grate:  metal frame on dogs or andirons

doghead:  hammer of a gunlock

doghole:  place fit only for dogs, mean and miserable abode

doghouse:  small house for dogs; caboose or shack for railroad workers; dog kennel

dog hysteria:  canine hysteria

dog killer:  person in charge of killing mad or unwanted dogs

dog Latin:  jargon imitating Latin

dog laurel:  evergreen shrub of southern U.S.A.

dogleg fence:  zigzag fence

dog-legged:  crooked or bent like a dog's leg

dog letter (dog's letter):  the letter "r," from resemblance of trilled "r" to dog's growl

dog lichen:  common foliose lichen, supposed cure of hydrophobia

dog meat (dog's meat):  inferior meat

dog mint:  wild basil

dog-nap (dog-sleep):  short sleep, often pretended and fitful

dog-napping:  stealing of dogs

dog nettle:  hemp nettle

dog out (dog up):  to dress up in one's best clothes; to dog it

# Dog

dog-paddle: simple swimming stroke

dog parsley (dog's parsley): fool's parsley; wild chervil; dog poison

dogplate: faceplate

dog plum: cape ash

dog-poor: destitute

dog pound: enclosure for stray dogs, etc.

dog robber: Army officers' orderly or servant

dog rose: European wild, prickly rose

dogs (hounds): human feet

dogs, the: the cat's meow

dog salmon: humpback salmon

dogs-and-cats: rabbit-foot clover

dog's death: miserable end

dog show: foot inspection

dog-sick: very sick

dogskin: skin of dog; fur

dog sled (dog sledge): sled drawn by dogs

dog's-nose: drink of beer or ale mixed with gin or rum

Dog Star: Sirius; sometimes called Procyon

dog tags: metal identification tags worn by soldiers and sailors on chain about their necks

Dog Tail (Dog's Tail): Polar Star, Ursa Minor

dog's tail (dog's-tail grass): any grass having spikelike panicles; yard grass species

dog tent (pup tent): military shelter tent

dog-tired (dog-weary): exhausted

dog's-tongue: hound's-tongue

dogtooth violet (dog's-tooth violet): European bulbous herb of lily family

dog-town: colony of prairie dogs

dogtrick: knavish act

dogtrot: gentle trot

dogvane: small vane on weather rail of vessel to indicate the direction of the wind

dog wagon: lunch wagon

dog warp: strong rope with hook used in logging

dogwatch: 4 to 6 p.m. or 6 to 8 p.m. watch on ship

dog whelk: any of certain thick-shelled marine snails

dogwood: tree having white or pink flowers; also wood of

dogwood winter: brief spell of wintry weather in spring

hound: hunting dog; contemptible person; one very fond of something; side bar of vehicle

hound: to pursue, chase, or attack

Hound of Heaven: Christ

houndsbane: horehound

hound's-tongue: coarse weed of the borage family

houndstooth check (hound's-tooth check): small broken-check textile pattern

pup: young dog, fox, wolf, seal, etc.; silly, conceited person; inexperienced person; wiener or hot dog on roll; to give birth to pups

puppy: young dog, shark, etc.; conceited young person

puppy-dog feet: clubs in playing cards

puppy love: preadolescent love, calf love

pup tents: overshoes used in circus; military shelter

slut: female dog; dirty, sloven, and immoral woman; bitch; drudge

sluttish: having qualities of slut

# Dog

## Proverbs and Proverbial Phrases

Alert (careful or busy) as a bird dog.

Crazy as Tom Tyler's old bitch.

Bitch the pot (to pour out the tea).

A cur will bite before he barks. Cf. Dog's barking (below).

A dog's age (long time). Cf. Coon's age.

Agree like dog and cat.

Two dogs over one bone seldom agree. Cf. Two cats and two dogs and a bone never agree.

Scratching and biting cats and dogs come together.

Dogs bark as they are bred.

A dog barks more out of custom than care of a house.

One barking dog sets all streets a-barking. Cf. When one dog barks, another begins.

A dog will bark ere he bite. Cf. Barking dogs seldom bite.

His bark is worse than his bite. Cf. Big bark and little bite. He is all bark and no bite.

A good dog never barketh about a bone. Cf. A good dog deserves a good bone. The dogs follow the man with the bone.

A good dog does not bark without cause.

All are not thieves that dogs bark at.

An old dog barks sitting down.

If the old dog bark, he gives counsel. Cf. An old dog does not bark for nothing.

You can't excuse a dog after he bites you.

There's no use to have a dog and bark yourself. Cf. Do not keep a dog and bark yourself.

He is barking up the wrong tree.

I'd rather be a dog and bay at the moon.

Even bad dogs shouldn't bite at Christmas.

A man may provoke his own dog to bite him.

If a man bites a dog, that is news.

Hold on like a bulldog.  Cf.  Spunky as a bulldog.

A mastiff grows fiercer for being tied up.

A dog's chance (bare chance in one's favor).

Crooked as a dog's (hind) legs.

It is an ill dog that deserves not a crust.

Every dog has his day.  Cf.  Every dog has his day and the bitch her evenings.

A dead dog will not bite.

Die like a dog.

Dog it (to dress up; to make slight effort; to flee or retreat; to travel at others' expense).  Cf. Put on the dog (below).

Dog in a doublet (mean creature or daring person; doublet originally dress worn on boar hunts in Flanders and Germany).

Proud as a dog in a doublet.

It would make a dog doff his doublet.

When a dog is drowning, everyone offers him drink.

Drunk as a dog (dog-drunk).  Cf.  Blind (drunk) as a pup.

It's so dry the trees are following the dogs around.

Women and dogs set men by the ears.

Dog eat dog (ruthless, savage competition).  Cf.  Dog does not eat dog.

Faithful as a dog.

For fashion's sake, as dogs go to church.

Ferocious as a mad dog.

The dog that fetches will carry.  Cf.  A dog that will carry a bone will bring a bone.

Not fit (weather, etc.) to turn a dog out in.

# Dog

Follow like a dog.

A dog is man's friend.  Cf.  The poor dog is the firmest friend in life.

Go to the dogs (be ruined).  Cf.  Gone to the dogs.

The guilty dog barks first.  Cf.  A hurt dog always barks.  The hit dog always hollers.

A hair of the dog cures the bite.

Hanged like a dog.

Don't stay until the last dog is killed.  Cf. ...until the last cat is hung (to the very end).

Honest as a house dog.

Humble as a dog.

Hungry as a dog.

Hunted like a dog.

In the doghouse (in disfavor or disgrace).

Keen as a hunting dog.

Don't kick a dead dog.  Cf.  Never kick a dog when he is down.

Any dog knows better than to chew a razor.

Enough to make a dog laugh.

Lazy as a dog (hound).

Lazy as the dog that leaned against the wall to bark.  Cf.  Lazy as Ludlam's dog that leaned against the fence to bark.

A lean dog for a long chase.  Cf.  A lean dog shames his master.

Lies like a dog.

A dog's life (wretched existence).

The dog that licks ashes, trust him not.

He that lies with dogs riseth with fleas.  Cf.  Many as a dog has fleas.

A living dog is better than a dead lion.  Cf.  A living ass is better than a dead doctor.

Every dog is a lion at home.  Cf.  A dog is valiant at his own door.

A dog has a good look at the bishop.

Love me, love my dog.

A dog in the manger that neither eats nor lets others eat.

Mean as a dog.

Naked as a yard dog.

If you give a dog a bad name, you might as well hang him.  Cf. Give a dog a bad name and everybody will want to kick him.

Keen as a beagle's nose.

The colder the dog's nose, the healthier the dog.

A dog's nose is ever cold.  Cf.  Cold as a dog's nose.  Note: Dog's nose (Brit.), a man addicted to whiskey.

Keep a dog tied up too long and he'll lose his nose for the trail.

A dog's nose and a maid's knees are always cold.

He is an old dog at it (expert).

Put on the dog (dress in fanciest clothes and best finery; put on airs).

Rain cats and dogs.

Ran like a scalded dog.  Cf.  The scalded dog fears cold water.

Dogs run with dogs.

Savage as a mad dog.

Go to see a man about a dog (as excuse).

Shaggy as a dog.

Like a sheep-killing (sheep-stealing) dog.

Sick as a dog.

Beware of a silent dog and still water.

Sitting like a wart on a dog's back.

Let sleeping dogs lie (let well enough alone).  Cf. It is nought good a slepying hound to wake. -- Chaucer, Troilus and Criseyde

Sneak away like a dog.

Stinks like a dog.

It's a poor dog that can't wag its own tail.

The sun won't shine on one dog's tail all the time.

Proud (pleased) as a dog that has two tails.

Cut off a dog's tail; he will still be a dog.

Talking like a dog trotting in dry leaves.

Thick as hairs on a dog's back.

He who ties a mad dog is likely to be bit.

Tired (weary) as a dog.

Treated like a dog.

That is a dog's trick.

You can't teach old dogs new tricks.

Try it on a dog (test it).

Every dog to his own vomit. Cf. The dog is turned to his own vomit again. -- 2 Peter, II, 22. Cf. The dog returns to his vomit or the sow to her wallowing in the mire.

Dog the watches (to change the order of night watches).

There are more ways to kill a dog than to choke him with butter. Cf. ... than choke him on biscuits, or by hanging.

Work like a dog.

It is a poor dog that is not worth the whistling.

Yellow dog under the wagon.

Clean as a hound's tooth.

A gentle hound should never play the cur.

To hold with the hare and run with the hound. Cf. Follow the hounds, or ride with the hounds (to hunt).

Hungry as a hound.

Quit kicking my hound (dog) around.

A man who kicks his hound will beat his wife.   Cf.   The man who strikes his horse strikes his wife too.

Sneaking as a hound.

Yellow as a suck-egg hound.   Cf.   Like a suck-egg dog.   Worse than a suck-egg hound.

Cute as a beagle pup.

Frisky as a pup.

Pretty as a speckled (spotted) pup (under a red wagon).

Take off like Snyder's pup.

Have pups (have kittens).

Friendly (pert, playful) as a puppy.

Weak as puppy water.   Cf.   Weak as water.

Tickled as a puppy dog.

Do not expect a good whelp from an ill dog.

The last whelp of a litter is best.   Cf.   The first pig, but the last whelp (puppy) of the litter, is the best.

Cowed like a whipped spaniel.

## Superstitions and Motifs

If a dog lies on its back, the weather will change.

### From Brown Collection

Death:   Cats and dogs know when death has come to the house. VII, 5186.   The barking of a dog before 10 p.m. is a sign of death.   VII, 5206.   If a dog howls near a sick person, that person will surely die.   VII, 5207.   If a dog lies with his head in his master's doorway, it is a sign of death. VII, 5216.   It is a common belief in North Carolina that death is foretold by a sound in the heavens like a pack of hounds at bay.   VII, 8557

Pregnancy:   Putting a hand on a dog will cause the child to be marked.   VI, 107ff.   If the afterbirth is gotten hold of by a dog, the woman will always have a weak back.   VI, 59

# Dog

Howling: Dogs' howls are evil omens. VII, 7167. The screech owl that howls at night is one of the worst harbingers of bad luck, second only to a howling dog. VII, 7259. The howling dog means the house will catch fire. VI, 3026.

Bite off the dog's tail to prevent infection from dog bite. VI, 1740

Against hydrophobia wear a dog's and a wolf's tooth. VI, 1694. Cf. Whiskey and turpentine salts are good to drive out poison caused by the bite of a mad dog. VI, 1695

If a child's tooth when extracted is put where a dog can get it, and a dog swallows it, a dog's tooth will grow in the child's mouth. VI, 391

If the roof of a dog's mouth is black, it is a sign of a good dog. VII, 7402

If you cut off a dog's tail and bury it under the front doorstep, your dog will stay home. VII, 7412

To cure indigestion, hold a piece of dried dog's excrement on the stomach for a few hours. VI, 1701

The hair of a dog draws lightning. VII, 7008

If you sit on a dog, you will have bad luck. VII, 7164

It is good luck for a dog to follow a person home. VII, 7163

Eat some dog grease if you want to get married. VI, 4471

Sleeping with a dog will cure rheumatism. The animal absorbs the rheumatism. VI, 1975

Grease stewed from a black dog, and applied in the dark of the moon, is a sure cure for rheumatism. VI, 1976

For snake bite, put grease on the wound and let a dog lick it. VI, 2146

To cure a sore, let a dog lick it. VI, 2175

The barking of a dog is the sign of someone's coming. VI, 3936

When dogs move about uneasily while lying down, look for rain. VII, 6670

If a dog eats grass, it is going to rain. VII, 6671

In hunting, a dog will often see a spirit or ghost. When he does, he will get behind his master and whimper. VII, 7873

The howling of dogs shows the presence of witches.  VII, 5617

The perfume of the fall (offal?) of a black dog and his blood on the posts and walls of the house prevents a witch's entrance. VII, 5626.

From Clark Collection

Dog days: If cut during dog days, the cut will not heal until dog days are over.  185.  Don't have a tooth pulled on dog days, or you will bleed to death.  819

Putting a piece of copper wire around a dog's neck will keep him from having distemper.  1312

Breed a female dog on the seventh day for more male puppies and on the third day for more female puppies.  1313

If dogs are barking and won't stop, take off your shoes and turn them upside down and side by side, and the dogs will stop. 1304

The hair of the dog is good for the bite.  1226

An asthma dog (Mexican chihuahua) will cure asthma when he takes it from a person.  169

If one urinates in his dog's food, the dog will not stray from home. 1310

Bad luck to buy a dog.  1311

If you cut a dog's tail off, he can't walk a log.  1305

From Motif-Index

Dogs track down law-breakers.  B578

Dog guards master's life and wealth.  A2223.5

Dog defends master's child.  B524.1.4.1

Dog follows master's corpse into river.  B301.1.1

Dog dies on mistress's grave.  B301.1.2

Dog refuses to help wolf.  K231.1.3

Sheep-dogs unite to hunt wolf.  J624.2

Wolf prefers liberty and hunger to dog's servitude with plenty. L451

Dog scares fox away from cock.   A1545.3.1

Dog granted patent of nobility.   A2546.1

Barking to dog in the moon.   K1735

Divination from dog's howling.   D1812.5.0.9

Bitches transformed to women.   D341.1.   Cf. Women transformed to bitches.   B297.2.1

Dog caresses sheep, hoping for sheep's death.   K2061.3

Dog with human head.   B25.2

Devil in form of dog.   G303.3.3.11

Witch in form of dog.   G211.1.8

Waste of time to make a bed for a dog.   J562

## Quotations--Literary and Otherwise

The dogs eat of the crumbs which fall from their masters' table. -- St. Matthew, XV, 27

Like the man who threw a stone at a bitch, but hit his stepmother, on which he exclaimed, "Not so bad!" -- Plutarch, Of Bashfulness

Men are generally more careful of the breed of their horses and dogs than of their children. -- William Penn, Fruits of Solitude

Sir, a woman preaching is like a dog's walking on his hind legs. It is not done well; but you are surprised to find it done at all. -- Boswell, Life of Johnson

>'Tis sweet to hear the watchdog's honest bark
>Bay deep-mouth'd welcome as we draw near home;
>'Tis sweet to know there is an eye will mark
>Our coming, and look brighter when we come.
>    -- Byron, Don Juan

The more I see of the representatives of the people, the more I admire my dogs. -- Alphonse De Lamartine, in letter to John Forster

Let sleeping dogs lie--who wants to rouse 'em. -- Dickens, David Copperfield

It's over the hills we'll bound, old hound,
Over the hills, and away.
-- George Meredith, "Over the Hills"

The biggest dog has been a pup.
-- Joaquin Miller, <u>William Brown of Oregon</u>

The Antiseptic Baby and the Prophylactic Pup
Were playing in the garden when the Bunny gamboled up;
They looked upon the Creature with a loathing undisguised;
It wasn't Disinfected and it wasn't Sterilized.
-- Arthur Guiterman, <u>Strictly Germ-Proof</u>

Oh, the saddest of sights in a world of sin
Is a little lost pup with his tail tucked in!
-- Arthur Guiterman, <u>Little Lost Pup</u>

Dogmatism is puppism come to its full growth.
-- Douglas Jerrold, <u>Wit and Opinions of Douglas Jerrold</u>

It is other folks' dogs and children that make most of the bad feelin's between neighbors. -- Ellis P. Butler, <u>Confessions of a Daddy</u>

What are little boys made of?
Snips and snails, and puppy-dogs' tails;
That's what little boys are made of.

Why does a dog wag his tail? -- The tail cannot wag the dog.

Me and my wife and a stump-tailed dog
Crossed Cane River on a hickory log.
The log did break and she fell in;
Lost my wife and a bottle of gin.
-- Brown Collection, I, 190


Old Blue

1.  I had a dog and his name was Blue.
    Just listen and I'll tell you what that dog would do.

    Chorus:
    Here, Blue, you rounder you!
    Here, Blue, you rounder you!

2.  One morning, whilst he was out with me,
    He treed a possum up a white oak tree.

3.  I took my ax and I cut him down
    And put sweet taters all around his ham.

4. Got up next morning; Blue was sick.
   I sent for the doctor to come here quick.

5. The doctor come, he come in a run,
   And he says, 'Old Blue, your hunting is done.'

6. Old Blue died; and he died so hard
   He dug little holes all around in the yard.

7. I dug his grave in a shady place,
   I kivered it over with a possum face.

8. I let him down with a golden chain;
   With every link I called his name.

9. Old Blue's dead, and he's gone to rest.
   He was jus' a dog, but he done his best.

10. When I gets to heaven, I know what I'll do;
    I'll grab my horn, and I'll blow for Blue.
    -- Brown Collection, III, 252

## The Way the Cat Jumps

Did you ever rescue a kitten, perchance an alley or mongrel sort, that was lean, frightened, and lost? You nourished it with warm milk and scraps of food, bundled it in a woollen blanket near a hearth or kitchen stove, and gave it plenty of love and attention. This waif grew and grew, began going out in the evening, met a tomcat and in a few weeks showed signs of expectancy.

One afternoon, after hearing strange meowing upstairs, you hurried up the steps to the guest room to find some unwelcome company. The big-sized tib-cat, once a mere plaything, was on the new bedspread, nursing some eight to ten white, black, and spotted kits. Now the children had a houseful of fluffy, soft, and silky images of heaven itself--to be clutched and squeezed, named in peculiar ways, and fed without limit. As these kittens increased in size and soon got in the way, the household had to come to some regretful decisions. Some were given to friends, some disposed of in best-unmentioned ways, and others turned loose on distant roads.

How many of these creatures survived or found merciful homes will never be known. However, nothing has been able to halt the explosive feline population. Cats in the house, cats on fences, cats in bushes and up trees, cats in the barns and garages, cats everywhere.

The feeding, clothing, housing, breeding, and medicating of cats runs into many million dollars each year. They no longer live chiefly on scraps--they eat luxury foods such as tuna and choice chicken parts, to say nothing of special cat snacks. They are shown in their Sunday best at special exhibits of the pedigreed, dressed in colorful robes, sweaters, bonnets and ties.

Cats today, as in olden times, are of both good and bad repute. In many parts of the world they are sacred and thus protected. Throughout Africa and Asia, and in scattered areas elsewhere, images of cats appear on gates and pillars to symbolize their guarding of the people. The cat sometimes represents the sun god, a token of fertility and prosperity. In heraldry the cat is a symbol of protective care and affection. Seamen of many nations carry cats aboard their vessels as harbingers of good luck, particularly because of their capacity to predict the weather. On the other hand, ever since the evil Hecate was transformed to a cat, cats have been associated with witchcraft and necromancy. In our country some think that the cat is a spellbinder and perpetrator of hoodoo. And rather widespread throughout the United States, the British Isles, and Germany is the notion that the black cat is a symbol of evil and bad luck.

The naming of this animal has evolved by a curious and varied course. Years before the Christian era, the Egyptians, who had a rich lore about the cat, called the male cat kut and the female cat kutta. Many years later the Turks called kittens kedi. The Egyptians also gave us the name puss or pussy, through the word Pascht, the name of one of their many goddesses. We are indebted to the weavers of Bagdad for the name tabby, from a special cloth labeled taffeta, characterized by being watered, waved or striped. The dialectal "tib-cat" comes from Tib, a nickname for Isabel. And as for the tomcat--it is just tom plus cat; when castrated it becomes a gib-cat.

The domesticated cat, Felis domesticus, is of the family Felidae. Up to this time no cat has let it out of the bag where it came from. It is assumed, however, that cats stemmed from ancient Egyptian connections, and perhaps in part from China. One view is that they are descendants of a North African wildcat (Felis ocreata maniculata), probably the Kaffir cat that was crossed with the European wildcat (Felis catus). The resultant species was taken to England in 936 A.D. to meet several needs, including the observation of and connivance with the kings. From the British Isles, as well as from the Continent, seamen and settlers took this beast to all parts of the globe. At the present time, according to the fanciers, there are fifty to sixty breeds, including about thirty in the United States. The principal categories are the following:

Striped Manx and White Manx (from the Isle of Man), almost tailless, usually short-haired, and related to the short-tailed or kink-tailed cats of Japan, Thailand, and China.
Abyssinian, usually short-haired.
Siamese, straight-tailed or kink-tailed, usually short-haired, and whose young are semi-albino, with white or blue eyes.
White Persian, Black Persian, and Silver Persian, usually long-haired.
Angora, usually long-haired.
Tabby and Red Tabby.
Pallas's Cat.
Striped domestic cat.

As predatory and carnivorous mammals, cats are chiefly nocturnal and terrestrial. Their bodies are lithe and supple, their muscles strong and flexible, their jaws powerful, their teeth and claws exceedingly sharp. They have five toes on each front paw and four toes on each rear paw. Their vision is very keen, their hearing highly sensitive. In color they vary from black to white or gray, from yellow to orange, from bluish to emerald. These pussyfooters, with soft and velvety soles, move at high speed. They have a longevity of fourteen to eighteen years, which can be astronomical when multiplied by nine. They are playful, graceful, often reserved, solitary, timid, and high-strung, and are reputed to have a well-developed sense of humor. They purr and meow, hiss and spit, howl and yell, scratch and bite, and screech and caterwaul as do no other animals.

Their primary sources of food are hares, rabbits, field mice, rats, moles, and birds. They stalk their victims with unusual patience, finally lunging at them with furious might. Although they destroy many useful and colorful birds, they are friendly partners with man in the elimination of rodents and controlling the birds that destroy the silk cocoons in Japan and China. The folk say that all cats like to nibble at the flickle (bacon), mess in the catsup or mustard, dabble in the lard or meal, eat the fish caught by others, lap milk until their sides almost burst, or get into the cream and smear it on their whiskers for later licking. Unless the maids are vigilant, cats will take whatever they want.

The big cats of Africa and Asia--the lion, leopard, jaguar,

cheetah, puma, tiger, lynx, ounce, ocelot, serval, panther, and wildcat--though sometimes tree climbers, are largely terrestrial like their small domesticated relatives. Very supple and highly vicious, they stealthily pursue baboons, antelopes, zebras, giraffes, ostriches, hogs, sheep, and goats. They kill their victims by choking them or breaking their necks. Even man himself, unless wary and armed, is subject to their awful tooth-and-claw preying.

Apart from the influences of these mighty predators, the domesticated cats have afforded the common folk, scientists, and dictionary makers a large number of useful and suggestive words. For instance, in plant life, we have the following samples: catberry, catbrier, catbird, cat-chop, cat-clover, catkin, catnip, cat's-ear, cat's-faces, cat's-foot, cat grape, cattail, cat's-tongue, cat thyme, cat willow, puss clover, pussy's-paws, pussytoe, and pussy willow. In the animal kingdom: catamount, catfish, cat louse, cat owl, cat shark, cat squirrel, bear cat, ram cat, tabby moth. In the human species: cat burglar, catskinner, cat's-paw, and tabby (old maid or gossip). In nautical devices: cat used as device to launch planes from ship or as anchor on logging and lumbering vessel, cat beam, cat block, cat boat, cat chain, cat fall, cat head, cat hook, cat rig, cat schooner, cattail, and catwalk. Other useful devices or gimmicks are the cat-o'-nine-tails, caterpillar tractor, cat ladder, catling, catpiece, catpipe, cat plant, and cat and clay. In children's games: tip cat, cat and dog, cat and mouse, cathop, cat's cradle, catling, catstick, and pussy in the corner. (See list below for explanations of these and other words.)

The tales of the folk show their awareness of the conceited and arrogant manners of cats and people. They shake with belly laughter when they hear of someone's being compared to Adam's house cat, or about the blustering chap that could not bell a clawing cat, or of the nervous and long-tailed cat acting up in a roomful of rocking chairs, or of the cat being bounced ceiling-high in a blanket, or about two cats with tails tied together and scratching at each other's posterior, or of the cat on a hot tin roof, or of the fellow that swung a cat high in the air to see which way he would jump, or of the old maid whose tongue the cat had silenced, or of the outlander trying to choke a cat with biscuits or butter instead of killing it with bullets, or of the cat that could look at a king and tickle his shins with a serpentine tail or push his whiskers into his beard.

These cat-eyed and cat-footed animals are as stubborn and independent as many of us. As catawampuses, they can be as quarrelsome and cross as a cat with a sore tail. On the whole, they are delightfully curious about life in all its varieties; in most matters they are somewhat radical, conservative only in their patience and caution. Contrary to one of the old beliefs, it is doubtful if curiosity has ever killed more than a few of them. They know when to jump the prey and when to avoid a superior enemy.

Their wiles and cunning are illustrated in the cat-and-mouse game, a drama that is motivated by hunger and carried out with bloody maneuvers. By natural training no mouse has ever built his nest in a cat's ear, and no rat has faced a cat muffled or gloved for battle. Mice and rats have learned to play only when the cat is blind, off on a spree, or dead. If the mouse or rat, however, assumes that the cat is not thinking, he is bound to be devoured sooner. The cat may take a catnap or wink momentarily, but he is simply playing his game with finesse. At the proper time he plunges, addles the mouse, rolls him over for awhile, and finally gulps him down. When he chases a big, hearty rat, he seems at his best. He doesn't waste time sporting with this fat and perhaps disease-ridden varmint--with a ferocity characteristic of the big cats, he gives the rat a neck-breaking coup de grace.

The cat does not include the dog among his close friends either. Oh, yes, before a cozy fire, they may lick one another in the presence of people. But just give them the door to the open air, and their ancient feud begins all over. They scratch and spit, meow and yell, bark and cry, and like the Kilkenny cats have it out in blood and tears. In most instances, the cat finally makes a quick retreat up a tree, and vows again that he will never be caught wandering in a dog factory.

Yet cats have also a brighter and jollier aspect. For example, the kitten, the least offensive of his tribe, is a fun-loving, good-natured, gentle plaything. But even this pesky imp can make you have kittens or throw a catfit or conniption.

   The endearing traits of the kitten linger on in the pussy cat or marbled tabby that likes to cuddle up in the lap of an old maid or to keep company a widower or old man. Very affectionate and well-disposed, she can purr and snore ever so gently in a snug place. She is fond of her daily allowance of milk and enjoys a brisk rubbing of her body. Though she may be fat, lazy, and greatly pampered, she never loses her cattish will. Unable to scream like a wildcat, she is still ready to take on a mouse, or rat, or dog should the opportunity arise. In subdued quality, her cattishness comes to the fore whenever there is game or adventure.

   On the other side of the coin is a much more aggressive and phenomenal cat, an astounding fellow called The Cat's Whiskers, known also as The Cat's Meow, The Cat's Pajamas, The Cat's Ankle, and sometimes The Pussy's Twister. He really knows how to put on the cat, and thus his reputation for being a glamor puss. In his makeup, there is nothing of the sourpuss or picklepuss. Folks say that he is a cat on wheels and also a hep cat, an expert in swing and jazz music. In finance and politics, he is a fat cat that prowls triumphantly along the alleys of the poor and the boulevards of the strong. Being an extraordinary performer, "He's a big shot where little shots ain't no more than kittens in a doghouse." Granted that he is often a fool and an egotist, never discount his power of persuasion--he can make others feel that his personal views are for their salvation. But remember--do not try to trick him! He will not be the cat's-paw for the selfish or irresponsible. If you try to thwart his inner purposes, he will cleverly insult you-- grin at you like a Cheshire cat, laugh in your face, spit at you, or thumb his tail under your nose. And if these tricks do not succeed, he'll hypnotize you before you know it.

   The most spectacular and cat-witted of the domesticated sort is the tomcat, occasionally called a ram cat by the folks. He is a sort of independent bear cat, who prides himself on having the best of saint and sinner. At the proper time he shows forth the virtues of The Cat's Whiskers, but for the most part he is Mr. Catso, a catlike Casanova or base adventurer, who has no scruples about flagrant tomcatting. He tolerates no other tomcat, he respects no pedigreed tib-cat, and he will not share any responsibility for his offspring. His plundering, so he thinks, is his divine prerogative. And a no-less-assumed privilege is his hell-raising at all hours on dark nights beneath the windows of the tired and restless. No cat-calls can stop his rashness, and no cat-o'-nine-tails can scare him away.

This tomcat is as persistent and fierce as old Tibert in the medieval romances or as quick on the draw as Tybalt in Romeo and Juliet. His arrogance is explosive. His aggressiveness is sustained by the accumulated traits of his forebears. He has a super-abundance of cattishness--flexibility of body, keen hearing, rapacious courage, tooth-and-claw excellence, immense patience, and glinting eyes with many colors that are reflections of mosaic gold (cat's gold), the silver in mica (cat silver), a variety of oxides in ironstones (cathead), and the charming effects of the cat's-eye, a gem that pours forth an opalescence along with the multicolored reflections of quartz and chrysoberyl. This monarch of domestic cats has filled a niche in the annals of political history, as recorded in a fifteenth-century couplet by Collingbourne:

> The catte, the ratte and Lovell our dogge
> Rulyth all England under a hogge.

This couplet, published first in Fabyan's Chronicle in 1516, satirized Richard the Third (the hogge), who usurped the throne in 1483, his chief butler and lord chamberlain, Viscount Lovell, and two other fellow conspirators, Sir William Catesby and Sir Richard Ratcliffe.

At this juncture you may be ready to ask some serious questions about the nature of a cat--as a fluffy pet for children, a quiet and faithful companion of the lonely, or a dependable killer of mice, rats, and destructive birds. The folks say that he is more than these: he is a first-class agent of the bad and the good, both in life and after death.

They advise you never to fear a white cat or a black cat with white paws--he's your friend. But be on the lookout for a wholly black cat, or thirteen black cats, especially on Friday the 13th. Trouble lies ahead if one of these black creatures crosses your path, unless you are alert enough to turn your hat around and walk back nine steps. If, however, he crosses from right to left in front of you, your luck will be good. On the other hand, beware of a cat looking into a mirror, or one sitting with his tail to the fire, or the one turned loose to be a stray. Your tragedies will be multiplied. Furthermore, do not pass a cat while you are pregnant--your child will have moles. Keep cats away from your sleeping baby--they will suck the breath out of it. At a wake, do not permit any cats near the corpse--they like and eat human flesh.

If you have any ailments, go to the cats for remedies. For appendicitis, kill a black cat on a night when the moon is full, split it down the spine, and apply its warm organs to the source of pain. For consumption, take a tablespoon of blood from the tail of a cat that has no black hair. For rheumatism, sleep with a cat and he'll draw out the pain. For shingles, bathe the affected parts with the warm blood of a black cat. To remove a sty, rub a black cat's tail across the eye. To get rid of warts, take a black cat into a graveyard at midnight; when you hear a strange noise, throw the cat as far as you can. For whooping cough, drink milk that a cat has lapped.

To forecast the weather, watch a cat washing himself behind the ears--it's a sure sign of rain; but if he washes the spot over and over again, the weather will be clearing soon. If you want to see devils or their imps, boil a cat and pour the contents into a spring. If you desire to be a witch in the form of a cat or a rabbit, drop a black cat into a kettle of boiling water. If you need to break the spell of a witch, turn your pockets inside out, or kiss your sleeve, or remove the black cat's bone from the hands of the witch.

For those who are anxious about love affairs, the folks' advice is to watch the cat that washes his face before a crowd--the person he looks at first will be the first to marry. Or go to a quilting party and request the ladies to bounce a cat in the quilt--the person at the place where the cat leaps out will be the first to get a husband. In these and other well-laid schemes for health and bliss, it is important that you know which way the cat may jump.

## Derivative Names

cat: short for catfish, cat-o'-nine-tails, catskin or fur

cat: prostitute; spiteful woman; person devoted to swing music

cat: the corn god

cat: game called tipcat (including stick to bat with, the bat itself), using words "one old cat, two old cat," etc.

cat: toy with elastic band used in throwing missiles from prongs of stick; device used in launching airplane from deck of ship

cat: double tripod for holding plate, etc.

cat: vessel used in coal and lumber trade in England; three-masted Deal lugger; strong anchor to hoist anchor to cat-head of ship; catboat

cat: medieval structure used as fortification, called cat house, cat castle

cat: caterpillar tractor

cat: part of first coat of plaster on laths

cat: European heraldic representation of wild cat or domestic cat

catamount (catamountain): any of several species of wild cat family such as cougar, lynx, etc.

cat and clay: straw and clay used as chinking material

cat and dog: game played with cat and dog

cat-and-dog: quarrelsome characteristic

cat and mouse (cat and dat): children's game; behavior like that of cat and mouse

cat-and-mouse: constant fight and pursuit

Cat-and-Mouse Act: law passed by British Parliament in 1913 to provide for temporary discharge of prisoners, especially aimed at militant suffragettes

catawampus (cattywampous): fierce, savage, askew, malicious; a hobgoblin

cat beam: broadest beam in a ship

cat back: hook of cat block used in hoisting an anchor

# Cat

catberry:  mountain holly

catbird:  slate-gray American songbird that makes sound like cat meowing

catbite fever:  rat-bite fever carried by cats

cat block:  block used in catting an anchor

catboat:  sailboat having cat rig

catbrier:  one of several prickly plants

cat burglar:  person who enters house by upper story or roof

catcall:  small instrument producing sound like cry of cat; call showing disapproval

cat chain:  small chain used in catting an anchor on ships with ram bows

cat-chop:  fig marigold

catclaw (cat's-claw):  climbing shrub

cat-clover (cat-in-clover):  bird's-foot trefoil

cat cracker:  catalytic cracker

caterwaul:  howl and cry like fighting cats, as in rutting period; to be lecherously inclined; act of a caterwauler

cat-eye (catface):  small knot or bruise in lumber; wrinkle in clothing when ironed too dry; quality of being catfaced

cat-eyed:  having eyes like cat's; able to see in dark

catfall:  rope or chain used to hoist anchor to cathead

catfight:  very rough-and-tumble argument

catfish:  any of various fish, with fancied resemblance to cat's teeth or ferocity

catfit:  fit of anger or emotional outburst, conniption

cat foot:  biennial cudweed

cat-foot:  short, round, compact foot like cat's

cat-footed:  soft-footed like a cat; stealthy or noiseless in walking

cat grape:  Missouri grape

catgut: tough cord made from intestines of animals, especially sheep, but never from cat--used in stringing violin, etc.; heavy linen or cotton fabric; also prostrate herb such as American goat's rue and wild sweet pea

cat hair (cat's hair): sore, tumor, or boil; hair of cat

cat ham: thin, flat thigh

cat-hammed: thin and flat from side to side, especially as said of horses and cattle

cat-haul: the subjecting of persons to long and severe questioning

cat haw: fruit of hawthorn

cathead (cat davit): protruding piece of timber or iron near bow of vessel for hoisting anchor; a sleeve attached to lathe to steady work or turning of lathe; a nodule of ironstone

cathole: small opening for cat to go through

cat hook: hook attached to a ship's cat block

cathop: part of the game of faro

cat house: cat of medieval warfare; brothel; cheap lodging house

ca'thro (ca'throw): disturbance or commotion

catkin: scaly spike, or inflorescence resembling cattail

cat ladder: ladder for scaling roof, placed perpendicularly to wall

catlap: weak drink

catlike: like a cat, stealthy and noiseless

catline: heavy line used in hoisting in oil-well drilling

catling: little cat; catgut; long surgical knife

cat-locks: cotton grass

cat louse (cat flea): biting louse or flea found on cats

catnap (cat sleep): short light sleep or nap, doze

catnip (catmint, catwort, cat's heal-all): well-known herb in England, liked by cats and used as medicine, having whorls of small blue flowers in terminal spike

cat-o'-nine-tails: whip made of usually nine knots or cords, used for flogging

cat owl: owl with ear tufts, such as great horned owl

catpiece: in logging, a stick with holes, used as upright in sluiceway entrance

cat pine: white pine

catpipe: device for making catcalls

cat plant: oil or gasoline refinery

cat rig: rig on single mast, for sails and long boom

cat-rigged: having cat rig

cat salt: finely granulated salt formed from bittern

cat schooner: cat-rigged boat

cat's cradle: children's game involving manipulation of strings on fingers

cat's-cradle: ribwort or ribgrass

cat's-ear: any of several American species of pussy's toe

cat's eye: marble game

cat's-eye: a mineral, a gem reflecting opalescent reflections from within, like eye of a cat; variety of chrysoberyl and also of quartz

cat's-faces: pansy

cat's-foot: ground ivy

cat's-foot, the: interjection showing disgust or disbelief

cat's gold: mosaic gold

cat'sgrass (cat's-hair, cat's-milk): sun spurge

cat shark: spotted dogfish

cat's ice: cat ice

cat silver: mica

catskin: skin or fur of cat

cat skinner: operator of caterpillar; a cat man

cat's meow, the: any remarkable person or thing, also cat's whiskers, cat's ankle, and cat's pajamas

catso: base fellow

cat's-paw: dupe or fool, from fable of monkey persuading cat to get chestnuts out of fire; light air ruffling water; hitch in rope

cat spruce: white spruce

cat's purr: murmur or purr of cat

cat squirrel: common European squirrel; cacomistle

cattail (cat's-tail, cattail rush, cattail grass): tall marsh grass or plant; timothy; catkin or ament; horsetail, blueweed, cotton grass; color musk; the inboard end of cathead

catstep: corbiestep

catstick: stick used in the game of tipcat

catstitch: decorative stitch in quilting

catstone: cairn to mark place of battle

cat's-tongue: velvet bur

cat stopper: cathead stopper

catsup (catch-up, ketchup, katsup): seasoned tomato sauce

cat's valerian: common valerian

cattail millet: Italian millet

catted: built up or bonded with clay or cat and clay

cattery: place for keeping cats

cat thyme: European germander, with aromatic foliage

cattish: catlike or feline; having quality of cattishness

catty: spiteful, stealthy, or treacherous

cattyman: expert logger

catwalk: narrow footway along bridge on ship or airplane

cat whisker: in a radio, a fine wire that makes contact with the crystal in the crystal detector cat-whistles:  the horsetail

cat willow:  false indigo

cat-witted:  unteachable or spiteful

cats and dogs:  describing heavy rain; low-priced stocks; odds and ends

bear cat:  panda; remarkable person or thing, with special power to get things done

civet cat:  one of various carnivores, such as cacomistle, little spotted skunk, etc.; producer of commercial civet

hep cat:  swing artist; jazz expert or enthusiast

kitten:  small or young cat; young and inexperienced person

kittenish:  playful; coquettish

puss:  mouth, face; grimace; effeminate man

puss:  cat, hare, or girl, often affectionately used

puss clover:  rabbit-foot clover

Puss in Boots:  nursery tale cat that secures princess and fortune for his master

pussy:  cat or pusscat; game of tipcat

pussyfoot:  to move cautiously to avoid being seen; being careful about revealing one's feelings or opinions; beating around the bush; to be a pussyfooter

pussy in the corner (puss in the corner, pussy wants a corner):  children's game

pussy's-paws:  California herb

pussytoe:  type of cat's-foot

pussy's twister:  the cat's meow

pussy willow:  small American willow with silky catkins

ram cat:  male cat

sourpuss:  grouch, killjoy; also picklepuss or drizzlepuss.  Cf. glamor-puss

tabby:  brown or gray cat; old maid or spiteful woman or female gossip; taffeta, watered, waved or striped fabric

tabby moth: grease moth

tabby weave: plain weave

tib cat: female cat

Tibert: name of cat in old tales such as Roman de Renard, known to be fiery, high-tempered, and explosive; probable origin of Tybalt in Shakespeare's Romeo and Juliet

tiger cat: any of various wildcats such as clouded leopard, marbled cat, etc.

tomcat: uncastrated male cat; promiscuous woman-chaser; man lacking sense of responsibility for offspring

## Proverbs and Proverbial Phrases

Active (agile, cross, curious, gentle, modest, nimble, quick, sees like, sleepy, sneaky, spry, still, supple, watches like, weak, or wild) as a cat.

Act like a cat in a gale of wind.

I wouldn't know him from Adam's house cat.

Let the cat out of the bag (reveal something inadvertently).

Who is to bell the cat? (It is easy to propose impossible remedies.) (Aesop's Belling the Cat) Cf. Who shall hang the bell about the cat's neck?

Busy as a cat on a tin roof trying to cover up.

Like a cat on hot bricks. Cf. Stick to one like a sick kitten to a hot brick. He takes to it like a kitten to a hot brick.

No more chance than a cat in hell without claws.

Curiosity killed the cat. Cf. Curiosity killed the cat, but satisfaction brought him back. Care killed the cat.

Black as a black cat (in a coal cellar).

Dog my cats!

Little by little the cat eateth the flickle (bacon).

The cat would eate fish, and would not wet her feete. -- John Heywood, 1497-1580

# Cat

It would make a cat laugh.  Cf. Enough to make a cat speak (sick).

He grins like a Cheshire cat.

He has cat eyes.

Fighting (agreeing, quarreling) like cats and dogs.  Cf. Raining cats and dogs.  Leading a cat-and-dog life.

Fighting like the Kilkenny cats (that is, to the death).

The cat and the dog may kiss, yet are none the better friends.

Funny (nervous) as a long-tailed cat in a room full of rocking chairs.

To see which way the cat jumps (to observe the course of events).

You kill my cat, and I'll kill your dog.

Cat will to kind.  Cf. Cat after kind, a good mouse hunt.  Kit after kind.

The cat is hungry when a crust contents her.

The cat has eaten her count (like a woman with child).

The cat is in the cream-pot.  Cf. As meek as a gray cat with a dab of cream in her whiskers.  The cat shuts its eyes when stealing cream.

That cat is out of kind that sweet milk will not lap.  Cf. The cat shuts its eye while it steals milk.  Like a cat around hot milk.  Take to warm milk like a kitten.

An old cat laps as much milk as a young one.

How can a cat help it when the maid is a fool?  Cf. The cat did it.

Send not a cat for the lard.

He is like a cat: fling him which way you will, he'll light on his legs (feet).

A cat may looke on a king. -- John Heywood.  Cf. A cat may look at a king and so may I at her.

The cat knows whose beard (lips) she will lick.

The liquorish cat gets many a rap.

A cat in the meal (something hidden).

Mean as a sore-tailed cat.

It had need to bee
A wylie mouse that should breed in the cat's eare. --John Heywood.
Cf. It's a bold mouse that breeds in a cat's ear.

Let the cat wink and let the mouse run. Cf. Though the cat winks,
 she is not blind. The cat sees not the mouse ever. When
 the cat winketh, little wots the mouse what the cat thinketh.
 The cat winked when her eyes were out.

Two cats and a mouse never agree.

Plays like a cat with a mouse.

An old cat sports not with her prey.

A cat in gloves (gloved, muffled) catches no mice.

While the cat is away, the mouse (mice) will play. Cf. When the
 cat's away, the rats come out to play.

Keep no more cats than will catch mice.

A good cat deserves a good rat.

As a cat loves mustard.

A cat has nine lives. Cf. As many lives as a cat.

Noisy as a sack of cats.

To make a cat's-paw of (get someone to do your dirty work).

Quicker than a cat can lick her paw.

Quiet as a cat in a dog factory.

You look like something the cat drug up.

Not room enough to swing a cat in. Cf. Far as you can swing a
 cat by the tail.

You got the cat by the tail.

The more you rub a cat on the rump, the higher she sets her tail.

You don't need it any more than a cat needs two tails.

The cat has his tongue. Cf. The cat got your tongue?

He takes to it like a cat to water. Cf. The scalded cat fears cold
 water.

There are more ways of killing (skinning) a cat than by choking her with bullets (biscuits or butter).

He is a cat on wheels (doing something extraordinary).

He is the cat's whiskers. Cf. He is the cat's meow (pajamas, ankle).

Cunning (cute, docile, funny, gentle, good-natured, lively, playful, purrs like, quiet, spry, still, tame, weaker than) as a kitten.

Have kittens (to be extremely upset or to have a nervous fit).

He's a big shot where little shots ain't more than kittens in a doghouse.

Affectionate (good-natured) as a pussy cat.

Loving as two pussy cats.

Eyeing each other like two tomcats.

Useless as tits on a tomcat.

Fierce (screamed like, sly, spry) as a wildcat.

## Superstitions and Motifs

Bad luck: If you meet a black cat in the road, you will have bad luck. Brown Collection, VI, 3813. Bad luck to have thirteen black cats. Clark Collection, 1218. Cf. Black cat or the number 13 means bad luck. Clark, 1217. It is bad luck to kill a cat. Clark, 1223. A cat looking in a mirror means bad luck. Coffin and Cohen. If you find a cat sitting with her tail to the fire, expect bad luck. Coffin and Cohen. If you turn a stray cat away from your door, you turn away your good luck. Clark, 1302. It is bad luck to move a cat from one house to another. Brown Collection, VI, 2955.
A cat leaving the place where born is a sign of the family breaking up. Clark, 1225.

Good luck: If a black cat crosses your path, turn your hat around and walk back nine steps. Clark, 638. Cf. If a black cat crosses your path from right to left, it is a sign of good luck. Brown Collection, VI, 3808. It is good luck to have a black cat come to your house and remain. Brown Collection, VII, 8562. A few joints of the backbone of a black cat, when carried in the pocket, will bring good luck. Brown Collection, VII, 5787. It is good luck to pull a black cat's tail. Brown Collection, VII, 7155. If a black cat with white paws crosses one's path, it is a sign of good luck. Brown

Collection, VI, 3811.

## From Brown Collection

For appendicitis, kill a black cat on a night when there is a full moon, split the cat down the spine, and apply the warm organs to the pain.  VI, 812

If a bird sings before breakfast, a cat will catch it before night. VII, 7219

If you whistle while you are in bed, a cat will bite you next morning.  VI, 3095

As a cure for consumption, find a cat without a white hair and take a tablespoon of blood from its tail.  VI, 1188

For a black cat to cross your path is a sure sign of death. VII, 5185.  Cf. If a black cat crosses the path of a funeral procession, another relative will die within a year. VII, 5456

Cats and dogs know when death has come to a house.  VII, 5186

The "setting up" or wake watch was observed not only through respect but also to keep away cats, which always try to get to the corpse. VII, 5427.  Cf. Black cats live on human flesh.  Clark, 1224.

Do not rub a cat's fur backwards because you are likely to get in a fight.  VI, 3608

If you keep black cats at home, you'll never marry. VI, 4695. Cf. If you walk on the tail of a cat, you will not marry during the year.  VI, 4637

If a cat washes her face near a crowd of people, the one she looks at first will be the next to marry. VI, 4469. Cf. If two persons shake a cat in a quilt, the one at whose end it runs out will marry first.  VI, 4470

If a black cat passes a pregnant woman, the baby will have moles on it.  VI, 105

If a black cat comes to your home and stays, it is a sign of prosperity.  VI, 3362

If a cat be allowed to sleep on the bed, it will cure a person of rheumatism by absorbing it.  VI, 1973.  Cf. Never kick a cat, or you'll get rheumatism.

To cure shingles, bathe parts in the warm blood of a fresh-killed black cat.  VI, 2096

# Cat

Use piece of tongue of young heifer to rub on smallpox sores; then give piece to cat to cure smallpox. VI, 2116

If you rub a black cat's tail across your eye, it will cure a sty. VI, 2277

A cat will suck a baby's breath if left alone in the room with the baby. VI, 267. Cf. Cat as vampire sucks breath of child; Hecate changed to cat as vampire.

A live cat is split open and applied warm to soothe a swollen knee. VI, 2313

If you pull an old tooth and a cat, a dog, or a hog finds it, the tooth that comes back will resemble the tooth of the animal that found it. VI, 393

By putting a dead cat in a tree stump, one can remove warts. VI, 2450. If one takes a dead black cat into a graveyard at midnight and, when he hears a noise, throws the cat by the tail at the sound--that will take warts off the hands. VI, 2451

You will not catch whooping cough if you drink the milk which a black cat has drunk of. VI, 2710

A cat washing her face indicates that somebody is coming. VI, 3934. Cf. When a cat rubs his paws over his ears when washing, visitors are coming. VI, 3935

If a cat carries her foot over her ear three times, there will be high water soon. VII, 6895

When a cat sits with its back to the fire, it is the sign of a storm. VII, 6917. A sneezing cat presages rain. VII, 6657. Cf. When cats wipe themselves behind the ears, you may expect rain. VII, 6659. Bathing a cat causes rain. VII, 6662. It is a sign of rain for a cat to eat grass. VII, 6663.

Cats running and playing is a sign of windy weather soon to follow. VII, 6977

If a cat washes her face o'er, 'tis a sign that the weather'll be fine and clear. VII, 6238

Witchcraft: The power of a witch or a wizard to banish at will is obtained from some bone of a black cat. VII, 5590. To become a witch, drop a live black cat into a black kettle of boiling water. VII, 5591. Black cats are witches. 5592. Black cats see ghosts and devils. When you see cat's eyes shine at night, you see a witch's eyes. 5593. To become a witch, eat grasshoppers or crickets. VII, 5594

Breaking charms of witch: To break charms from witch rabbits, or witch cats, turn all pockets inside out. VII, 5659. Cf. ...prevent bad luck by kissing the sleeve. VII, 5661. Take the witch's magic black cat's bone away from her, and she cannot cast any more spells.

By boiling cat and pouring contents into spring, you can thus see devils and imps. VII, 5771

If you are awake at eleven, you will see witches and black cats at twelve. VII, 5605

## From Clark Collection

If you butter a cat's feet, it won't leave home. 1300. Cf. To keep the cat at home, grease its forepaws and rake them down the back of the chimney. 1301

To dream of a cat is a sign of a bad enemy. 1220

A cat has nine lives. 1222. Cf. It is believed that if you take one of these lives it will haunt you.

A cat can see well in the dark. 1303

If a cat meows it is a sign of a birth. 30. Cf. The howling of a cat is a sign of new life. 1219.

## From Motif-Index

A cat is a beast of ill-omen. B147.1.2.2

Cat chooses rat meat at a feast. U135.1

Cat curses woman eating the fish that the cat caught. Q281.3

Cat is of divine origin; it prays when it purrs. A1811.3

Cat harms dead and dying. B766.1ff

Cat invites hens to a feast and kills them. K815.4

Cat makes truce with mice and then eats them. K815.13

Mouse teaches her child to fear quiet cat. J132.

Cat unjustly accuses a cock and then eats him. U31.1

Giant tickled into becoming a mouse and then eaten by cat. K722

Killing a cat is taboo. C841.11

Why cat hides its excreta. A2385.4

Cat

A deity has a cat's head.   A131.3.1

Cats crossing one's path a sign of ghosts.   E436.2

Witches as cats and rabbits.   G211.2 and G211.4

## Quotations--Literary and Otherwise

When I play with my cat, who knows whether I do not make her more sport than she makes me?-- M. Montaigne, Essays

Those who'll play with cats must expect to be scratched.--Cervantes, Don Quixote

> Let Hercules himself do what he may,
> The cat will meow and dog will have his day.
> -- Shakespeare, Hamlet

> But thousands die without or this or that,
> Die, and endow a college or a cat.
> -- A. Pope, Epistle III

There wasn't room to swing a cat there. -- C. Dickens, David Copperfield

More ways of killing a cat than choking her with cream. -- Charles Kingsley, Westward Ho

> The Owl and the Pussy-cat went to sea
>   In a beautiful pea-green boat,
> They took some honey, and plenty of money,
>   Wrapped up in a five-pound note.
> The owl looked up to the stars above,
>   And sang to a small guitar,
> 'O lovely Pussy! O Pussy, my love,
> What a beautiful Pussy you are,
>     You are,
>     You are!
> What a beautiful Pussy you are!"
> -- Edward Lear, Nonsense Songs

> The gingham dog went "Bow-wow-wow!"
> And the calico cat replied "Mee-ow!"
> The air was littered, an hour or so,
> With bits of gingham and calico!
> -- Eugene Field, The Duel

> My love she is a kitten,
> And my heart's a ball of string.
> -- Henry S. Leigh, My Love and My Heart

Pussy cat, pussy cat,
  Where have you been?
I've been to London
  To see the queen.
    -- Nursery rhyme

Hey diddle diddle
The cat and the fiddle,
The cow jumped over the moon;
The little dog laughed
To see such sport,
And the dish ran away with the spoon.
    -- Nursery rhyme

As I was going to St. Ives,
I met a man with seven wives,
Each wife had seven sacks,
Each sack had seven cats,
Each cat had seven kits;
Kits, cats, sacks, and wives,
How many were there going to St. Ives?
    -- Nursery rhyme

How I Love the Old Black Cat

1   Who so full of fun and glee?
    Happy as a cat can be,
    Polished sides so nice and fat,
    How I love the old black cat!
    Yes, I do.

    Chorus:
        Poor kitty, oh, poor kitty,
        Sitting so cozy close to the fire,
        Pleasant, purring, pretty pussy,
        Frisky, full of fun and fussy,
        Mortal full of mouse and rat,
        How I love the old black cat!
        Yes, I do.

2   And the boys, to have some fun,
    Call the dogs to set them on.
    Quickly I jump on my hat
    And try to save the old black cat.
    Yes, I did.

3   Some may choose tartar shell,
    Others like the white so well.
    Let them choose of this or that,
    But give to me the old black cat.
    Oh, please do!
        -- Brown Collection, III, 195f

## Rats

For hundreds of years man has been smelling and seeing rats, along with a multitude of mice. And he is not particularly fond of them, even though he may concede that they are useful as pets for children and as experimental animals in research laboratories. Once in a while some Robert Burns will pour out his sympathy for the "timrous beastie," but by and large mice and rats are unwelcomed guests.

To prove this, merely whisper the word mouse or rat in a roomful of ladies, and watch them jump with horror. Or just recount the old story told by Thomas Coryat in his Crudities (1611) about Hatto's being chased and devoured by rats in his castle on the Rhine during the famine of 914 A.D. Then can come the tales about a dynamite-laden vessel that wrecked a harbor after the rats gnawed away its retaining hawsers, or about the entire population of a city being wiped out by the bubonic plague that the rats brought in, or about the rats that chewed up little children.

It is no wonder that these animals are considered to be ill-omens, to have evil eyes, and to make their exits from the houses of the dying. In view of the mystery that shrouds their exact origin, some folk believe that they pelted from the skies during nightmarish storms, or that when Noah was preoccupied as skipper of the Ark the devil created them to divert the paired-off couples on the dull forty-day voyage, or that they were mothered by witches to prey on mankind. But these and other theories did not scare the ancients of Greece, Rome, and the East: they glorified rats as sacred and deified them as companions to the gods and goddesses, particularly Apollo, Horus, Ganesa, and Isis.

Some students state that mice and rats had invaded all of Europe by the 13th century after a long and circuitous trek from China; by some quirk they bypassed Russia until 1727.

Rats belong to the genus Rattus of the family Muridae, which also includes mice, hamsters, voles and lemmings. The chief types are the Norway brown rat (Rattus norvegicus), with long and lithe body, pointed head, beady eyes, short and rounded ears, and an almost hairless tail; and the black rat (Rattus rattus or Musrattus), with grayish color sometimes mixed with the black, a light and slender body, and large and thin ears. This species is smaller than the brown rat; it is also less numerous because its fertility is 20 to 50 per cent less. Both types begin breeding after six months, have a gestation period of twenty days, and produce several litters yearly. Found all over the world, they are far more aggressive than mice and are known to be furious attackers and highly destructive nuisances.

Their little relatives, mice, belong to the genus Mus of the family Muridae. The many species differ in size, color, shape of ears, and limbs; all have velvety and hairy bodies, pointed heads, dun eyes, almost hairless tails, and sometimes white bellies. They too start raising their young after six months and multiply very rapidly. The best known of the several hundred breeds is the field mouse (Mus musculus).

Rats and mice, which create much loathsome rattage, live on grain, insects, small birds, lizards, frogs, one another, and other small animals. They are noted for scurrying and frisking about on floors, over bins of corn and wheat, and in the open fields. They tunnel under the foundations of buildings and burrow in the earth to escape the rigors of changing weather as well as the attacks of their traditional enemies.

The mouse is meek, quiet, still, and timid. It is said that he becomes extremely melancholy in a church or an empty mill, but in a churn he can be as snug as any old bug in a rug. He is a quick mover, especially when pursued by a tomcat or owl. The folk say that no mouse ever builds its nest in a cat's ear, it never plays with kittens, and it follows the advice of its mother to fear all cats. The rat also knows after reading the biographies of his deceased relatives that he has no more chance with the cat than the proverbial snowball in hell. And, according to the evidence, no rat has ever been able to persuade a cat to wash his face before eating. Unless the rat has several holes wide apart from one another, his escape from the cat is highly improbable.

Some of this tooth-and-claw business has been carried over into the naming of mousey and rattish animals, such as rat bandicoot, ratcatcher, mouser, ratfish, rat flea, rat goose, rat hare, rat kangaroo, rat louse, rat mole, rat snake, ratter, rat terrier, ratton, dock rat, mousebird, mouse deer, mousefish, mouse opossum, and a fairly sizable number of human beings, as hereafter specified. There are only a few plants named after these animals, namely, rat pineapple, rattail, ratwood, mouse-ear, mouse-ear chickweed, and mousetail.

The contributions of these rodents to the English language reach their peak in satiric comparisons with the human race. In rapier thrusts by the folk, they puncture the ego of man and make him yell: "Am I man or mouse?" The cry of "Rat!" heaps upon him all that is villainous: scoundrel, saboteur, deserter, spy, ratfink, scab, loose woman, harlot, or wencher. A rat plays loose in his loyalty, has no principles to speak of.

A guy can be mouse-trapped like the football player on a field. In his desperate competition with his neighbors in business or the social whirl, he can be caught in the notorious rat race, meaningless and worthless. Ultimately he may be down a rathole-- a single one, too--drowned, poisoned, or mad. And there he sees and smells rats--well-known symptom of delirium tremens. If crazy, he has rats in his garret or upper story, and the doctors may recommend to his relatives that he be confined in the traditional rathouse, a filthy and bottomless pit prepared for the damned.

Dare you offer a defense of the mouse or the rat that destroys so much grain, undermines buildings, wrecks vessels in harbors, infects the land with mortal diseases, and in many ways makes himself an object of fear and contempt? You may claim that he is an excellent scavenger in sewers, that he does eliminate a large number of animals that are as bad as he is, that he is important to laboratory research, and that he instinctively warns people to vacate sinking ships and tumbling buildings.

You may support the folk view that a mouse or a rat, dead or living, can do a lot for the common weal. Suppose you want to plant corn, do so when the oak leaves are as big as a mouse's ear. If perchance you are trying to get rid of your rats, feed them a greasy paper on which you have written the name of the owner of the house to which you want them to go: your neighbors will get your rats. But avoid dreaming about rats, for that means that you have a host of personal enemies. And for goodness' sake, do not darn garments gnawed by a mouse; otherwise some member of your family will die.

That's not all the invaluable help. For baldness, eat fresh mouse meat. For bed wetting, feed a child a sandwich made of mouse meat. For epilepsy, swallow mouse fat. For fever, use mouse-ear made into a tea. For rattlesnake bite, eat mouse flesh. Cooked mouse and rat flesh are also recommended to cure smallpox, whooping cough, measles, and earache. And if your child will put a freshly pulled tooth under her pillow, she will find a dime left by a mouse.

Should these remedies prove ineffective, you will find comfort in dispatching all mice and rats on a long voyage with the witch that mothered them.

### Derivative Names

rat:  mean person, scoundrel; one who abandons party or associates, especially in time of trouble; an informer; scab laborer working for less pay; printer not approved by trade union; loose woman

rat:  to hunt rats; to desert like rats leaving ship; to behave in mean and disloyal manner

rat:  pad in woman's hair to give greater thickness; railroad train

rat:  student, especially freshman

rat:  olive gray

rats: contemptuous retort or exclamation showing disappointment; delirium tremens

rats in the garret (or loft or upper story): mad, eccentric. Cf.

Rat

    Rats in the belfry.   Bats in the belfry.

rat bandicoot:  ratlike bandicoot related to rabbit bandicoot, but having shorter ears and legs

rat-bite fever:  infectious human disease caused by rat bite, characterized by ulcerations, rash, muscular pains, and relapsing fever

ratcatcher:  one who catches and exterminates rats; in Britain an informal fox-hunting costume, such as tweed jacket and tan riding breeches

rat cheese:  common yellow cheese in uncut bulk

rat claw foot:  in furniture, an elongated foot having form of a thin claw grasping a ball

ratfink:  informer or squealer; scab worker

ratfish:  one of several rat-tailed fish in Pacific

rat flea:  any of several kinds of fleas, some being known as carriers of bubonic plague, etc.

rat goose:  common brant

rat guard:  disk of sheet metal fitted around hawsers to prevent rats from boarding vessels

rat hare:  pika

rathole:  burrow or hole gnawed by rat; filthy quarters; seemingly endless or bottomless place where all is lost

rat-house:  asylum for insane in Australia

rat kangaroo:  any of several Australian and Tasmanian kangaroos

ratlike:  like a rat

ratline (ratling):  on ships, any of small ropes, usually tarred, that transverse and surround horizontally and thus serving as steps for going aloft

rat louse:  sucking louse on parasitic rats

rat mole:  mole rat

rat pineapple:  pinguin

rat race:  frantic scurry or mad scramble; meaningless pursuit like trying to keep up with neighbors

rat rhyme: nonsense or doggerel verse

ratsbane (raticide): rat poison

rat snake: Old and New World snake feeding on small mammals and birds

rat stop: projection outside masonry foundation to keep out rats

rattage: damage and filth caused by rats

rattail: rat's tail; grenadier

rattail (rattailed): resembling a rat's tail

rattail comb: comb with narrow pointed handle for setting hair

rattail file: long, narrow file having circular cross section

rattail spoon: spoon with tapered rib running beneath bowl

ratten: in Britain, to destroy or remove machinery, tools, etc. to compel employer to meet union demands; sabotage

ratter: dog or cat or person that catches rats; deserter or traitor

rat terrier: one of several terriers used in catching rats

rattery: place where rats are kept

ratton: small rat (Scottish and English)

rattrap: device for catching rats; run-down, filthy place; difficult or hopeless situation; balloon barrage (British)

ratty (rattish): full of rats; characteristic of rats; wretched or shabby

ratwood: West Indian shrub or small tree

dock rat: bum hanging around docks

mouse: rock-and-roll dance in which dancer places his thumbs in his ears and flaps his fingers back and forth

mouse: to hunt or mouse or prowl; to seek stealthily

mouse: black eye; disgrace or shame; harlot

mousebird: coly

mouse deer: chevrotain

mouse-dun: dark brownish-gray color

mouse-ear: any of various plants with small leaves, such as forget-me-not

mouse-ear chickweed: any of several weedy herbs of genus <u>Cerastium</u>

mousefish: sargassumfish, so-called from size and habitat similar to that of field mouse

mousehole: burrow of mouse, or hole to its burrow

mouse-hunter: wencher

mouse opossum: murine opossum

mouser: an animal that catches mice; person that hunts for or prowls for prey

mousetail: plant of the genus <u>Myosurus</u>

mousetrap: trap for mice; defensive play in football; in Britain, a submarine

mousey (mousy): mouse-like; drab and colorless; quiet and noiseless; infested with mice

mousing: on ships, a wrapping of several turns of small materials around the shank end of a hook

## Proverbs and Proverbial Phrases

A mouse in time may bite in two a cable.

Mice do not play with the cat's son.

What can the mouse do against the cat?

Let the cat wink and the mouse run.

To speak like a mouse in the cheese.

Drunk as a mouse (very drunk).

Flee like rats from a sinking ship. Cf. Flee like mine rats from a mine.

When a house is ready to tumble down, the mice go out of it before. Cf. They say a falling house is best known by the rats leaving it--a falling state by the desertion of confederates or allies.

Fight like a cornered rat.

Gray as a rat.  Cf. Dun's the mouse.

The mouse that has but one hole is quickly taken.

Die like a rat (in a hole).

I gave the mouse a hole and she is become my heir.

Hungry (poor) as a church mouse.

Today a man, tomorrow a mouse.  Cf. Man or mouse?

Meek as a mouse.  Cf. Quiet (still or timid) as a mouse.

Like a mouse in the mill.  Cf.  Melancholy as mice in an empty mill.

Poor as any rat.

Quick as a rat that runs through a kitchen.

Down the rathole (useless or worthless).

Round as a pregnant mouse.

To have or see rats (have delirium tremens, to be crazy or foolish).

To smell a rat (to suspect treachery, to have suspicion).

Sure as a mouse tied with a thread (far from sure).

Let not the mousetrap smell of blood.

Like a rattrap, easier to get into than out of.  Cf. Trapped (caught) like a rat in a trap.

It is like giving advice to a rat when his leg is in the trap.

Warm as a mouse in a churn (very snug).

Wet as a drowned rat.  Cf. Dead as a drowned rat.

Pour not water on a drowning rat.

## Superstitions and Motifs

From Brown Collection

It is bad luck to patch a tablecloth that has been gnawed by rats. VI, 3291.  If a rat gnaws a hole in a garment, the owner must not darn it himself. If he does someone of his immediate family will surely die. VII, 5243

To dream of rats is a sign of great trouble. VII, 7179. To dream about rats indicates many enemies. VI, 3609

If rats come up to the deck of a ship, it is a sign the ship is leaking. VI, 3464. Cf. Mine rats leave a mine flooding with water or gases.

If a house is infested with rats, take a piece of greasy paper and write the name of the house to which you want the rats to go. They will eat the paper and go immediately to that house. VI, 2991

Fresh mouse meat is a cure for baldness. VI, 848

For bed wetting, cook a mouse, preferably by boiling, and make a sandwich of it and feed it to a child. VI, 279. Cf. Fried rat is said to be a cure for children who wet their beds. VI, 280

Corn has to be planted as soon as oak leaves are as big as a mouse's ears. VII, 8137

Mouse fat is a dependable cure for epilepsy. VI, 1346

Mouse-ear is made into a tea for fever. VI, 1436

Mouse flesh is used as a cure for rattlesnake bites. VI, 2136

If a child pulls a tooth and puts it under his pillow, a mouse will carry it off and leave a dime. VI, 388

From Motif-Index

Rat gnaws a net. B545.2

Rat persuades cat to wash face before eating, and then escapes. K562

Association of rat with cat ceases when mutual danger has passed. J426

The owl's wings borrowed from rat. A2241.2

Witch as rat. G211.2.6

Mouse teaches her child to fear quiet cat, but not noisy cocks. J132

Giant tricked into becoming a mouse. K722

Lawsuit between owl and mouse.   B270.2

Man transformed to a mouse.   D117.1

Mountain in labor brings forth mouse.   U114

Witch in the form of a mouse.   J211.2.5

### Quotations--Literary and Otherwise

A huge gap appeared in the side of the mountains.  At last a tiny mouse poked its little head out of the gap. -- Aesop

The lab'ring mountain scarce brings forth a mouse. -- Horace, Ars Poetica

I begin to smell a rat. -- Cervantes, Don Quixote

The mouse that hath but one hole is quickly taken. --George Herbert, Jacula Prudentum

It had need to bee a wylie mouse that should breed in the cat's ear. -- John Heywood, Proverbs

Not a mouse stirring. -- Shakespeare, Hamlet

She watches him as a cat would watch a mouse. -- Jonathan Swift, Polite Conversation

Not die here in a rage, like a poisoned rat in a hole. -- Jonathan Swift, Letter to Bolingbroke

>The best laid schemes o' mice and men
>  Gang aft a-gley;
>an lea'e us nought but grief and pain,
>  For promis'd joy.
>     -- Robert Burns, To a Mouse

He who builds a better mouse-trap will have the world beating a path to his door. (Summary)-- Authorship uncertain, but attributed to Ralph W. Emerson

In baiting a mouse-trap with cheese, always leave room for the mouse. --Hector H. Munro, The Square Egg

Life goes on forever like the gnawing of a mouse. -- Edna St. Vincent Millay, Ashes of Life

> Three blind mice, see how they run,
> They all ran after the farmer's wife,
> She cut off their tails with a carving-knife,
> Did you ever see such a sight in your life,
> As three blind mice? -- Nursery rhyme

> Hickory, dickory dock,
> The mouse ran up the clock,
> The clock struck one,
> The mouse ran down;
> Hickory, dickory dock. -- Nursery rhyme

> Pussy cat, pussy cat, where have you been?
> I've been to London to look at the queen.
> Pussy cat, pussy cat, what did you there?
> I frightened a little mouse under the chair.
> -- Nursery rhyme

## The Trail of the Serpent

Serpents, snakes, vipers, adders, and reptiles are found up trees, under rocks, in the grass, in beds, in asylums, and ever in the soul of man. According to one legend, the earth rests upon a serpent, a tortoise, and an elephant.

Most frequently called snakes, the awful and mysterious serpents (Serpentes) belong to the large family of reptiles and are of the genus Ophidia, the majority of which are classified as Colubridae. Some reproduce themselves by laying eggs, but most give birth to their young. In all there are thirteen general categories, one of them extinct. Although the exact number of species has never been determined, there are thought to be approximately 2500, of which about 600 are dangerous and only a few deadly.

Snakes are scaly, long, slender, cylindrical creatures without limbs. They vary in length from about one foot to thirty feet and have up to 435 vertebrae. Many of them have pointed, recurved teeth; they depend largely upon their olfactory sense to run down their prey. They move by serpentine locomotion, that is, by muscular contraction and expansion, usually pushing forward by gripping or stationary rears. They have forked, slender tongues and hiss without voices. Their colors are marvelously beautiful and handsome, with numerous glossy varieties of yellow, black, green, red, brown, pink, purple. The venomous types kill by using their fangs to inject poison into the nervous systems of their victims; the non-poisonous constrictive kinds wrap themselves around their prey and crush it to death. Coldblooded animals, whose temperatures adjust to the environment, they hibernate in severe winters and estivate during very dry summers.

Snakes are carnivorous and feed chiefly at night when it is cool; some are terrestrial, some aquatic, some arboreal, some burrowing. They live on insects, birds, small animals like pigs and

Serpent

deer, mice, rats, moles, fish, lizards, frogs, and other snakes. In most instances they swallow their dead or living victims. Their viciousness is balanced by their usefulness in destroying rodents and other pests. And their fishlike flesh is prized as a gourmet delicacy.

Although the vast majority of snakes are utterly harmless, you had better beware of the following deadly types:

Vipers or adders (Vipera berus of the family Viperidae) are observed in Africa, Eurasia, and Australia; very venomous, especially the puff-adder, sometimes called the death adder. In most instances they give birth to their young, which when adult are about two feet long and are reddish-brown, variegated with black.

Pit vipers (Crotalinae of the family Viperidae), distinguished by a pit between their eyes and nostrils, are found in America and other parts east toward Asia. Excepting the American puff-adder or hognose, which is harmless, they are highly venomous, and include the following subgroups: 1. Rattlesnakes, subclassified as massasauga, pigmy, diamond-back, timber, and canebrake, all of which are found in the Americas. 2. Water moccasins, or cottonmouths, usually observed not far from water and having no rattles; frequently give birth to their young. 3. Highland moccasins, or copperheads, having no rattles and usually giving birth to their young.

Coral snakes (of family Elapidae), about four feet in length when adult, usually laying eggs, and highly secretive and venomous.

Cobras (of the family Colubridae), closely related to the coral snakes.

Boidae in two classifications: 1. Python, of tropical Old World, being about 20 to 30 feet long, living 15 to 30 years; powerful teeth, non-poisonous, uses constriction to kill prey. It is doubtful if it is able to kill cattle and horses. It lays eggs and incubates them with its coils. 2. Boa, of which there are 40 species in America, the Mediterranean basin, Madagascar, and Polynesia. It has no teeth, is non-poisonous, and kills by constriction. The boa constrictor of South America is related to this species.

Dragons, of the genus Frightful Bugaboo, and reputed to be really lizards. Huge-winged and fire-breathing, traditional guardians of stolen hordes. Supposed to be protective, but always terror-inspiring; often depicted on shields, banners, and other nationalistic implements. Found mainly in literature, painting, and sculpture. Dragons have never been known to poison anybody, but they have scared the hell out of a lot of the simple-minded.

Regardless of what the scientists have recorded, the folk hold on to their traditional misconceptions about snakes. The most common erroneous beliefs: most snakes are harmful, especially the black and green types; they can be charmed by music and incantations; they milk cows and other animals; the mothers of snakes swallow their young to protect them; a rattlesnake always rattles before it bites; snakebites can be cured by using snake oil, snakeskin, snakeroot, or other useless concoctions.

The snake has played a long and glamorous role in the religious, nationalistic, artistic, and recreational aspects of civilization. Particularly in the East, Near East, and areas near the Mediterranean Sea, the serpent once held a respected position, though seldom worshipped. The ancient Cretans worshipped a snake goddess, who had snakes coiled around her arms and sometimes about her waist. The ancient Egyptians likened the snake to the spirit of the universe, and the Buddhists considered it an emblem of anger. Among the Greeks, reptiles were sacred to Apollo, Athena, and some of the water gods; the adder was a supporter of Eris, the goddess of discord. The Romans glorified snakes as symbols of authority and dominance, carving or painting them on shields and other implements of war. The great Roman writer Virgil depicted the traitorous and treacherous in the figures of the serpent-bound Laocoon and those depraved, filthy, snaky sisters, the Furies. In Palestine the ancient Hebrews transformed a rod into a snake and contended that a serpent caused the fall of man; the early Christians promised that redeeming love as expressed by the Messiah would bruise the head of this beguiling force. In more recent times African tribes have venerated the snake as an object of great power; in Dahomey, where snakes are supposed to be the robbers of the wealthy, they represent the beauty and promise of the rainbow. In America some folk respect snakes as supernatural influences for

Serpent

good or evil.

The beauty of the serpent was celebrated by the ancient Greeks in serpent columns erected as tokens of victory. Serpentine motifs have been widely used in the decoration of buildings and furniture. Craftsmen have transmitted the serpent X-stretcher and the snake or serpent star with its brittle central disk and outstretched arms. Gunsmiths have placed serpentine hammers on guns; plumbers have contrived snakes to clean out clogged sewers; loggers have developed snakes to pull logs through forests; manufacturers have produced skeins of silk called snakes; and some over-enthusiastic patriots have bought fireworks that burn with brilliant serpentine flame.

For recreation in these times, crap shooters can keep watch on snake eyes, that is, the point of two, with each die showing one. In a popular song-game in which the snake is "It," the children cry out, "Black snake, where are you hiding?" The American Hopi Indians enact yearly snake dances, with dangling snakes or their representations, that are spectacular exhibitions of fun and fury.

In mineralogy, there are descriptions of the addar (adder or snake) stone as an ammonite resembling a coiled snake and of serpentine as a hydrous magnesium silicate with oily, green, and spotted colors and much like the imitation serpentine jade. In geography, we have the Snake River; on the moon is the Serpent Sea. Numbered among the constellations are the Serpent Bearer (Ophiuchus) and its neighbor Serpens.

The botanists have aptly named at least thirty flowers or plants after snakes, such as adder's-tongue, snakeberry, snake cucumber, snake flower, snake lily, snake melon, snake nut, snake palm, snake violet, snakewood, and the intriguing viper's bugloss. The zoologists have designated the snakebird, snake buzzard, snake charmer, snake doctor, snake eel, snakefly, snake hawk, snake mackerel, and other animals.

But according to the folk and their literature, man himself is the serpent. From the time of the Scriptures, writers have stumbled often over the snake, held to be the cause of original sin. Milton's explanation was that "foul concupiscence," unholy lustfulness, was created by Satan (the snake) who injected it into the mind of Eve; she in turn contaminated Adam and their children forever. Man thus became snake-headed, snakelike, viperine, and serpentine-- cunning and knowledgeable, sinuous and deadly. The fruit of the tree of knowledge had corrupted him by destroying his innocence.

Man has ever since been desperately seeking more facts about himself and his environment, at first through yardsticks and plumb lines, now by a fast array of jet propulsion, cybernetics, and electronics. By these devices and speculations mankind has been forced more and more to stand before his looking glass, which the British call "the snake in the grass." In this mirror man can see himself as a turncoat copperhead, hidden and secretive, a treacherous viper although apparently harmless. The folk, who know him by experience, declare that he is coldblooded, crooked, low, mad, poisonous, sinuous and insinuating as any coiled snake or its winding path. They say that he excels in hurting others: he uses his enemy's hand to strike the viper's head; he can outdo any parlor snake with all his fickleness and deceit. This guy, they declare, thinks himself to be the snake's hips just as much as the tomcat prides himself on being the cat's whiskers.

This fellow can also cherish a serpent or viper deep down in his bosom. He is bitterly ungrateful and ultimately strikes his benefactors. Having long participated in despicable actions and the handling of snakes' tails, he has become uncertain about his own wits: he jumps when he sees a lizard, or rope, or whip. In his convulsions he sees snakes as others see rats--his madness may send him to a snake pit, an asylum for the mentally disturbed.

This dark character, however, is not without his admirable traits. With the status of a magician, he is a charming fellow. On the stock markets, he works for windfalls; he is loaded with a huge bag of tricks, trite sayings, amulets, charms, remedies, tonics, trinkets, and nosegays, which eager buyers grab as bargains of a lifetime. He sells rattles of snakes and little red celluloid bracelets, coiled like serpents, as sure-fire tokens of good luck. At the fair he convinces a pregnant woman to buy a snakeskin, which when placed around her thighs will speed up a safe delivery; then he induces her to purchase five more snakeskins--to avoid breaking her dishes, to stop the earaches of her children, to rid her husband of the rheumatism, to ward off snakebites when she goes blackberrying, and to rout the "hants" and other demons.

At another stall on the midway this charmer's lieutenant sells snakeroot, used in making teas to cure snakebites, fever, and headaches. He also makes hauls with snake oil to stop earache, and gallons of rattlesnake fat to cure the phthisic. He convinces all the stutterers present to gobble down his supply of snake eggs to relieve them of their ailment. And to the lovelorn, he offers all sorts of concoctions for conjuring their beloveds; one such is composed of the hair of the blood snake, the scales of a rattlesnake, the feathers of an owl, the parings of fingernails, and one hair from the head of the one to be conjured. Between sales he throws in some naughty stories, sings a few bawdy jingles, and advises some red-necked farmers to watch the peculiar movements of snakes in order to foretell the weather. Just when he is ready to close up shop for the day, he sees a kid having a fit of whooping cough. He reaches for his jar crammed full of small, green snakes, yanks out a lively one, and says, "Son, swallow this at once. It will stop any cough before you can say Jack Robinson!"

From the primordial ooze of life to the spangled chambers of gods and men, the serpent's trail has spread its power over the universe. It is restless and endless, open and concealed, moving warily, twisting, turning, coiling, striking, or constricting. Time and again the serpent has displayed its force, only to have its head bruised. It has been scotched, but never killed. In the long eons ahead it will continue to threaten and challenge the hopes of an evolving humanity as a colorful and respected villain.

## Derivative Names

addar stone: perforated stone whose properties were supposed to cure adder bite; worn by druids as charm

adder-mouth (adder's-mouth): delicate North American orchid having small greenish flowers adder's-tongue: cosmopolitan fern with spike of fruit; rattlesnake plantain; one of several flowering plants such as dog-tooth violet

copperhead: North American venomous pit viper; during Civil War a Northerner in sympathy with the Confederacy

reptile: animal that crawls on belly like snake; person of low and despicable character

reptilelike: having character of reptile, mean, treacherous

Serpens: constellation adjoining Ophiuchus, the Serpent Bearer

serpent: wily, treacherous, or malicious person; the Devil; a firework that burns with serpentine motion or flame

Serpent Bearer: constellation in northern and southern skies, called Ophiuchus

serpent column: three bronzed snakes intertwined, a symbol of victory in Greece

serpentiform: shaped like a snake

serpentine: like snake in form or movement; winding like a road; shrewd, wily, or cunning; device on a harquebus lock for holding match; cannon of several sizes used from 15th to 17th century; common mineral, hydrous magnesium silicate, usually oily green and sometimes spotted

serpentine front: curved front of chest of drawers, etc.

serpentine jade: green variety of serpentine used as substitute for true jade

serpentine stretcher: in furniture, an X-stretcher having curved lines

serpentenize: convert a mineral or rock into serpentine

Serpent Sea: the Mare Angius, a dark plain on the face of the moon

serpent star (snake star): brittle star, with central disk from which radiate long, slender, fragile arms

snake: treacherous or insinuating person; male who deceives girls; one who excels

snake (parlor snake): a ladies' man; a would-be seducer

snake: to wind, wriggle, or curve like a snake; especially when

Serpent

trying to evade action; to steal warily

snake: plumbing device used to open clogged pipe; a length of resilient steel wire for threading through electrical conduit; to drag or haul in serpentine manner, as logs, etc.

snake: member of any of various Shoshonean tribes in North America; railroad switchman

snake: arrow buried in grass; hose; skein of silk; whiskey or snake poison of inferior kind

snakebark: medium-sized timber tree in sub-tropics

snakeberry: bryony; bittersweet; red baneberry

snakebird: one of several swimming birds with long, slender or snaky necks found in southern swamps

snakebite: bite of snake, especially of the venomous type; the resulting painful, toxic condition; bloodroot

snakebite remedy: hard liquor

snakeblenny: any of several pricklebacks of genus Lumpenus

snake buzzard: serpent eagle

snake cane: tropical South American palm

snake charmer: entertainer who supposedly charms snakes; catbird; British bugler

snake cucumber: snake melon

snake dance: ceremonial dance of American Hopi Indians, in which snakes or their representations are handled or imitated by the dancers; a parade in serpentine line; a prayer for rain

snake doctor: dragonfly; hell-grammite; snake feeder

snake-eater: markhor; dragonfly

snake eel: any of several tropical eels

snake eggplant: a species of common eggplant

snake eyes: in dice, the point of two

snake fence: zigzag or worm fence, made of rails placed at angles to one another

snake fern: deer fern; royal fern

snakefish:   ribbonfish; lizard fish

snakeflower:   blueweed; greater stitchwort; white campion

snakefly:   any neuropterous insect with elongated neck

snakefoot:   in furniture, elongated foot or short leg, Dutch foot

snake-footed:   serpent-footed

snake-goddess:   Cretan goddess

snake-grass:   greater stitchwort; common forget-me-not

snake hawk:   swallow-tailed kite

snakehead:   herb or turtlehead plant; an elongated fish

snake-headed:   annoyed, vindictive

snake-hipped:   having thin, sinuous hips and usually mobile; sometimes said about agile dancer

snake in the grass:   mirror in England; a hidden danger

snake juice:   strong drink, or bad whiskey

snake killer:   secretary bird; road runner

snake lily:   a herb having twining stem and rose-bud or pink flowers; blue flag

snake line:   small line passed between two ropes

snake mackerel:   long, silvery deep-sea fish

snake melon:   a gourd and its fruit; snake gentian; snake gourd

snake-milk:   flowering spurge

snake moss:   common club moss

snakemouth:   terrestrial orchid, native of North America, with fragrant rose-pink flowers

snakeneck:   snakebird

snake nut:   fruit of tree native to Guinea; its embryo resembles coiled snake

snake off:   to slip quietly away

snake oil:   any of various concoctions sold as remedies, usually of questionable value

snake palm: Asiatic evil-smelling aroid; devil's-tongue

snakepipe: horsetail

snake pit: mental hospital marked by squalor and inhumane conditions

snake-plantain: ribwort

snake ranch: cheap, dirty saloon or bar

Snake River: principal tributary of the Columbia River, flowing through Wyoming, Idaho, Oregon, and Washington

snakeroot: any of various plants whose roots are supposed to be remedies for snakebite

snakery: house for snakes

snake's-beard: Asiatic herb

snake's-head: guinea-hen flower; toad lily

snake's hips, the: any superior or remarkable person or thing

snakeskin: skin of snake; leather made from skin of snake

snakestone: ammonite resembling coiled snake; addar stone, porous material supposed to neutralize the toxic effect of snakebite

snake's-tongue: adder's-tongue; a fern; moonwort

snake-tart: eel pie

snake violet: bird's-foot violet

snakeweed: bistort; Virginia snakeroot

snakewood: East Indian vine; trumpetwood

snakeworm: traveling mass of army worms

snakewort: bistort

snaky: of or pertaining to snakes; abounding in snakes; treacherous or insidious; bearing likeness to serpentine nature of snakes

Snaky Sisters: the mythological Furies

viper: malicious, repulsive or treacherous person; marijuana smoker

viperous, viperine, viperish: venomous, snakelike

viper's bugloss: blue weed, a coarse and bristly plant

### Proverbs and Proverbial Phrases

If the adder could hear, and the blindworm could see,
Neither man nor beast would ever go free.

Whom a serpent has bitten a lizard alarms.

He that hath been bitten by a snake is afraid of a rope.

Cherish a serpent in one's bosom. Cf. Viper in the bosom (showing ingratitude and treachery). Put a snake in the bosom, and it will sting when it is warm.

A caution to snakes (something very surprising, odd, eccentric, or unusual).

Cold as a coiling water-snake.

Coldblooded (crooked, hissing, low, mean, poisonous, poor, sinuous, treacherous) as a snake. Cf. Crooked as a blacksnake. Lower than a snake. Mean as a striped snake.

Crooked as a snake's path.

To have more of the serpent than the dove.

Unless a serpent has devoured a serpent, a serpent does not become a dragon.

Snake in the grass. Cf. Viper in the grass (concealed danger; treacherous person; dangerous but apparently harmless). Slick as a snake in the grass.

Hard to see as a green snake in the grass.

Hate 'em like snakes. Cf. Hateful as a serpent.

Low-down as a snake's belly. Cf. Lower than a snake's belly.

Mad as a one-eyed rattlesnake.

See snakes (to have delirium tremens).

Treading on reptiles (according to Christian tradition, to crush false doctrine or heresy).

# Serpent

No more sense (money, etc.) than a snake has hips.

Don't stir up more snakes than you can kill.  Cf. Kindle not a fire that you cannot extinguish.  Raise no more spirits than you can conjure down.

It is good to strike the serpent's head with your enemy's hand.

Hung by a serpent (that is, got with child).

Hold a serpent by the tail (to act foolishly).

The trail of the serpent (is over all of us).

No viper so little but hath its venom.  Cf. Snake (viper) in the bosom.

### Superstitions and Motifs

The tree into which a coachwhip snake fastens itself to whip its victim to death also dies.

A snake tooth is a good charm.

Saliva from person is poisonous and deadly when spit into mouth of serpents.  Pliny the Elder, Natural History

#### From Clark Collection

Snakes swallow their young to protect them.  1267

A whip snake can beat an individual to death.  1251

Snakes go into barns and milk cows.  1323

A rattlesnake's rattles are sign of good luck.  1258

A hoop-snake can take its tail in its mouth and roll speedily toward its victim.  1254

A snake can strike a distance three times its length.  1249

#### From Brown Collection

A child whose mother killed a snake a few days before the child was born resembled and acted like a snake.  VI, 112

Look at a snake and your eyes will cross.  VI, 1392

If you hang up a horsehair, it will turn into a snake the first time it rains.  VII, 7300.  Cf. 7301-7

Snake eggs will cure stutterers. VI, 2273

If you have started somewhere and see a snake, you will have good luck. VI, 3880

Dreaming: To dream of snakes is a sign of sickness. VI, 717. When you dream about a snake, it is a sign that you have a (dangerous) enemy. VI, 3614. If you kill the first snake you see at the beginning of the new year, you will conquer all of your enemies; but if it gets away, your enemies will conquer you. VII, 8543

Little red celluloid bracelets which are coiled to resemble a serpent are often worn for luck. VII, 7324

Charms: Finding a shed skin of a snake is a sign of luck. VII, 7294. Cf. It is bad luck to handle a snakeskin. VII, 7299. If the skin shed by a snake is placed around the thigh of a woman in labor, she will have a speedy recovery. VI, 37. While walking along, if you see a snake shed (shedded skin), pick it up, rub your hands with it, and you will break no more dishes. VI, 2895. If you wear a snakeskin in your hat, you won't have the headache. VI, 1589. Three drops of blood taken from a snake while it is still alive, mixed with a small pinch of spider dust (ground spider) and stirred in a cup of green corn, will kill any rival who drinks it and will bring back the loved one. VI, 4265. A snakeskin belt, or a snakeskin around the waist, will cure rheumatism. VI, 1987. A snakeskin bag with a toad's eye in it is worn to ward off the hants. VII, 5760. A snakeskin around the body will prevent evil spirits from troubling the wearer. VII, 5746. A snakeskin bag and toad's eye in it are worn to ward off swamp fever. VI, 2306.

Conjuring: When a snake is found in a bed (of someone), it is a sign that that person is conjured. VII, 5552. Take seven hairs from a blood snake, seven scales from a rattlesnake, seven bits of feathers from an owl, add a hair from the head of the person you desire, and a bit of nail paring, and cook these for seven minutes over a hot fire in the first rain water caught in April. Sprinkle the concoction on the clothes of the person to be charmed. It cannot fail. VII, 5555

If a snake track is seen across one's track, one must stoop down and rub it out with his cheek to break the spell. VII, 5573. A dried lizard pounded makes a powder which, when thrown on a person, makes a snake come in him. VI, 719

Remedies: Swallowing a live snake will cure whooping cough. VI, 2718. Sterility in women is often treated with flesh of various kinds of snakes. VI, 10. For earache, drop snake oil in one's ear. VI, 1330. For phthisic, eat the fat of a dead rattlesnake which did not bite itself. VII, 1917. Powdered snakeroot is a cure for coughs. VI, 213. Snakeroot tea is good for fever. VI, 1450. Powdered snakeroot is a cure for headaches. VI, 1601.

Death: One who has been bitten by a snake has a snake hanging to his liver. As soon as the snake has eaten the liver up, the person dies. VI, 721. If the first snake you see in the year is a dead one, some member of your family or a friend will die during the year. VII, 5244. A snake never dies till sundown. VII, 7317.

Snakebite: If you step on a snake's track, the snake will return to bite you. VII, 7321. To cure snakebite, cut the snake up which bit you and place it over the bite. VI, 2141. Cf. To cure the bite of a snake, kill the snake, and apply some of its fat to the wound. Drinking tea made from snakeroot will drive out the poison from the body after the snake bites. VI, 2154. There is a snakeweed which, if bruised and placed on the snake bite, will draw out the poison. VI, 2155. If a snake bites a person that has eaten onions a day or two before, the person will die. VII, 5245. A dried snake's skin is used as a protection against snakebites. VI, 2139.

Weather: If you kill a snake and leave it lying on the ground, it will be a sign of bad weather. VII, 6196. The first thunder in the spring wakens snakes. VII, 7290. When terrapins and snakes are seen crawling across roads and other unusual places in dry weather, it is a sign of rain very soon. VII, 6759. When you kill a snake, be sure you leave him lying on his stomach, or it will rain. VII, 6889. If you kill a snake and want fair weather, be sure to bury it. VII, 6377. Leaving a dead snake turned downward brings sunshine. VII, 6256. If snakes and toads are late disappearing, look for a mild winter. VII, 6107.

From Motif-Index

Snakes issue from dragon's shoulders. B11.2.7

Witch transforms self into snake when she bathes. G245.1

Devil in form of snake. G303.3.3.15

Seven-headed serpent. B15.1.2.6.1. (Many others with varying number of heads.)

Adder transforms self to blindworm (that is, lizard, sometimes called slow worm). A2145.5

Serpent supports sky. A665.6. Cf. Serpent supports earth. A842.1

Earth rests on tortoise, serpent, and elephant. A844.6

Serpent with human head. B29.2.1

Soul in form of reptile. E733. Cf. Wise reptile. B123

Adder grows in heart of man. F559.7.2

Child born with serpent in caul. T551.8. Cf. Child born with viper in heart. T557

Reptile leaps into unjust bishop's throat. V229.2.11.1

Viper as magician's familiar. G225.7.2. Cf. Magic reptile. B176

Animal languages learned from serpent. B217.1.1

Serpent steals from God's coat a stick for his sack. A2262.3

Snake around neck as chastity test. H412.5

Bridal chamber filled with coiled snakes. T172.1

Treasure-guarding snake around princess's chamber. H335.3.4

Serpent asks victim to feed him honey. K815.18

Snake sucks woman's milk. B765.4.1

Serpent carried by bird lets poison drop in milk and poisons drinkers. N332.3

Man fears snake like rope. J11.1

Snake mistaken for whip. J1761.6.1

Serpent charmed into helplessness by magic formula. D1410.5

Snake put to sleep by music. D1962.5

Snake swallows young to protect them. B751.1

Snake complains to Zeus that people step on him. J623.1

Origin of death: serpent immortal instead of man. A1335.5

## Quotations--Literary and Otherwise

Now the serpent was more subtile than any beast of the field. -- Genesis, III, 1

The serpent beguiled me and I did eat. -- Genesis, III, 13

For they cast down every man his rod, and they became serpents;

but Aaron's rod swallowed up their rods. -- Exodus, VII, 12

At the last it (liquor) biteth like a serpent, and stingeth like an
    adder. -- Proverbs, XXIII, 32

In that day the Lord with his sore and great and strong sword shall
    punish Leviathan the piercing serpent, even Leviathan that
    crooked serpent; and he shall slay the dragon that is in the
    sea. -- Isaiah, XXVII, 1

O generation of vipers, who hath warned you to flee from the wrath
    to come. -- Matthew, III, 7

Be ye therefore wise as serpents, and harmless as doves.
    Matthew, X, 16

Now will I show myself to have more of the serpent than the dove;
    that is, more knave than fool. -- Marlowe, The Jew of
    Malta

> To beguile the time,
> Look like the time; bear welcome in your eye,
> Your hand, your tongue; look like the innocent flower,
> But be the serpent under it. -- Shakespeare, Macbeth

We have scotched the snake, not killed it. -- Shakespeare, Macbeth

Where's my serpent of old Nile? -- Shakespeare, Anthony and Cleopatra

> How sharper than a serpent's tooth it is
> To have a thankless child. -- Shakespeare, King Lear

> The infernal serpent; he it was whose guile
> Stirred up with envy and revenge, deceived
> The mother of mankind. -- Milton, Paradise Lost

> The world's great age begins anew,
>   The golden years return,
> The earth doth like a snake renew
>   Her winter weeds outworn. -- Shelley, Hellas

The cradle of every science is surrounded by dead theologians as
    that of Hercules was with strangled serpents. -- Thomas H.
    Huxley

## A Horse of Another Color

About fifty million years ago--as indicated by fossils found in England and in the United States--the probable ancestor of today's horse got started. The dawn horse (Eohippus) was a herbivore, foxlike in appearance, about twelve inches high. He had a long body, long tail, short teeth, tiny ears, five-toed front feet and four-toed hind feet. After many aeons he evolved as the Mesohippus (middle horse) and finally the Merychippus (grass eater), always growing in size and strength but gradually losing his toes. Then, for unknown reasons, he became extinct.

Ultimately there appeared some connecting links between the foregoing species and the modern horse: the wild ass, the zebra, and Przewalski's horse (Equus przewalskii). The last, native to the Gobi desert, was a sort of pony, twelve hands high, and rather mulish with his stiff and rough coating of hair. A likely successor of these links is the asslike onager now found in parts of Africa.

Finally there developed what we presently call the horse (Equus caballus of the family Equidae, which includes the horse, zebra, ass, mule, and hinny). By the beginning of historic records this animal was twelve to fourteen hands high and possessed one toe or hoof on each leg. Over the centuries he was highly domesticated and bred into what is called the Arabian horse, in recognition of the loving care bestowed by the Arabs, Berbers, and Moors. He was popular in Assyria about 4000 B.C., in Babylonia about 2000 B.C., in Egypt about 1650 B.C., and not long thereafter in Greece and Rome. The stallions of this breed modified numerous species in the East, Near East, Europe, and North Africa. The Arabian horse was the backbone of the farflung conquests of Alexander the Great, Mohammed, Charlemagne, and Genghis Khan. It came to the New World with the Spanish invaders.

Our modern breeds have been developed by much crossbreeding and inbreeding, particularly with Arabian stock. The principal classifications are as follows:

1. Draft Horses (descendants of the big Flemish horses of the Middle Ages)
   Percheron of France, gray, highly spirited like the Arabian.
   Belgian, chestnut or sorrel, developed in Belgium and very popular in America.
   Clydesdale of Scotland, feathered below the knees and usually having a white blaze.
   English Shire, bay and brown, feathered below the knees, the heaviest and tallest of the four.

2. Harness Breeds
   Hackney, Yorkshire, Hanoverian, and Oldenberg.
   American Standardbred, an excellent trotter and pacer.

3. Roadsters--Riding and Saddle Horses (with three to five gaits-- walk, single-foot, pace, trot, canter or gallop)
   Thoroughbred, English breed with notable quality.
   Arabian, the aristocrat in appearance, stamina, and speed.
   American Quarter, an all-purpose animal used for polo, cattle herding, rodeos.
   Tennessee Walking, well-known as a brisk walker.

4. Ponies (from 9 to 13 hands high)
   Shetland, Highland, Dale, and Fell.

Horses have strong and rounded bodies, supported by graceful and finely shaped legs; they have large eyes, soft lips, flaring nostrils, flowing manes. They are chestnut, palomino, albino, black, or gray, or they can be spotted or splotched (piebalds and skewbalds). They give birth to their colts after eleven months of pregnancy. They live from twenty to forty years, provided they don't become victims of distemper, glanders, heaves, or spavin.

Horses eat corn, oats, barley, wheat, hay and grasses. They need thoughtful masters to see that they are bred properly, fed and watered, exercised daily, groomed often, shod to protect their hoofs, housed in dry and cool stables, and blanketed when necessary.

Horses have always been a part of history--its mythologies, religions, and arts. The Greeks, always proud of their war horses, attributed equine traits to gods such as Poseidon, Athena, Aphrodite, and Cronus. Horses were carved high on the capitals of the Parthenon and other structures. An important deity was the swift flying horse named Pegasus, who has given his name to a satellite launched at Cape Kennedy. Helios and Thor drove horses through the skies. The ancient Semites consecrated their horses to God. The Hindus recognized the keen intellect of the horse by putting Aries into the Zodiac. The Hebrews, who suffered much from military conquests, thought of horses as symbols of war. The Four Horsemen of the Apocalypse represented conquest, death, pestilence, and war. The Celts, Danes, and Saxons venerated their horses and often buried them with their owners.

Throughout the world, one can find the grand equestrian image, raised high on a pedestal, bearing on his back an equally grand person. The horse is glorified in the galloping meter (anapest) of "Lochinvar," "The Destruction of Sennacherib," "How They Brought the News from Ghent to Aix," and "The Charge of the Light Brigade." He is portrayed in famous paintings like "The Horse Fair" and "Hay Harvest in Auvergne."

This lovable and cheerful animal plays a significant role in the language of the people, as the appended list indicates. There is an extensive vocabulary relating to the care, management, and working of horses. Some twenty-five plants owe their names to the horse--such as horse balm, horse mushroom, horse nettle, horse radish, etc. In the animal kingdom are the horse ant, horse crab, horsefly, and many others. There are numerous useful devices too, like the sawhorse, haircloth, horse pistol, horse rake, and pony engine. And in the literature cited below, it is obvious that horsemanship is associated with good living, pride of ownership, joyous and spirited sport, and social importance.

Since the invention of the horseless carriage, the horse, like the mule, has been receding from the human scene. In primitive nations the horse is still the prime source of heavy and burdensome labor, but in industrialized countries the horse's traditional jobs have been taken over by machinery. The glorious heyday of the cavalry mounts and chariot horses is reflected in the prominent position horses hold in sports today. Witness the colorful steeplechases, the sportsmen riding off in pursuit of foxes, the races at hundreds of tracks, the polo contests, the rodeos, the spirited horse shows, and the just plain horseback riding.

Despite all the fun engendered by these pastimes, the folk, often frustrated by balky and kicking horses, and with a sharp dislike of unexpected dark horses, hurl their barbs at those with too much of the horse in their make-up. A man can work or eat like a horse; he can be just as sick, long-faced, stubborn, or strong. He can indulge in horse play, then let out an explosive horse laugh at his victim's plight. It all amounts to a mare's nest, or maybe only a horrible nightmare. Still horsing around, man is compared to a high-stepping stallion or stud-horse, if his activities warrant, or reverenced as much as an old war horse.

In further jibing, the folk say that an ass who goes traveling in the realms of gold will never come home looking like a horse. The idiot is always one, especially if he spouts a lot of nonsense, politely called horsefeathers or horse collar.

Another murky character is the horse trader, who used to be a common sight around the countryside. He was seldom accused of being a horse beater, but his ways were tricky. By the time he finished his inspection of a horse, a free horse or a gift horse, he had convinced the gaping crowd that he was the horse's mouth, the unquestioned source of authority. When he sold, bought or swapped, he always got the better bargain.

We still have with us, as in the days of old, the rider that does not know where he is going, the sort that mounts on the off side and has been known to look for his mare at the time he is astride her. Such a one might as well be riding a shank's mare or a staff or a hobbyhorse, for he is bound to gallop off in all directions at once.

Then there is the impatient guy at whom the folk yell: "Hold your horses, buddy." Or the one that wastes his time singing psalms over dead horses, or continuing to beat a gone horse. Or the simpleton that tries forcing a balky nag to drink water. Or the farmer that locks the stable door after the horse thief has long since cantered away. Or the college student who uses a pony for exams instead of his own good horse sense.

The helpful horse also provides a bag of remedies for assorted problems and ailments. The folk say that chilblains can be cured by soaking your feet in warm water to which horse dung has been added, and that this same substance, when fresh, will heal an open wound. If you carry a buckeye in your pocket, you can ward off coughs, shortness of breath, and rheumatism. You can also rid yourself of rheumatism by clutching a horseshoe in your pocket. They say that a horse hair placed in a barrel of water will become a snake or worm; that it will remove your moles; and that it will, when drawn across the bridge of your nose, stop nosebleeding. Moreover, if your child has whooping cough, have him drink mare's milk, or force him to drink from a vessel used by a white horse, or allow a stallion to breathe into his throat. Just drinking after any horse is sure to stop the toothache.

Horses are reliable forecasters of the weather too. A horse draws lightning; if he shakes his harness, it will rain in three days; if he sweats in his stable, or sniffs loudly and switches his tail violently, it will rain. If he runs, kicks, or plays much, strong winds are in store.

To enjoy good fortune, hang up horseshoes over the doors of houses and barns, or in fruit trees, or over hog troughs, or in fireplaces, or throw them over your left shoulder. Soon money will pour in, fruit will be more plentiful, hawks won't attack your chickens, hogs will fatten more readily, witches will not come nigh, and favorable marriages will take place. Seeing a white horse also will promote good luck and prosperity. Should you ever see 100 white horses, count them and you'll get some silver. If you buy a white horse, be sure that he has one white foot; otherwise luck will elude you.

Among all domesticated animals, the horse is pre-eminent, whether he be colt or old gray mare. Through the centuries he has marched in triumph--the farmer's ally, the child's companion, the soldier's fiery steed, the circuit rider's carrier, the country doctor's trusty transportation.

## Derivative Names

colt: young horse up to three years old; sometimes known as male foal to distinguish from filly; inexperienced person

colt: (nautical) rope's end used for chastising or flogging

coltpixie (coltpixy): mischievous hobgoblin in guise of colt, leads men or horses into bogs

coltsfoot: cow perennial herb of the composite family, bearing yellow flowers and used as medicine

coltskin: skin of colt, sometimes used as leather

colt's-tail: horseweed; field horsetail

colt's tooth: wolf tooth in horses; youthful wantonness

filly: female foal or colt; lively young woman, sometimes wanton

filly-hunting: amorous searching for women

gelding: castrated animal, especially a castrated horse; a eunuch

horse: male of the horse, gelding or stallion; horses collectively; horseflesh; cavalry; to go by horseback

horse: athletic apparatus

horse: diligent, able student; a grind; a pony, a literal translation

horse: joke, especially as played on a person; horse play; stupid, contemptible person

horse: mass of rock; truck or tractor. Cf. iron horse and military tank

horse: peculiar name for man such as an old horse; knight in chess

horse: $1,000, circus use; heroin; meat, especially corned beef; mud-bank

horse: to possess a woman; prostitute's customer

horse, stud: man who has fathered many children

horse aloes: caballine aloes

horse-and-buggy: old-fashioned

horse ant: large mound-building ant of North America and Europe horse apple: feces of horse

horse around: to joke, to indulge in horseplay, to fool around

horseback: natural bridge; to do quickly

horse balm: richweed

horsebane: European water dropwort

horsebean: broad bean; Jerusalem thorn

horse-beast: horse

horse block: block or platform for mounting or dismounting a horse

horseboat: boat moved by horsepower; boat for carrying horses

horseboot: leather covering to protect a horse's pastern

horsebot: botfly or its larva

horse box: railroad car for transporting horses

horseboy: stableboy

horse brass: brass instrument, originally for the harness of a horse

horsebreaker: one who trains horses

horse briar: greenbriar; cat briar

horsebrush: low, tough, hoary, sometimes spiny shrub of western U.S.A.

horse-buss: resounding kiss. Cf. horse-kiss

horsecar: railroad or street car pulled by horses; car for transporting horses

horse cavalry: cavalry mounted on horses

horse-chestnut: a tree or its large nutlike seed

horsecloth: cloth for covering or trapping of a horse

horse collar: score of zero

horse conch: marine gastropod

horse coper: horse trader, especially the tricky sort

# Horse

horse crab (horsefoot): king crab; colt'sfoot

horse-critter: horse

horse daisy: mayweed

horse dance: Indian dance imitating raising of horse

horse doctor: medical officer; veterinarian

horsedrench: dose for a horse, or instrument by which it is given

horse devil: wild indigo

horse-eye: oxeye bean

horseface: long homely face

horse fair: fair for sale or showing of horses

horsefeathers: expression of disbelief or disgust; nonsense

horsefish: moonfish

horseflesh: flesh of horse, especially when slaughtered for food; horses collectively

horsefly: gadfly, usually bloodsucking

horse furniture: harness or housing of horse; horse-gear

horse gentian: plant of honeysuckle family

horse gowan: daisy; dandelion; camomile

horse guard: black and yellow sand wasp

Horse Guards: English cavalry brigade

horsehair: hair of horse; haircloth

horsehead: tropical American moonfish

horse hoe: horse-drawn hoe

horsehide: baseball

horsejockey: professional rider of race horses

horse latitudes: calm regions lying 30 degrees north and south of equator

horselaugh: boisterous laugh

horseleech (formerly horse leach): veterinary surgeon; common leech attacking noses and mouths of horses; insatiable person; whore

horseless carriage: automobile

horse louse: sucking louse

horse-mackerel: common tunny or tuna

horseman: skilled rider or caretaker of horses

horsemanship: skill in care, training, and riding of horses

horse marine: legendary marine cavalryman; man out of his element

horsemint: any of several European and American mints

horse mushroom: coarse edible mushroom

horse mussel: large, coarse marine mussel

horse nails: money

horse's neck: derogatory characterization

horse nettle: prickly weed of the nightshade family

horse, old (hoss): familiar term for addressing another

horse opera: cheap, stereotyped movie or thriller about cowboys

horse parlor: place where betting on horses is carried on

horsepiano: calliope

horse pistol: large pistol

horseplay: boisterous play

horseplayer: habitual bettor on horse races

horse plum: American plum

horsepond: pond for watering horses

horsepost: hitching post

horsepower: power exerted by pulling horses: unit of power of 33,000 footpounds of work per minute

horsepox: acute infectious disease of horses

# Horse

horse purslane: coarse tropical American fleshy weed

horse race: contest of uncertain outcome

horseradish: plant of mustard family

horse rake: large wheeled rake drawn by a horse

horse room: bookmaking establishment

horse-sense: common sense

horseshoe: shoe for horse; game played with horseshoes

horseshoe crab: marine animal, regarded as a crustacean

horse show: public competitive showing of horses and horsemanship

horse-sugar: sweetleaf, an American shrub

horsetail: flowerless fern; tail of horse; style of hairdo

horse-tamer: horsebreaker

horse-tick: forest fly

horse-trade: shrewd bargaining

horsetree: whiffletree

Horse, Trojan: wooden horse used as ruse in capturing Troy

horseweed: North American weed of aster family

horsewhip: to whip or flog brutally

horsewoman: skilled woman rider of horses

horse-wrangler: herdsman in charge of horses on ranch

hoss: to annoy; a horse

mare: female of horse, ass, zebra, etc.

mare: evil spirit supposed to cause bad dreams, as in nightmare

mare's nest (mare's tail): a supposed great discovery that turns out to be a hoax

mare, shank's: one's own legs

mare's tail: slender cirrus cloud; an erect, aquatic Old World plant

pony: small horse not more than thirteen hands in height; race horse

pony: small glass for liquor

pony: chorus girl, burlesque dancer

pony: literal translation; any unethical aid; a crutch

pony: English sum of money, 25 pounds

pony cart: donkey cart

pony engine: small switching locomotive

pony express: first rapid-transit postal and express system in western U.S.A.

pony grass: perennial grass in Rocky Mountains

pony mixer: small machine used for mixing pastes, paints, etc.

pony tail: style of hairdo. Cf. horse tail

pony truck: two-wheeled swivel truck

pony truss: truss used in bridge building

pony up: to pay

stallion: male horse used as stud in breeding; piebald horse; prostitute's customer; vigorous man

stud: any male person, especially a dude, sport, or roué

stud: collection of horses, kept for breeding; also at stud

stud book: record of pedigrees

studhorse: male horse kept for breeding

## Proverbs and Proverbial Phrases

If an ass goes a-traveling, he'll not come home a horse.

Better ride an ass that carries us than a horse that throws us.

Better ride a lame horse than go on foot.

Who hath no horse may ride on a staff.

Have a horse of thine own and thou may'st borrow another.

# Horse

A horse, a wife, and a sword may be shewed, but not lent.

Back the wrong horse.

Balky (buckeyed, holy, sick, strong) as a horse.

Eats (works) like a horse.

A balking horse will not pull.  Cf. Balky horse'll always take a hill.

Don't beat a dead horse (useless effort).

Broke (ran) like a quarter horse.

Put the cart before the horse (proceed in wrong order).

A horse of another color (an entirely different matter).

A good horse can never be of bad color.

Scared as a year-old colt.

To have a colt's tooth.

As much out of place as a colt in a flower garden.

A colt is worth nothing unless he breaks his cord.

The wildest colt makes the best horse.

You may break a colt but never an old horse.

That horse is troubled with corns.

Crazy as a horse in a windstorm.

Die the death of a trooper's horse with your shoes on (to be hanged).

One horse is allowed to eat grass and the other is not allowed to look over the fence.

Fast as a horse can trot.

When the filly will have a blaze, the mare hath a bald face.

Don't ride a free horse to death.

A galled horse cannot endure a conch.

Never look a gift horse in the mouth.  (One implication is that teeth may be bad.)

Never kick a gift horse in the mouth.

A gone horse.

Where the horse lies down, there some hair will be found.

The horse that draws after him his halter is not altogether escaped.

It would have made a horse break his halter (bridle).

Know the horse by his harness.

A good horse often needs a good spur. Cf. A good horse has no need of a spur. A bridle and spur make a good horse.

A good horse must smell to the pixy.

It's a good horse that never stumbles.

A golden bit does not make a horse any better.

The best horse needs breaking, and the aptest child needs teaching.

To ride the high horse. Cf. To be on one's high horse. (To be arrogant or put on airs.)

When one is on horseback, he knows all things.

He who is carried by horses must deal with rogues.

A hired horse never tires.

To hold one's horses (to be patient).

Horse and horse (equally matched).

Horse and man (or foot). (Overthrown together.)

A horse made and a man to make. (Best when man unarmed.)

Send for a horse ladder (a fool's errand).

The horseshoe that clatters wants a nail. Cf. Your horse cast a shoe.

A jade will eat as much as a good horse.

Better a lean jade than an empty halter.

A horse grown fat kicks.

Enough to make a horse laugh.

# Horse

A lean horse for a long race.  Cf. A lean dog for a long chase.

He lied as fast as a horse could trot.

There's no use to lock the barn after the horse has been stolen.

She looked like death on a pale horse.

Mad on a horse; sho's proud on a pony.

The grey mare is the better horse.  (John Heywood, 1497-1580)

Like a man who sought his mare and he was riding on her.  Cf. He looks for the horse he rides on.

To find a mare's nest.  Cf. To find a mare's nest with a teehee's egg in it.

Go before one's mare to market, or lose the halter.  Cf. Run before one's horse to market.  (To play doubles or quits; to count on unhatched chickens.)

Money makes the mare go.

Ride a shank's mare (to walk).

A mare's shoe and a horse's shoe are both alike.

Steady as a mill horse.  Cf. Like a horse in the mill.

The horse next the mill carries all the grist.

A horse is his who mounts him.

Out of (from) the horse's mouth (authoritative).

An off horse.  (Side farther away, right side.)

A one-horse town (small, simple place).

It is a proud horse that will not carry his provender.

Every horse thinks his pack is the heaviest.

If two men ride a horse, one must ride behind.

You can't ride two horses at one time.

A running horse is an open tomb (sepulcher).

Better lose saddle than the horse.

A short horse is soone currid.  (John Heywood)

Enough to make a horse sick.

A skittish horse won't carry double.

One horse stays for another.

Steal the horse, and carry home the bridle.

In the stud book (of ancient lineage).

Don't swap horses while crossing a stream.   Cf. Don't swap horses in the middle of a stream.

Swell like a horse with the colic.

Horses sweat, men perspire, and women glow.

Tell that to the horse marines!   (Don't be silly.)

To horse!   (To mount.)

Trust not the horse, ye Trojans.   (Virgil)

I wouldn't trust him as far as you could throw a horse by the tail.

It is easy to walk when one leads a horse by the bridle.

A man may bring a horse to water, but he cannot make him drink without he will.   (John Heywood)   Cf. You can take (lead) a horse to water, but you can't make him drink.

Let a horse drink when he will, not what he will.

Whip the horse with oats, not with a whip.

One white foot--buy him; two white feet--try him; three white feet--look well about him; four white feet--do without him. Cf. One white foot, keep him to the end.

## Superstitions and Motifs

From Brown Collection

For a balky horse, take a hair from his tail and tie it around the leg.   This breaks the spell and he goes on.   VII, 7636.
A horse can see a ghost and will balk.   VII, 5721

Put a rusty axe in the feed trough to cure a horse of blood humor. VII, 7651

For chilblain, soak the feet in warm water to which horse dung has been added.   VI, 1041

# Horse

Horses talk at Old Christmas. VII, 6015. Exactly at midnight of Old Christmas, all cattle and horses everywhere stand up and then lie down on the other side. VII, 6012

Fresh horse manure is applied to cuts. VI, 1263

If you carry a buckeye in your pocket, you will not have diseases. VI, 755. Cf. A horse chestnut in the pocket will prevent infectious diseases. VI, 1741

If you dream of a red horse, you will be angry soon. VII, 7113

Horsemint will cure fever. VI, 1429

Do not trot the horse across the bridge going to a funeral. VII, 5458

If you walk through a place where a horse wallows, you will have a headache. VI, 1585

If you hang up a horsehair, it will turn into a snake the first time it rains. VII, 7300. Cf. Put a horsehair into a bottle of water, and it will turn into a little, long worm (snake). VII, 7385. Others say into eel.

If a person finds a horseshoe and throws it over his left shoulder, this will bring good luck. VII, 7120

Put (Keep) horseshoe in the fire to keep hawks away from your chickens. VII, 7488.

Horseshoes nailed over the door will keep off conjuring influences. VII, 5569. To keep witches away from the house, hang a horseshoe over the door. VII, 5627. Carrying a horseshoe nail will keep the influence of the witches away. VII, 5683. Horseshoes are tacked up over the stable door to ward off witches. VII, 7661. Put a horseshoe in the fire if your butter won't come and gather. This kills the witches. VII, 7551

Man and wagon mired in sand and thought to be conjured. Man took axe and drove it into one log on the wagon. As supposed conjurer passed, axe flew out and man with wagon drove on. VII, 5556 (summarized).

Hang a horseshoe in fruit trees, and you will have a heavy crop. VII, 8412

If a horseshoe is nailed to the hog trough, no ill luck will befall the fattening hogs. VII, 7690

For rheumatism, carry a horseshoe nail in the pocket. VI, 2050

Hang a horseshoe over the door, and the first man that enters will marry you. VI, 4479

Nosebleed is cured by drawing a horse hair tightly across the bridge of the nose. VI, 1863

To find a penny in a horse's track is good luck. VI, 3446

If baby has the stretches, pass a horse collar over the baby's head seven times. This cures it. VI, 348

To cure toothache, drink after a horse. VI, 2349.

Take a hair from a horse's mane and wind it around the wart (to remove it). VI, 2432. Take a piece of horse manure and put it on a stump; when the manure is gone, the wart will be gone. VI, 2457. Count the number of warts you have, and get an equal number of gravels; put them into a cloth and tie them up. Then throw it into the road where the horses will travel over them, and the warts will disappear. VI, 2634

A horse or mule draws lightning. VII, 7009

When horses sweat in the stable, sniff loudly, and switch their tails violently, you may expect rain. VII, 6672

Horses, cows, and pigs running, kicking, and being especially playful is a sign of wind. VII, 6988

Death is conceived as riding a white horse. VII, 5234

Whenever you see a white horse, look for a red-headed woman to pass. VI, 3804

If you count one hundred white horses, you will find some silver. VI, 3415. Cf. To count gray horses brings good luck. VII, 7110

If you "stamp" a hundred gray horses, you will find some money. VI, 3418

The first man whom you meet after counting one hundred gray horses is the one you will marry. VI, 4474

It is bad luck for a man to take his bride home behind on a white horse. VI, 4860

A white-footed horse is likely to be a cheat. VII, 7633

A horse is worth as many hundred dollars as times he can roll over when he wallows. VII, 7637

Mare's milk will cure whooping cough.  VI, 2716

If a stallion breathes into the throat of a child with whooping cough, the child will soon become well.  VI, 2717

For whooping cough, let a child drink water out of a vessel just used by a white horse.  VI, 2714

From Clark Collection

Your horse will die if you kill a frog. 1283

Horses foal only at night. 1330

Where a horse or mule wallowed, dig a well for good water. 1025

If one dreams about white horses, there will be a death in the family. 877. Cf. A dream of a white horse is a sign of a hard blow. (Brown Collection, VII, 6987). Dreaming of a white horse means good luck; dreaming of black horse means bad luck. 1211

Horses have night eyes. 1329. Cf. White horses can see in the dark. 1331

A horse's hair removes moles. 148

Horseshoe over the door for good luck, and turned up so the luck won't run out. 370

Rain three days when a horse shakes with gears on. 1173

From Motif-Index

Colt, mistaken for devil, is addressed. J1785.4.1

Real mother of colt will swim to it. J1171.4

Treasure found if one goes with one-night-old colt onto one-night-old ice. N542.1

Untrained colt is result of master's neglect. J143

Knight protects colt from storm. Q51.1

Witch drowns foal. G265.2

Horse so enchanted that he stands still. D2072.0.2.1

Horse with golden mane. B19.5

Horse kicks murderer to death. B591.2

Horse-nail stumps bewitch. G224.13.1

Horse recognizes false rider and throws him. H62.2

Horse requests wolf to start eating at rear and kicks him to death. K555

Horse transformed to another animal. D412.4

Horse wading in blood at Armageddon. A1080.1

Horse in wild hunt breathes fire. E501.4.2.4

Do not cross bridge without dismounting from your horse. J21.7

Devil in the stable wrapped in horsehide. G303.8.12

Dragon becomes horse. D49.1.2

Dwarf rides through air on wooden horse. F451.6.2.2

Gorgon's blood becomes flying horse. D447.3.2

Rainbow is rain-god's horse. A791.7

Fairies milk mortal's mare. F366.1.1

God as mare seduces a stallion. D658.3.1.2

Strong man as son of man and mare. F611.1.6

Devil as a white stallion. G303.3.3.5.3

Neighing of stallion in Assyria impregnates mares in Egypt. B741.2 and H572

Tabu to eat horsemeat. C221.1.2

Loss of horseshoe nails brings train of troubles. N258

### Quotations--Literary and Otherwise

A pale horse: and his name that sat on him was Death. --Revelations, VI, 8

No man ought to looke a given horse in the mouth. -- John Heywood, Proverbes, Cf. He always looked a given horse in the mouth. Rabelais, Works

... ride not a free horse to death. --Cervantes, Don Quixote

He doth nothing but talk of his horse. -- Shakespeare, The Mer-

Horse 323

       chant of Venice

A horse! a horse! My kingdom for a horse. -- Shakespeare, King Richard III

My purpose is, indeed, a horse of that colour. -- Shakespeare, Twelfth Night

For want of a nail the shoe is lost, for want of a shoe the horse is lost, for want of a horse the rider is lost. -- George Herbert, Jacula Prudentum

I am sick as a horse. -- L. Sterne, Tristram Shandy

Spur not an unbroken horse; put not your ploughshare too deep into new land. -- Sir Walter Scott, The Monastery

It makes men imperious to sit a horse. -- O.W. Holmes, Elsie Venner

> But, once in a way, there will come a day
> When the colt must be taught to feel
> The lash that falls and the curb that galls
>   and the sting of the rowelled steel.
> -- Kipling, Plain Tales from the Hills

In the choice of a horse and a wife, a man must please himself, ignoring the opinion and advice of friends. -- G. J. Whyte-Melville, Riding Recollections

His screaming stallions maned with whistling wind. -- Anna H. Branch, Nimrod Wars With the Angels

He flung himself from the room, flung himself upon his horse and rode madly off in all directions. -- Stephen Leacock, Gertrude the Governess

What is dead in the middle and live at both ends? -- Man and horse plowing.

> Jeff Davis rode a white horse,
> Lincoln rode a mule;
> Jeff Davis was a gentleman,
> Lincoln was a fool. -- Brown Collection, III, 387

> Two white horses side by side,
> None can ride but the sanctified.
> Hallelujah! I belong to that throng.
> -- Brown Collection, III, 645

### The Old Grey Mare

Oh, the old grey mare she ain't what she used to be,
She ain't what she used to be, she ain't what she used to be,
Oh, the old grey mare she ain't what she used to be
Ten or twenty years ago. -- Brown Collection, III, 174

## Bibliography

Bartlett, John, Familiar Quotations. Boston and Toronto, Little, Brown and Company, 1951.

Benham, Gurney, Benham's Book of Quotations. London and Melbourne, Coard, Lock & Company, 1907.

Frank C. Brown Collection of North Carolina Folklore, I-VII. Durham, North Carolina, Duke University Press, 1952-1964.

Clark, J.D., "Similes from the Folk Speech of the South," Southern Folklore Quarterly, 4:119-133, September 1940 and 4:205-226, December, 1940.

Clark, Joseph D., "North Carolina Superstitions," North Carolina Folklore, 4:3-40, July, 1966.

Coffin, Tristram P., and Hennig Cohen, Folklore in America. New York, Doubleday and Company, 1966.

Coutant, Frank R., The A B C of Goat Dairying. Fairburg, Nebraska, Dairy Goat Journal, 1941.

Encyclopedia Americana, 30 volumes. New York, Americana Corporation, 1964.

Encyclopaedia Britannica, 24 volumes. London, New York, Chicago, and Toronto, The Encyclopaedia Company, 1936.

Evans, Bergen and Cornelia, A Dictionary of Contemporary American Usage. New York, Random House, 1957.

Henry, Marguerite, All About Horses. New York, Random House, 1962.

Jobes, Gertrude, Dictionary of Mythology, Folklore and Symbols. Metuchen, N.J., The Scarecrow Press, 1961.

Mathews, Mitford M., A Dictionary of Americanisms, I-II. Chicago, The University of Chicago Press, 1951.

New Standard Dictionary of the English Language. New York, Funk and Wagnalls Company, 1955.

Partridge, Eric, A Dictionary of Slang and Unconventional English. New York, The Macmillan Company, 1961.

Random House Dictionary of the English Language. New York, Random House, 1966.

Smith, William George, and Paul Harvey, The Oxford Dictionary of English Proverbs. Oxford, Clarenden Press, 1957.

Standard Dictionary of Folklore, Mythology and Legend. New York, Funk & Wagnalls, 1949.

The Story of Pork. Chicago, American Meat Institute. n.d.

Taylor, Archer, and B. J. Whiting, A Dictionary of American Proverbs and Proverbial Phrases. Cambridge, Belknap Press of Harvard University, 1958.

Thompson, Stith, Motif-Index of Folk Literature, I-VI. Bloomington, Indiana, Indiana University Press, 1955-1958.

Webster's New International Dictionary of the English Language. Springfield, Mass., G. & C. Merriam, Publishers, 1935 and 1961.

Wentworth, Harold, and Stuart Berg Flexner. Dictionary of American Slang. New York, Thomas Y. Crowell Company, 1960.

Wilstach, Frank J., A Dictionary of Similes, Revised Edition. New York, Grosset and Dunlap, 1924.